FOURTH, FIRST + FULHAM
The Golden Era of Carlisle United

FOURTH, FIRST + FULHAM

The Golden Era of Carlisle United

MARTIN DALEY

PUBLISHING

Martin Daley was born in Carlisle in 1964. He originally began writing after studying the life and times of his own ancestors. A writer of both fiction and non-fiction, another inspiration is his home city and its history, which always features heavily in his books.

Martin is a member of the Crime Writers' Association and in 2011 he completed the first volume of stories featuring his own local fictional detective – the Edwardian policeman, Inspector Cornelius Armstrong.

As an avid historian and football fan, there was a certain inevitability about Martin turning his attention to his hometown football club *Carlisle United – Fourth, First + Fulham* is the result.

First published in Great Britain in 2012 by The Derby Books Publishing Company Limited, 3 The Parker Centre, Derby, DE21 4SZ.

ISBN 978-1-78091-032-1

CONTENTS

For my brother Mark
Forever Blue

INTRODUCTION

I am starting this book by taking a major risk and confessing: *I'm a Gooner!* For those who are not fluent in footballese that means I have followed the fortunes of Arsenal Football Club since I was a kid; but before all Blues' fans throw this volume on the fire in disgust, I can explain – I was young! I was impressionable! Every small boy has to pick a glamour/fantasy team almost as a rite of passage!

Making a snivelling apology is one thing, explaining why I chose that particular club is another; what drew me to Arsenal when all of my childhood peers were jumping on the Liverpool, Leeds and Manchester United bandwagons, remains a bit of a mystery. Maybe it was those unusual white sleeves that set them apart from the rest; or perhaps because they hailed from the mysterious South; or maybe it was just because I was an awkward little sod who refused to conform. Whatever the reason, like all the other small boys barely out of infants' school, I picked my glamour/fantasy team and stuck to them. My only crime is, 40 years later, I'm still at it!

That's not to say I ever disowned my home-town club. You see Carlisle United were always my everyday team; the team that Dad used to talk about; the team that were always in the local paper; the team that we went to watch every week.

As a young supporter, you quickly understand that your glamour/fantasy team operate in a completely different universe to your everyday day team, and this somehow allows you to legitimately lead this mysterious double life.

Then there is the other layer of lunacy, the International game: this allows you to bizarrely cheer on the same player you inwardly loath and pillory to your mates on a regular basis throughout the season.

As you grow you become to understand the meaning of seemingly ridiculous random words or phrases: the 12th man, he gave him the eyes, stonewall, good feet, park the bus, handbags, nutmeg, the Makalele role, in the hole, they've got the cigars out, tea cups, the hairdryer, row Z; a 50–50, (and my own particular favourite) he's havin' one. So it is, after several decades of such irrational, monomaniacal, and at times shameful behaviour, I can claim with some authority to be…*a football fan.*

The inspiration for this particular book came from a casual conversation I was having with my brother Mark one day, when we were recalling our first experiences (starting in

1970) of witnessing live football at Brunton Park. Midway through the conversation, it suddenly dawned on me that, unknown to us at the time, we were witnessing some of the greatest games the club had ever played in and watching some of the greatest players in the likes of McIlmoyle, Ross, Balderstone, Bowles and Gorman, ever to pull on a Carlisle jersey.

When you add to the mix my dad (himself a Blues' fan since he was a boy) who had witnessed some of the incredible achievements of the 1960s (back-to-back promotions, great Cup games etc.), I felt compelled to get down in print what the three of us have talked about for years since.

The book is, therefore, part conventional history, part commentary on the period – in comparison to the game today – and part memoir, as told through the eyes of a small boy taking his first steps on the strange planet they call 'football'.

The story essentially begins in the early '60s: National Service was over and the maximum [football] wage was abolished; short, back and sides gradually turned into mop-heads; and in this broadcasting age of innocence, television programmes consisted of staples like *The Good Old Days* and *Dixon of Dock Green*. As the '60s morphed into the '70s, mop-heads became mullets and every weekend would start on Friday nights when the whole country tuned in to see if Stuart Hall could actually avoid wetting himself, as he tried to commentate on some British town's feeble attempt to outdo the highly drilled French and Germans in the European version of *It's a Knockout*.

It was an era long before the saturation of football coverage we know on satellite TV today. In the '70s there were only two major TV channels and live games were restricted to the FA Cup Final, the European Cup Final and the end of season England/Scotland International. In short, if you wanted to see the live game, you had to go your local ground (note ground, not stadium).

These were the days before the do-gooders stipulated that children could not participate in outdoor, unsupervised breathing without having first undergone a full risk assessment; dads therefore took their kids to matches packed with thousands of adults without a second thought given to crowd safety.

Looking back, I am not sure if things generally were better or worse – probably just different. Having said that we all have a nostalgic hankering for times long since past, and we invariably view them with rosy retrospection (you know the sort of thing: 'the summers were so much longer when we were kids, and Granny used to make a pan of broth out of the sole of me granddad's old boot that would feed the whole street for a week'). Notwithstanding such sentimental reverie, I soberly state that for Carlisle United most of the '60s and '70s *really were* special. The whole period would eventually be recognised as the club's greatest, and considering the financial constraints of today's game, it is one that will never be repeated.

The club was essentially formed at a rowdy Annual General Meeting of *Shaddongate* United on 17 May 1904, at the Temperance Hall, in the heart of the small impoverished area of the city. Heated discussion led to fierce debate, which in turn led to violent disagreement; eventually the reformists won out, and it was decided to change the name of the club in order to attract a wider interest and income from followers right across the city. Carlisle United was born.

As the shareholders and supporters trudged away from the meeting that night they could never have imaged that one day, their embryonic team would be standing toe-to-toe with the great and the good of the game, giving as good as they got. But 60 years later, that is exactly what happened for much of the two subsequent decades.

During my research I realised that this 'golden era' was virtually sandwiched between two infamous FA Cup ties: one in 1963, the other in 1975. Whereas the two do not *exactly* act as bookends in this volume (periods slightly before and after are covered) they do offer a certain symmetry. Both were at Brunton Park; both to lower League opposition; both ended in ignominious 1–0 defeats. But as for the 12 years in between – what an adventure that was!

The book does not follow in strict chronology, but is rather laid out in themes. For example in one chapter, the big Cup ties are all grouped together across the period in question; as are the seasons when the club came close to promotion to the top division in another. That said, the themes do essentially start in the early 1960s and run through to the mid-1970s, and the endless cross-references give the reader the choice to take the themes in isolation, or accept them as one long story, as I have.

Of course, the game played 40 to 50 years ago is very different to the one played today, as is the structure of the Leagues. Just in case you have not worked it out yet, the 'Fourth' mentioned in the title refers to the Fourth Division (today, it no longer exists); the 'First' is a reference to the First Division or League Division One as it was often called (today Carlisle actually *play* in League One – which is two Divisions *below* the top flight!). I conclude that it will be confusing all round (not least for me) if I constantly try to 'translate' the Leagues as they were at the time in question to what they are now. In an effort to place the club's position in context at any one time, therefore, in the main, I simply make references to the Fourth, Third, Second and First tiers of the English League.

Similarly with the positions on the field of play: the old-style positions were just a little bit before my time and I must confess that I do not really know my half-backs from my elbow; I hope my elders and betters will therefore forgive me for using some modern-day terminology to describe where a particular player plied his trade or what his attributes were.

I do not doubt for a moment that I have missed out someone's favourite player or skirted over someone else's favourite match, but as with all histories, this one is subjective.

So, if you are a relatively young Carlisle fan, I hope you find some interest in learning a little bit about your club's heritage; if you are a supporter of another club, I'm sure you can relate to some of the adventures told in this book as you serve your own particular life sentence; and if you are a Carlisle United fan of, say, 45 and over – I hope I have done your club justice. Enjoy!

Martin Daley
Carlisle 2012

ACKNOWLEDGEMENTS

The list of players, officials, supporters, journalists and family members who took time to give their own perspective on the period in question is lengthy, and they are listed in the Principle Sources section at the back of the book. Typical of the Carlisle family, everyone was courteous, welcoming and genuinely interested in a project about their club. I cannot thank them enough for their time and I hope I have done them justice. I also thank ex-Arsenal captain Frank McLintock who kindly shared his recollections of an epic game at Brunton Park in 1973. I must confess to being a little awestruck at interviewing some of the players I idolised as a kid – I conclude they are sporting legends and absolute gentlemen to boot. Also in the latter category is former work colleague and United historian David Steele who kindly went through the manuscript and checked for any howlers.

My dad is also mentioned among this list but a special note of thanks must go to him for taking me and my brother along to Brunton Park in the first place, and introducing us to a game that has caused us joy and heartache in equal measure ever since. Like all kids of that age, I was oblivious to time and expense, so I take the opportunity now to also acknowledge the hundreds of pounds he must have spent on paying for his two lads to get into the match season after season. Thanks Dad. Similarly, Mam must have spent hundreds more on half-time apples! Thanks Mam.

As usual, I owe a debt of gratitude to Stephen White and his colleagues at Carlisle Library for their help, support and use of facilities. Similarly, Stewart Blair, Photo Editor at the *Cumberland News*, was equally supportive and obliging when searching for, and allowing me to use some of the images from the archives. Most of the images in the book are from the Cumberland Newspaper Group or from Carlisle United, who also allowed use of the old club crest on the front cover. Others who have helped with the collection of pictures and who deserve my appreciation are: Ian Gray, Linda Mattinson, Peter McConnell, Norman and Peter Richardson, and Brenda and Tommy Styles. If I have missed crediting anyone else, I apologise.

Thanks as ever to my wife Wendy who puts up with me locking myself in my study for hours on end working on my latest project (although when I take a break and find her with a glass of wine in front of a favourite DVD, I'm not so sure this is the hardship she sometimes makes out!). Wendy also read the manuscript and suggested changes, as did my dad and proofreading pal Christophe Vever. Thanks again.

Finally, thanks must also go to my friend and colleague Janet Wainwright and her graphic-designing skills, in making my random thoughts on the front and rear cover a stunning reality; and to Laura and the team at DB Publishing for producing such an impressive book. Thanks to everyone concerned.

ONE STEP BACK

The great thing about football is that everybody has their own, inevitably different, opinions. Everyone watches the same game and disagrees about who played well and who was the most influential. From the most learned of journalists who have followed the game around the world for decades, to the two blokes in a pub; we constantly disagree over the most searching of questions: if that Russian linesman was not on duty that day would the Germans have beaten us again? How come the teams at the top of the League get all the good luck, and all the teams at the bottom get all the bad luck? Was Chris Waddle a mercurial midfield genius or just a big idle streak? And many more besides.

So, now that the scene is set, let's get straight down to it. Who was the best ever Carlisle United manager – Broadis? Shankly? Stokoe? Collins? (Okay, that was just to make sure you were paying attention.) Maybe some of the club's younger fans would plump for one of the latter-day operatives who achieved relative success in difficult circumstances, such as Wadsworth or Atkins. But in my view there can be only one true contender: George Alan Ashman.

You could certainly make a strong case for some of the others listed above, and I'm sure many Carlisle fans would, although Ivor Broadis's undoubted greatness was surely displayed *on* the field and not necessarily *off* it (due mainly, it should be said, to the fact that the then board did not share the same vision for the club as Ivor did).

The reverse is probably true of Bill Shankly: he was acknowledged as a good player and won five Scottish International caps as a result, but he will always be remembered for his work in the dug out. Despite Carlisle being his first managerial position, even at that early stage he was never one to hide his light under a bushel, and it could be viewed that during Shankly's tenure, his unswerving self-belief rubbed off on this tiny provincial club over half a century ago – making it and its supporters believe that great things can be achieved against all the odds. (Shanks, of course, would go on to plough a greater furrow and become a legend of the game by creating his '...bastion of invincibility' at Liverpool.)

Bob Stokoe meanwhile, like Ashman, had more than one spell at the club. Whereas Stokoe is certainly a controversial figure, there is no doubt he is respected by many a true Blue. Whatever contentions there are about his man-management skills or his playing style, his achievement in the 1968–69 season, when he took over a club that was languishing at the bottom of the League and steered them to safety, should not be overlooked. And the following year, when he took the Blues further in a major Cup competition than they have ever gone before or since should (and will be in this book) also be championed. For me, however, Stokoe will always be remembered predominantly for his success elsewhere, most notably with Sunderland who created one of the biggest shocks in FA Cup Final history when they beat the mighty Leeds United in 1973. (But come on Bob, as great as that achievement was what were you thinking about with that track suit/trench coat/trilby combo?)

Like Shankly and Stokoe, Alan Ashman achieved major managerial success away from Brunton Park (all three won the FA Cup for example after leaving Carlisle), but his achievements with the Cumbrian side were equally remarkable; his list of 'firsts' is unsurpassed: first time the club achieved back-to-back promotions; first League Championship (Third Division) for the club, and with it, the first ever promotion to the second tier of the Football League (1965), first time the club reached the fifth round of the FA Cup (1964), first time the club racked up over 100 goals in a season (1964), first time the club reached the sixth round of the FA Cup (1975), and, of course, the first time the club reached the top flight of English football (1974).

As I said earlier, football is very subjective and in relation to Ashman, I use the word 'best'; perhaps others would simply say he was the most successful – end of. There may even be those less generous who would say things fell into place as he was in the right place at the right time and therefore he was just lucky (a word Ashman himself once used in self analysis later in his career). But for me, I am happy to go with, *the best.*

Researching this book has been an absolute joy for me, as it takes me back to my childhood and my introduction to the game I have followed ever since. But as well as being a self-indulgent trip down memory lane, it has also been an education, as I have learned much about the club I grew up watching, and some of its stars. For example, (and true Blue historians might want to skip this bit as I show my ignorance), whereas I will always champion the achievements of Alan Ashman the manager, I am ashamed to say I did not realise he was such a star player for Carlisle in his day. I was vaguely aware that he played for the club but was totally unaware of his playing achievements, long before he ever dreamt of managing the club.

Fred Emery was the Carlisle United manager (1951–58) who signed Alan Ashman – a young centre-forward – after seeing him score six goals in one game for Nottingham Forest reserves. Emery paid the East Midlands club £5,500 for the services of the centre-forward – a record fee for Carlisle at the time. Ashman did not disappoint, scoring a hat-trick on his debut against Rochdale in a 4–0 win (he remains the only Carlisle player ever to achieve the feat on debut – another first!).

He was an ever-present in his first season and finished with an impressive 20 goals. It was the mark of things to come from Ashman, who reached double figures in four of his seven seasons with the club. He reached his high point in the 1953–54 season with 29 goals – matching Jimmy Whitehouse's tally of the previous campaign – but that season was also significant for the player as he picked up a serious knee injury.

In those days there was no flying off to the world's leading knee specialist in Colorado, or partaking in a few weeks rehabilitation in Dubai; you were either fit to play or you were not. And if you were not then you were on the footballing scrapheap. The best a player could hope for was to stay with a club for 10 years and get a testimonial that would give him enough money to buy a milk round or cover the lease on a pub. Ashman soldiered for another four years before he had to succumb to the inevitable in 1958; he retired aged 29, with an outstanding record of 99 goals in 207 games.

Like many players and managers who have come to Carlisle throughout the generations, Ashman grew to love this footballing outpost: not only the club and its fans, but also the city and its rural hinterlands. He decided therefore to settle in the area when he was forced to hang up his boots.

Jim Monkhouse was a club director and offered his former centre-forward a job looking after chickens on his farm at Langwathby, near Penrith. The market town itself have always had a good amateur football team and they approached Ashman and offered him the manager's job, in the summer of 1959. It was the Blues of *Penrith*, therefore, that became Alan Ashman's first managerial appointment.

Back at Brunton Park meanwhile the Blues of Carlisle were going through a fallow period in their history. In 1958 they became founder members of the then new Fourth Division after finishing in the lower half of the Third Division (North) the previous season. Fred Emery – the manager who signed Ashman, the player – lost his job as a result and was replaced by former Scotland manager Andy Beattie. Around the same time there were changes in the boardroom that would ultimately prove significant.

The archetypal Board of Directors in those days were made up of the local wealthy land owner, the butcher, the baker and the candlestick maker. Percy Sharp was chairman of Carlisle United and in November 1959 he resigned and was replaced by fellow director Edmund George Sheffield (E.G., George or Mr, depending on where you were in the pecking order). By the time Sheffield had joined the board in February 1958, he was already considered a lifelong supporter of the club, having attended Carlisle United's first ever League match in 1928. With the club in a poor financial position, the new chairman of 1959 made it known that a priority was to put the club on a sound financial footing.

As his appointment created a spare seat around the table, the directors asked Bob Jenkins if he would like to join the board. Jenkins ran the Pioneer Food Company that had been in his family for generations and had done the catering at Brunton Park for many years. (Typically – and in the true spirit of the community club – he had provided Bill Shankly and his players with a piece of meat if they were struggling financially a decade earlier.) Whereas Bob was flattered by the offer of a director's position, he was not really that interested; however, he suggested that his 23-year-old son Andrew, who had been hooked on United for some years, *would* be interested in the role. The Board therefore agreed to the almost unprecedented move of offering young Jenkins the position.

Andrew's dad had not mentioned anything to him, so the first he knew about it was when George Sheffield, the new chairman, rang him up to offer him the position – it was November 1959. The following February, the board repeated the move when they offered 23-year-old David Dent the position of full-time secretary; he became the youngest person to hold such a post in the whole of the Football League. The two young men – who were junior to their colleagues by some 30 to 40 years – became friends instantly and set about introducing some innovative ideas to the club. (Over 50 years later, Andrew Jenkins is chairman of the club and David Dent is life President.)

Andy Beattie's reign as manager only lasted two years and the club saw little in the way of improvement; he left his post in April of 1960. The current chairman recalls the unscientific approach to appointing Beattie's successor:

> 'They decided to get a selection committee together and interviewed [former Welsh international and Leeds United coach] Ivor Powell. I remember one of the directors told me he sensed he was a real tough guy when he shook hands – I think that's the way they judged it in those days!'

While the more senior members of the board were working on the immediate needs of the club, Jenkins and Dent were looking for ways of generating more income that would enable a change in strategy when it came to the playing staff.

Players were on a 12-month contract and each May clubs drew up a 'retained' list and a 'transfer' list that had essentially been in place since the late 19th century. For small clubs like Carlisle United this invariably led to a high turnover of players each season, as managers scrambled round in the bargain basement with their contemporaries for the best deal that could appease the frugal board members

The early years of the new decade would see greater change in the game than the previous 60 combined. The Professional Footballers' Association successfully campaigned for the end of the maximum wage. And if that was not enough, the real players' pioneer stepped forward in the shape of Newcastle United's George Eastham. First of all Eastham disputed with his club the habitability of the home they provided for him and his family, and then complained about the secondary [summer] job they had provided for him. He then successfully challenged the retain-and-transfer system which meant that clubs could keep a player's registration (thus preventing him from moving to another club) with a double whammy of refusing to pay his wages if he had requested a transfer. The so-called 'slavery contracts' were coming to an end.

Jenkins and especially Dent recognised that Carlisle's strategy adopted hitherto of turning over a high number of low-paid players each season had not brought any sustained success, so the aim was to bring more funds into the club to give the manager a chance of attracting a better quality of player to this footballing outpost. Andrew Jenkins again:

'The real success started when we decided to create a commercial department to raise money for better players, instead of getting free transfers and this 'in and out' all the time. Amongst other things we introduced a weekly draw. It started off generating about £350 a week, and before long, it was making £700 per week. This allowed us to start buying a few players in the £4k–£5k bracket.'

The newly generated income was not only to be spent on players – another key part of the vision was to start purchasing good quality semi-detached 'club' houses in the suburbs of Carlisle to allow new players to move their families to the geographically isolated city and settle them down in some comfort immediately. Such foresight would lead to a steady stream of excellent players arriving from the hot-bed areas of the North East, Yorkshire and Scotland. (The best the club previously offered its staff was a large soulless property on Goschen Road that was split into several poorly-equipped flats. It was known, disparagingly, by the players throughout the '40s and '50s as 'Hatter's Castle', after the 1931 novel by A.J. Cronin.)

On the playing side meanwhile, Powell took advantage of the increasing revenue streams by attracting good players like wingers Sammy Taylor and Les Dagger, centre-half Jackie Marsden and full-backs Hughie Neil and former England Youth International Terry Caldwell. Powell also tempted back the classy David Oliphant to his home-town club on loan after the former England schoolboy trialist had spent two years at First Division Wolves. These gradual shoots of hope culminated in the club winning its first ever promotion, from the fourth tier of the game to the third in season 1961–62.

Any success looks good on a club's role of honour but you do not have to look too far under the surface of this particular triumph to see that it was arguably the least distinguished promotion in Football League history.

Accrington Stanley went out of the League part way through the season and had their games and points expunged from the record. This resulted in a recalculation of points among the remaining teams, which benefited Carlisle greatly, as they were one of the few teams to have been beaten by Stanley. The Cumbrians did enjoy a better-than-average season but they only finished one point ahead of Bradford and two ahead of York.

Carlisle and Bradford both beat and lost to Accrington (in two games) but York only played one against them which they won. Because Carlisle and Bradford's results cancel each other out, it was York who were the big losers when the points

Ivor Powell and his 1962 promotion winning team.

were totted up, as their two point 'deduction' cost them promotion as they had a better goal difference than the two teams above them. (The counter argument would obviously be that it was the lesser of two evils, precisely *because* some teams had only played one game against Stanley and therefore it was not a like for like comparison.) Because of Stanley's demise, and despite having the worst goal average in the history of the game, Carlisle sneaked into fourth place and won promotion to the third tier of the League.

On the eve of the 1962–63 season, the manager returned to Leeds and talked a young combative half-back into joining him in Cumbria. Peter McConnell was a solid squad member at Leeds and he got on well with their new manager Don Revie, but Powell's promise of regular first team football plus the club captaincy proved an enticing prospect for the Yorkshire lad and he decided to make the move north in August 1962, where he joined five other new recruits. All was set fair for the new era in the higher division but things got off to a fairly inauspicious start.

The pre-season fixtures included the traditional reserve 'possibles' versus the first team 'probables' in a warm up for the big kick off. In those days, Carlisle played in blue and white hoops, while the reserves were in all red. Playing for the reserves that day was one of the summer signings – a young Scottish centre-forward called Bobby Grant; if William Heath Robinson ever designed and built a footballer, he would probably have looked something like Bobby Grant. Bobby was a big, top-heavy lad with all the fleet-footedness of Frankenstein's Monster. Grant had originally been picked up by Glasgow Rangers but after only one game he had been moved on to St

Johnstone, where he fared twice as well (playing two games). Ivor Powell obviously saw something in him and brought him to Carlisle from the Saints in the close season.

On this August afternoon, Bobby lumbered forward in the 10th minute and swung a giant pendulum leg at the ball that just happened to appear in front of him. Connecting with the toe-end of his enormous boot, the ball flew like a leather missile into the top corner of the Hoops' net. Fortunately, first-team goalie Jim Harkness only felt the wind of the ball as it whizzed passed his left ear-hole – if he had been in the way it would have probably killed him!

By the time the game finished, the Reds had stuffed the Hoops 4–2, with another summer-signing, goalkeeper Joe Dean performing particularly well at the other end. It is never a good omen to be beaten by your own reserves, and when – a fortnight later – the reserves themselves were beaten in their opening fixture by South Shields, there seemed to be more questions than answers around the club and on the terraces.

All the fears were realised when the season proper got under way and United made a dreadful start. The first game resulted in a 4–1 hammering at home to Peterborough United. Three days' later, Peter McConnell made his debut: another home game and another thrashing – this time 5–2 at the hands of QPR. Two home games played: two defeats and nine goals conceded.

Even at this early stage and on the back of a disastrous pre-season, confidence was beginning to wane. Harkness was relieved of the number-one jersey as the team travelled to Peterborough for the reverse opening day fixture, with his place taken by new signing Joe Dean. Dean had been brought through the ranks at Bolton Wanderers, playing for the England Schools and England Youth teams along the way. He also became the youngest ever First Division goalkeeper when he made his debut for the Trotters against Wolves aged just 16 in 1955. His Blues' debut at London Road signalled the end of Harkness's career – Joe would be an ever-present for the rest of the season.

The change of 'keeper halted the maulings received at Brunton Park but only succeeded in gaining a point. Still without a win by game five, Powell was so desperate he called up Bobby Grant for the home game with Crystal Palace. Bobby rewarded his manager with a goal but it was only enough to secure a draw. And so it went on for another month. It was not until 22 September – Carlisle's ninth game of the season – when they managed a victory: 1–0 at home to (the eventual bottom team) Halifax Town with a goal from George Walker. By this time, Powell realised that Bobby Grant was not the answer and he was moved on to Gloucester City.

The agony went on for the home fans as winter drew in and the team stumbled on towards the end of the year. The final game of the year came at Watford on 29 December 1962. The game ended in another ignominious defeat, this time 5–1.

As could be imagined, the mood on the returning coach was sombre. It was not helped by an incident which took place between the manager and one of the directors. Powell apparently overheard Jim Monkhouse criticising the players' ability and attitude to another club official. Ivor leaped from his seat and tore into Monkhouse: 'You could see the vein's on Ivor's neck sticking out, he was so angry,' recalls Peter McConnell, 'I'm not sure it was the wisest thing to do, given the position the team were in.'

The defeat at Vicarage Road sent the Cumbrians to the bottom of the League with a miserable 15 points from 24 games played.

For the skipper it was a desperate time and in a moment of naivety, he gave what he thought was an 'off the record' interview to North-East reporter Doug Weatherall. Weatherall asked McConnell about his move and – as Leeds were doing well in his absence – did he regret making it. McConnell said he obviously did at that point; Weatherall published the story and the captain was slaughtered by the local fans.

If things were tough for the skipper, they were worse for the manager. The season was proving to be death by a thousand cuts for Powell and his nadir was reached in the first month of 1963.

After gaining some respite in the FA Cup with victories against Hartlepools United (the 's' was dropped in 1968) and Blyth Spartans in previous rounds, Carlisle had been drawn at home in round three to lowly Southern League side Gravesend and Northfleet. The winter of 1962–63 was the worst on record and as January wore on the tie had suffered three postponements due to the weather. Such were the rock-hard conditions of Brunton Park and the neighbouring parklands, Powell had to take his players out to Silloth to train on the beach.

In the meantime the draw was made for the fourth round and the winners pulled out a plumb home draw against First Division Sunderland. With everyone assuming the Cumbrians would get past the non-Leaguers, supporters and club officials were no doubt looking forward to a full house against the Wearsiders.

Carlisle (in hoops) press to no avail through Les Dagger...

…and then Ginger Thompson during the infamous Gravesend defeat.

With still no apparent end to the desperate weather conditions – and after a further four postponements – the game was scheduled again for Tuesday 29 January 1963. The afternoon before the match, Carlisle winger Sammy Taylor was ordered home to bed by the club doctor after suffering from a viral infection. No doubt Sammy would end up thankful for the illness.

The following day showed no let up in the weather. But after a pitch inspection on another atrocious afternoon the game got the green light from referee Bill Downey. Fog descended and more icy rain fell during late afternoon. By kick off, the pitch was virtually unplayable, but calendar pressures and the fact that the Kent side had made the long trip north convinced Downey to let the game go ahead.

It was the first game the Blues had played since the ill-fated trip to Watford – Ivor must have hoped it would never take place at all. In the 20th minute, one giant lump up-field from Gravesend defender, Bob McNicol led to the ball breaking to forward Tony Sitford to hammer in what was to be the only goal of the game. David Oliphant was marking Sitford and later recalled, '…the guy I was marking got the ball and hammered it from – I'm not joking – easily 40 yards. Of course it flew in the net and I got the blame!'

Carlisle huffed and puffed through the snow and fog but could not find an equaliser. At the final whistle, over 9,000 depressed supporters made their misery known before trudging away into the murky night.

Peter McConnell still remembers the mood in the dressing room afterwards: 'It was sheer desolation really, we just felt ashamed.' Upstairs meanwhile, board members were exchanging knowing looks and a meeting was hastily called for the following morning: the humiliation was to seal Powell's fate.

To compound Oliphant's misery, it was his 21st birthday and he had a party booked at the Central Plaza Hotel to celebrate following the game. He remembered the infamous event:

'We were all embarrassed about the defeat but it was booked so we went. Halfway through the night a bloke wandered over and started having a go "what the bloody hell are you doing after that shambles tonight, you should be ashamed". I told him it was my birthday and he calmed down but everyone was sick about the defeat.'

The following night the *Evening News* reflected the irate fan's mood: 'Carlisle United's performance last night will go down in local soccer history as one of the blackest ever.' A picture of Ron 'Ginger' Thompson trying his best to plough through the slush and mud, as fog descended told whole story.

The extraordinary board meeting of Wednesday 30 January 1963 took place away from prying eyes at club director Christopher Chance's office at the Holme Head site of his Ferguson factory. The board unanimously agreed to ask Powell to resign – if he refused, his contract would be terminated.

Pointing out how well Alan Ashman had done with the Penrith Blues, Jim Monkhouse suggested he approach his chief chicken looker-afterer, to see if he would consider taking over the hot seat at Brunton Park. In his four years with the Penrith Blues, Ashman had guided the amateur side from the bottom of the Northern League to the runners'-up spot, as well as overseeing their best ever run in the Amateur Cup. 'If things don't work out,' said Monkhouse, 'I'll take him back at the end of the season and we can look elsewhere.'

Ashman was known to the board members as a terrific player for the club during the '50s and the Jenkins family had employed the centre-forward at their Pioneer Foods Company during the close season. He obviously knew the club, was available, and equally important – given that it was his first professional managerial post – he was cheap. All things considered, Monkhouse's suggestion went down well with his colleagues and the director was tasked with approaching Ashman.

Most people knew that as soon as the final whistle blew on the Cup upset, poor old Ivor was a dead man walking; but when the board offered the Welshman a dignified exit, Powell refused – he was adamant he would not resign. The directors felt they had no choice: after 72 hours following the defeat, the inevitable news was released on the Friday night that Powell had been relieved of his position. (Powell would go on to achieve fame as the oldest working football coach – finally 'retiring' aged 93 in 2010. He was awarded an MBE in 2008 for services to coaching.)

Peter McConnell and his colleagues knew the writing was on the wall for the boss and recalls his coach with some affection:

'I wouldn't have come to Carlisle if it wasn't for Ivor Powell who had been my coach at Leeds. Don Revie was our new manager and although he didn't push me out, I wanted first team football. I was offered an opportunity at Bournemouth but the wife wouldn't have wanted to go that far south, so I owe Carlisle and Ivor a lot really.'

Another extraordinary board meeting was held on Monday 4 February 1963 where Monkhouse reported back that Ashman was delighted to take the position. No time was wasted in announcing him as the new man, but characteristically, in making the announcement, the wily chairman George Sheffield kept his options open by pointing out the rookie manager was being appointed on a temporary basis, '…it is possible however,' said the chairman, 'that we may offer the job permanently to Mr Ashman.'

With the Blues languishing at the bottom of the third tier of the Football League, and facing almost certain relegation, Ashman was under no illusions about the task he faced, 'It is going to be a hard job pulling things round, and one of the first things to be done is to dispel very quickly any reaction that may have set in as a result of the League position'.

There may have been a change in the hot seat, but the new manager was inheriting a trainer who would continue to be a constant at the club that would last for two or three generations. Dick Young never played for Carlisle but joined the coaching team in 1956; such was his passion for the game in general and the club in particular, he was another figure who became loved by the fans and the many players and managers he would work with.

Young was born in the North East mining village of Wardley in 1918 and had enjoyed a reasonable playing career either side of the War with Sheffield United and Lincoln City. In 1949 he found himself in a player/coaching role with the Imps and in 1955, he moved to Brunton Park to succeed Tommy Dawson as the trainer of Carlisle United.

Thus began a love affair with the club that would last over 25 years. His simplistic style of push and run football would gain the respect of scores of players that were to work with Young during that time. His enthusiasm for the club also extended to cleaning out dressing rooms and doing various bits of handy-man work around the ground.

Dick's down-time almost became as legendary with the locals as his achievements with the squad. He may have been ahead of his time with some of his training methods, but he remained a man of his generation through his love of his pigeons and his allotment. If Jenkins and Dent had a vision for the club and were destined to alter the direction it was taking in the Boardroom, then Ashman and Young were destined to realise that vision on the field.

But that was all in the future; Ashman clearly had a job on, despite inheriting a playing staff that was not the worst the game had ever seen. The main problem was, as with most teams at the foot of any League, and fresh from the humiliation of losing to Gravesend and Northfleet, they desperately lacked confidence, as Ashman himself had alluded to in his comments to the press.

The team were led, of course, by skipper Peter McConnell, who had signed from Leeds in August 1962 for £4,000. McConnell was renowned for his leadership qualities but even his confidence was dented by the time the new manager arrived. His colleagues included decent forward men, Reg Davies, Sammy Taylor and Les Dagger, while classy right-back Hugh Neil was ahead of his time: in an era when full-backs were renowned for their hard tackling and blasting long balls downfield, Neil prided himself on reading the game well, intercepting the opposition's attacks and playing his way out from the back.

The club also had its fair share of local born players. As well as Oliphant, Ginger Thompson was another local hero, a tough tackling midfield player. At the time of Ashman's arrival, Thompson was the club's longest serving player and had actually captained Ivor Powell's side to promotion in 1961–62. A further sign of the times is illustrated by clubs having good amateur players on their books – local boy Barry Brayton was an example in Carlisle's case and it was the likes of Brayton who complemented former Middlesbrough centre-forward Joe Livingston in attack.

It's fair to say that some of the senior pros had their reservations about the new appointment. In his autobiography, Peter McConnell recalled the players' puzzlement shortly after Ashman's arrival:

'The thing that amazed me about Alan was that it quickly became apparent that his tactical awareness was non-existent! If a game was going badly, he didn't seem to have the ability to make the changes that would matter, and that could be very frustrating. Sometimes we would look to him for guidance, or in expectation of a change, and it wasn't forthcoming. That did cause some amount of consternation for a while, but we got used to it and besides, we all thought he was just a temporary appointment at the time, so we weren't worried about it.'

Before his new team kicked a ball in anger under his stewardship, there were two main frustrations for Ashman: first there was the need to acquire more players, with a top striker being priority, as the goals tally of just over one goal per game was proving woefully inadequate; the second problem he faced was actually getting a game *played*. The winter of 1963 continued to be desperately bitter and – with many games postponed due to the weather – the new boss had to wait a full month before getting down to business. He spent the long month of inertia, looking at what striking options were available. Whatever tactical shortcomings he may have displayed later, he was about to win any doubters over with his skill in the transfer market.

First he travelled to Oakwell, to watch Barnsley v Preston North End – the purpose of the visit was to watch Barnsley's Ken Oliver; the visit proved unsuccessful with Oliver having a 'mare. Oliver's striking partner, however, Tony Leighton starred in the 2–0 victory but Ashman found his enquires about him were given short shrift. The Carlisle manager then turned his attention to Hull City's Dave King: no luck; then Lincoln City's Jim Campbell: likewise.

Back at Brunton Park meanwhile, Ashman did make his first signing. He signed the club's three young apprentices on as professionals. One of them was George

McVitie and by the end of his career, he would play over 300 games for the club and be adored by its fans as one of the greats.

Another of that category was also about to join the club. In March 1963, Ashman finally succeeded in his quest to sign a striker, when he made a chance call to his father, who still lived in Ashman's hometown of Rotherham. Ashman junior had been lamenting his recent misfortune in the transfer market to his dad when Ashman senior suggested his son might want to come down to Millmoor and look at the Millers' centre-forward, who had scored four goals in 12 games, and who might just fit the bill.

Hughie McIlmoyle was the latest of a seemingly endless production line of great Glaswegian footballers. Raised on a Glasgow-staple of street fitba' (kicking a tin around the streets of the Scottish footballing capital), Hughie originally played for his local amateur side Port Glasgow Rovers, before he was snapped up by Leicester City, where he caused a sensation in May 1961 when he was selected to play ahead of established Scottish International Ken Leek, in the FA Cup Final against Tottenham Hotspur after just seven first-team appearances. A year later he was transferred to Rotherham United.

On 12 March 1963, Ashman secured McIlmoyle's services for Carlisle for £5,000. Later that day the *Evening News* carried a seemingly innocent picture of a football manager and his new signing on the pitch. Little did anyone know at the time that the youthful looking duo of Alan Ashman and Hughie McIlmoyle would be marked down years later as the greatest manager and player respectively the club had ever seen (the striker was destined – 40 years on – to have a statue of him erected outside the entrance to Brunton Park to celebrate the fact). Hughie philosophically recalls the series of events that took him to Brunton Park for the first time:

> 'I was in training one day when the manager called me into the office and said he had an offer from Carlisle United and was I interested. I said yes – if Rotherham didn't want me it was time to move on. The following day E.G. Sheffield came down to see me – a real gentleman – and I signed right away. My view was there was no point in staying at a club if they don't want you.'

Hughie did not disappoint: from the get-go it looked as though he had found his spiritual home as he scored on his debut in a 4–2 victory over Notts County. Ashman and McIlmoyle appeared to instil some confidence throughout the dressing room, as consecutive victories were achieved for the first time, when the Blues beat Shrewsbury on the following Saturday, with the skipper McConnell scoring the winner. Before the month was out, McIlmoyle had inspired the only away win of the season with two of Carlisle's four goals at Halifax Town.

The final 18 games of the season developed into a strange roller-coaster win-loss-win-loss sequence (only two games were drawn during this period). By the season's end, Ashman had succeeded in improving the form of the team from that in the first two-thirds of the campaign (Powell: 4 wins, 7 draws, 13 defeats; Ashman 9 wins, 2 draws, 11 defeats). But it proved not to be enough to save the club; the disastrous first few months of the season had given the club too much to do – although they clawed their way off the bottom (the hapless Halifax finished below them), they finished five points from safety and were relegated with a modest 35 points from 46 games. The empty (but often used) football adage of 'too good to go down' proved no consolation to players and fans as the inevitable became a reality. McConnell recalls his shock at being relegated:

> *'It had to be one of the worst feelings I have ever had, when it was finally confirmed that we were going down. Not only do you feel disappointed for yourself, but there is a horrible feeling in the pit of your stomach that you have let the fans down. You start to look at the games that were drawn and you can pick out incidents in each one of them that had it been done differently, it may just have changed the end result. You also look closely at the defeats, especially the ones against the teams that were also struggling along at the bottom of the table, and they are the ones that hurt most and cut deepest.'*

George Sheffield and his director colleagues, however, were more philosophical about the events of the season and had seen enough potential in the young temporary manager they had appointed in February. Ashman was given the manager's job on a permanent basis in May 1963.

The great American crooner Tony Bennett – when asked how he became so good – once said, 'It was down to my humble beginnings. You have to start somewhere, and you have to get bad before you can get good'. So it was with Carlisle United: the 'golden era' all began with relegation to the Fourth Division. But bad times were about to get good.

THE ADVENTURE BEGINS

Newly appointed manager Alan Ashman knew that the close season of 1963 had to be used to tweak the squad to his own liking in preparation for the upcoming campaign. With Hughie McIlmoyle settled at the club and the signs of a promising partnership with former Middlesbrough striker Joe Livingston already taking shape during the final third of the previous ill-fated season, the boss turned his attention to other areas of the team.

For his first summer signing he contacted an old friend and former Carlisle teammate. Geoff Twentyman was a local lad, born in Brampton in 1930; he was a good all-round athlete as a youngster (including being a Cumberland Wrestling champion) and was signed by Carlisle's player-manager Ivor Broadis as a 17-year-old.

The Brunton Park that Geoff arrived at in 1947 could best be described as 'austere'. Twentyman's manager Broadis had joined the club a year earlier after playing for Tottenham Hotspur for several months following the war. His RAF posting to the airfield at Crosby in 1946 brought the international-class footballer to the doorstep of Carlisle United. Broadis recalls his first impressions of the ground upon his arrival:

'Stepping from the comparative grandeur of White Hart Lane to the shabby surroundings of Brunton Park was like leaving the Savoy for the Jungle Cafe. An old wooden stand leaned drunkenly under the weight of the years, while switchback sleepers formed terracing in a bed of ashes.'

The old wooden stand Ivor refers to burned down (before it fell down) in 1953 and the sale of Twentyman to Liverpool for £12,500 a few months later enabled the club to build a new one in its place. Now in 1963, the skilful centre-half was in the autumn of his career and working as player-manager of Irish side Ballymena United. Ashman felt his experience and leadership qualities would be invaluable as the club prepared to bounce back from the disappointment of relegation and enticed him back to Carlisle for one last hurrah. (The stand incidentally, had now been finished off with some fascia from Director Jim Monkhouse's old farm buildings that had been painted blue and white!)

Days after the Twentyman-signing, another player joined the club almost unnoticed, and more by chance than design; he was a simple makeweight in a deal

Oh no, the grandstand's burned down. Never mind, we can always sell Geoff Twentyman.

involving two other players and Luton Town. His name, however, was destined to live in the memory far longer than the two other more illustrious players involved in the deal.

The story began towards the end of the previous season when Second Division Luton Town had their eye on one of the more decent Carlisle players from Powell's team – classy full-back Alan McBain. McBain himself got wind of the Hatters' interest and by the time the season had ended, he put in a transfer request, but his appeal fell on unsympathetic ears and the board rejected it in late May 1963. Ashman, however, knew that it does not matter who the player is – if he is unhappy, he has to be moved on, so he suggested to the board that it might be in Carlisle's best interest to do a deal.

The board acquiesced and Ashman brokered a deal to swap McBain with Luton winger Jack Lornie plus a cash adjustment. In those footballing hard times, the Kenilworth Road club told Carlisle they would prefer it if the Cumbrians took one of their reserve team players instead of cash. Ashman and Dick Young assessed the players available and decided to plump for their 21-year-old reserve team goalkeeper, Allan Ross.

Ross had been at Luton less than 18 months, coincidentally signed for the Hatters at the same time Carlisle signed 'keeper Joe Dean from Bolton Wanderers. The makeweight in the McBain/Lornie deal later described his first impressions:

> '*When I came to Carlisle I fell in love with the place. Dick Young really influenced me to join. He was a straight-talking and honest man and told me that the club was looking to progress in the right direction.*'

Rossy would go on to become the all-time appearance record holder for the club, finally hanging up his gloves 466 appearances and 16 years later. He would also be the only player to remain at the club throughout the rise from the fourth tier of the League to the first.

Another player signing that summer was winger Eric Johnstone; with his arrival and that of Lornie, one of the established players to leave Brunton Park was fellow wide man Les Dagger.

A couple of other squad players were also added; perhaps the most intriguing was Bob McNichol, the Gravesend and Northfleet defender who launched the long ball forward to his centre-forward to score and knock Carlisle out of the Cup some months earlier. McNichol was destined only to play one game for the Blues but unknown to him at the time, his speculative punt up-field into the January gloom of 1963 was the catalyst for the sequence of events that led to the success that was to follow over the next 12 years.

The 1963–64 season started with two home games – first against Darlington and then Exeter City, two days' later, from which the Blues returned a draw and a victory respectively. The steady start as far as points were concerned was almost outdone by the six goals Carlisle scored in the process. Ashman and Young's attacking approach brought two goals for Hughie McIlmoyle and one for his strike partner Joe Livingston in each game.

The first away game of the season, however, put a massive dent in the Cumbrians' campaign: a trip to Tranmere Rovers resulted in a 6–1 hammering and after suffering another two defeats from the next three games, the dark clouds that hung gloomily over the club for most of the previous season threatened to return. Peter McConnell remembers the sequence:

'We were beaten quite comprehensively in our first away game when Tranmere ran riot in a 6–1 win. As with all big defeats, it stung a bit, and we thought it was going to be another one of those seasons where we wouldn't be able to pick up points on the road, as we lost our next two away games to Exeter and Torquay.'

The team travelled to Hartlepools United on 16 September, for their third consecutive away fixture, and in need of an away victory to boost their delicate confidence. The home side themselves had made a poor start to the season and were already struggling near the bottom of the League. A crowd of under 4,000 turned up for the 'derby' game, presumably prepared to see two teams who were unlikely to threaten the promotion positions come the end of the season.

Despite the season being less than 10 games old, the match proved to be a turning point in Carlisle's fortunes. McIlmoyle caused havoc in the Pools' defence from the off. By half-time, the Blues were two-up. The second half produced more of the same with wave after wave of attacks. By the end of the game, McIlmoyle had helped himself to two goals and had a hand in others for Eric Johnstone, Reg Davies and Barry Brayton; Hartlepools' misery was complete when Hughie Hamilton put through his own goal, to complete a comprehensive 6–0 demolition job.

Two more victories followed against Oxford and Aldershot and the Blues found themselves in fourth place in the League. Sandwiched between the two victories was an away tie to Manchester City in the League Cup. The Fourth Division side acquitted themselves well against their illustrious opponents but went down 2–0. The defeat was in part due to a broken thumb sustained by 'keeper Joe Dean who had to leave the field. The Aldershot game therefore, two days' later saw the debut of young goalkeeper Allan Ross who would retain the gloves for the most of the season. A clean sheet in his first game and a Frank Kirkup hat-trick made it a day to remember for all concerned.

Then Hartlepools United travelled to Brunton Park for their return fixture with Carlisle on 1 October 1963. Just 15 days after the McIlmoyle-inspired mauling on their own pitch, the Pools might have been forgiven for thinking their luck had turned as Barry Brayton saw two first half efforts come back off the crossbar with the score still goalless. At half-time, however, they were probably revising that view: they went into the dressing room 6–0 down.

McIlmoyle had been at it again with no less than four goals, while the skipper McConnell and deservedly Brayton had also helped themselves. Carlisle were profligate in the second half and the final score ended 7–1; McConnell recalls the two games with relish: 'We won 6–0 at their place, and 7–1 in Carlisle, and we could easily have reached double figures in both games if we had taken some of the other excellent chances that we created.'

McIlmoyle scored again at Bradford in the following game, taking his tally to an incredible 15 goals by the first week in October. According to skipper McConnell – even at this relatively early stage – the players sensed they were going places and in with a real chance of promotion back to the Third Division. The club sat in fourth place in the division with 13 points.

But as Carlisle dreamed of bigger things on 1 October, remarkably they were not the highest placed Cumbrian club. In the early 1960s Workington Reds had a decent team and, having also made a good start to the season the West Cumbrians found themselves a point clear of their East Cumbrian rivals and looking down on their near neighbours from the lofty position of joint top. The Reds were being marshalled by player-manager Ken Furphy – like Ashman – in his first full season in the hot seat.

Carlisle's away trip to Bradford was followed by games in quick succession – one against Newport County which was sandwiched between two with the team that sat above both Cumbrian sides – Gillingham. The top-of-the-table clash was the first Gills' League game played under floodlights and attracted a season's-best crowd of over 17,000. Perhaps it was, therefore, appropriate that the home side came out on top on their big night (2–0), despite Carlisle playing the neater football. But the Blues

Hughie completes his hat-trick against Gillingham in 1963.

quickly put the reversal out of their system by warming up for the return with a 4–1 demolition job of the Welsh side. The scene was then set for one of the biggest home games of the season against the team from Kent – and it did not disappoint.

Almost 12,000 fans saw the fixture that brought the two top teams together. From the off Carlisle took the game to the visitors; with the game not 15 minutes old winger Sammy Taylor went on one of his trademark catch-me-if-you-can runs down the left wing (they never caught him!); a low cross found the master-marksman Hughie McIlmoyle and his left foot sweep into the net to set the scene for a memorable night. Peter McConnell recalled the seminal games with Gillingham well:

'We played really well down at their place and were unlucky not to get something. They were a strong defensive team but didn't have our pace and skill. When they came up to Brunton Park a couple of weeks later we were determined to put matters straight. We were fantastic on the night, none more so than Hughie. He ran them ragged – they just couldn't handle him. We knew after that game we had a great chance of going straight back up.'

By the end of the night McIlmoyle had helped himself to a left foot, right foot, headed hat-trick and the League leaders had suffered their first defeat of the season. His performance would be marked down by many as one of his finest in a Carlisle shirt (praise indeed considering his many achievements).

The Blues kept their unbeaten run going for a further six games (during which time Joe Livingston helped himself to a hat-trick in a 5–0 mauling of Lincoln City) until it was time for the annual sortie into the FA Cup. Another five goals were bagged in the first round away to York City (with all five forwards getting on the score sheet) before the second round threw up an interesting home clash with non-League Gateshead.

Although in the semi-professional League below Carlisle, Gateshead had invested heavily in an effort to gain promotion to the Football League; you need look no further than the player-manager for evidence of this. Bobby Mitchell had spent most of his playing career on the north side of the River Tyne at St James' Park. A hero of the Magpie hoards, the striker made over 400 appearances for the club. He also knew a bit about the FA Cup, having been instrumental in Newcastle's three Wembley

McIlmoyle again at York in the Cup.

victories in the 1950s (he actually scored in the 1955 Final). His team had already despatched Darlington in the previous round and made the trip west with plenty of confidence.

As the game approached, the club were firing on all cylinders: the team were going well in the League and Cup, the supporters were loving watching every minute of the free-scoring campaign, and the board were counting the burgeoning coffers from the increased gates. The game against Gateshead took the total number of spectators at Brunton Park to over 100,000 for the season so far. The five-figure crowd that crammed into The Brunt on the afternoon of Saturday 7 December 1963 were about to see another classic.

After only eight minutes on the clock, sections of the home crowd must have been recalling the anxieties of 10 months earlier when Gravesend dumped the Cumbrians out of the same competition: Gateshead winger Bob Lindsay scored for the North East side.

Nerves were eased somewhat by the tried and trusted Taylor-McIlmoyle formula: Sammy won, and then took a corner, Reg Davies flicked it on and there was Hughie in the right place at the right time to hook in the equaliser.

The game opened up still further and developed into an end to end affair with both teams creating plenty of chances before the interval. Any thought of the League side controlling the second period were blown away when Gateshead scored twice in three minutes before the hour mark – the first a result of a mix up between Allan Ross and full-back Terry Caldwell.

As a famous football manager once said: 'Cometh the hour, cometh the man.' Or was it Sir Walter Scott? Either way, it was quarter past four and time for you-know-who to cometh and take control – big style. By this point in the season Hughie McIlmoyle was virtually walking around with a giant H on his chest, such were his powers; and he was not about to disappoint now.

Virtually from the restart after Gateshead's third, Carlisle won a throw in midway inside the opposition half; McIlmoyle went short to the receive it; he controlled it, turned, and hit a blistering left foot drive from over 30 yards out into the top corner of Tony Stafford's net. Two minutes later, Stafford pulled off a brilliant save from the Carlisle centre-forward to deny him his hat-trick and the equaliser.

The sequence was enough to swing the momentum the Blues' way and with their tails well and truly up, wave after wave of attacks ensued. As the game moved into the final quarter, Joe Livingston crossed for Sammy Taylor to ghost in and square things up. The crowd were in frenzy by this point and dozens of home supporters ran on to the pitch as Taylor's effort hit the back of the net. If they thought it was all over, it was on 79 minutes, and there was a certain inevitability about how it would be achieved. Taylor swung over another corner kick and there he was, sailing through the air to meet it head-on to secure yet another hat-trick and the spoils. If a few dozen had ventured onto the pitch after Taylor's equaliser, it seemed the whole crowd now piled on after McIlmoyle's winner. Taking several minutes to clear the playing surface, referee Alex Edge threatened to abandon the match if there were further disturbances. There were not and the Blue hoards went home happy. Now *that* is entertainment!

As the weeks drew towards Christmas, Ashman reviewed his playing staff and this prompted further activity in the transfer market. By this time, the makeweight in the Lornie/McBain deal, Allan Ross was holding down his place in the first team; Jack Lornie meanwhile was not. Bizarrely, after only four games for the Blues, he was transferred to Tranmere. A fortnight after Lornie's departure, Ashman used the money to strengthen his defence. With the short-term Twentyman unable to play every game, the manager bought centre-half Tommy Passmoor from Scunthorpe United. Passmoor was another product from the North East footballing hotbed, serving his time at Sunderland before moving on to South Shields and then Scunthorpe in 1959. He was destined to become a stalwart of the team throughout the decade.

As Passmoor was settling into defence during the final month of the year, fans' attention was focussed on the other end of the field; Darlington were hammered 6–1 a week after the Gateshead thriller (Livingston this time getting a hat-trick); and then Tranmere being taken apart 5–2 with incredibly yet another hat-trick from McIlmoyle (all headed on this occasion).

Christmas itself brought the traditional holiday fixtures against Workington. The fierce rivalry between the two clubs had existed for some years but now for the first time, both clubs simultaneously had cause for optimism as far as the achievement on the field was concerned.

Over 35,000 Cumbrians witnessed the two encounters with the Reds hosting the Blues on Boxing Day and the reverse fixture taking place two days later. The first game was an entertaining open affair with both teams giving as good as they got; the home side probably shaded it in terms of a performance but the spoils were shared two apiece.

Forty-eight hours later it was a different affair with the East Cumbrians seeking to assert their authority on their local and promotion rivals; it was wide man Reg Davies who caught the eye that afternoon scoring one and making two others for Taylor and McIlmoyle. The 3–1 victory left Carlisle in second place at the end of the year, one point behind Gillingham.

The New Year started where the old one had left off – regardless of the competition, or the opposition, the results kept coming. Queen's Park Rangers visited Brunton Park in the third round of the FA Cup. Third Division Rangers went in as favourites but by this point in the season, Carlisle feared no one and set about putting the Londoners to the sword. Over 15,000 fans initially saw McIlmoyle the provider, as he linked with Frank Kirkup who set up Joe Livingston for the opener. Then the striker reverted to type just before the hour mark when he weaved past three defenders and rifled a shot beyond the QPR 'keeper. It could have been more had Reg Davies's penalty gone in and another McIlmoyle effort not rebounded off the post, but two was enough to send the Blues into round four where they faced more non-League opposition.

Bedford Town had created a sensation in the previous round when they had pulled off one of the biggest shocks in the competition's history by beating Newcastle at St James's Park. Now they fancied their chances with a home draw against Newcastle's modest neighbours. The game proved an entertaining affair both on and off the pitch for the 4,000 travelling Blues' fans.

Firstly, they were entertained when the [then] well-known Carlislean Boulevardier Ginger Mulholland, decided to run along the grandstand roof and fell through the asbestos sheeting (my dad still cannot retell the tale without howling with laughter). The second interesting fact about the game involves the television coverage. In those days, regional television was in its infancy and Border TV travelled to Bedford to cover the game (probably one of the first such ventures by the local station). Sadly they did not cover themselves in glory as they managed to miss all three Carlisle goals – including Reg Davies's penalty! (It could only happen to Border Telly.)

United found themselves in the fifth round of the FA Cup for the first time in the club's history.

Their opponents? Cup traditionalists and six-time finalists Preston North End but with the Lancashire club now in the Second Division and Carlisle riding high in the Fourth, it was not inconceivable that the Blues could cause another upset.

United made the journey to Deepdale on 15 February 1964 in a strangely subdued mood after suffering back-to-back defeats against a Stan Harland-inspired Bradford City and Aldershot. But as the old saying goes 'form is temporary, class is permanent.'

Over 37,000 saw the visitors take the game to their illustrious opponents from the start with McIlmoyle going close straight from the kick off before North End took the lead against the run of play. The Cumbrians continued to outplay their hosts throughout; but luck evaded them as Sammy Taylor hit the post. With the game moving into injury time another slick move ended when McIlmoyle connected sweetly from the edge of the box; Carlisle's luck was summed up when his goal-bound shot hit Joe Livingston and bounced away to safety. The Blues left the field to a standing ovation after being forced to concentrate on the League run in. (Preston went on to reach the Final without having played a top flight team.)

With time to pause for breath following the Cup exit, Alan Ashman sought to bolster his squad for the all-important run with the signing of front-man Johnny Evans from Stockport County. Evans was a Liverpudlian who was adept at linking the play as well as weighing in with his fair share of goals; like many an Ashman signing, it proved inspired.

But if Evans was one of the new breed, one of the old stagers was coming towards the end of his career. Carlisle born Ron Thompson – 'Ginger' to everybody – made his 359th appearance for the club in Evans's first game at Bradford City on 4 February 1964. Ginger had made his debut way back on 27 October 1951 against the same team in a 1–0 victory. Evans scored his first Carlisle goal at Valley Parade and Ginger scored what would prove to be his last for the club three weeks later at Stockport in a 3–0 win.

As the season entered its final quarter, Carlisle and Gillingham were still neck and neck with Workington close behind. The Blues showed no signs of letting up when they followed the Stockport victory by banging in four more against Bradford Park Avenue the following week. Evans scored twice in the game and then continued his form with a hat-trick in a 6–0 humiliation of Doncaster and then two more as United put five past Southport, and in doing so, broke the 100 League goals barrier for the first time in the club's history.

Southport had their revenge on the Cumbrians two weeks later with a 3–0 victory, and with Gillingham drawing 1–1 at Aldershot on the same day, there was all to play for in the final month of the season. Carlisle were a point clear of the Kent side at the top of the League but the Gills had played three games less.

McIlmoyle helped himself to two more and Evans scored again in a 3–1 victory over Chester, but then a rare goalless game at York put everything back in the melting pot. With three games left (two at home and one away) in the final week of the season only one point separated five teams. With only four going up, Carlisle knew that only three wins would do if they were to win promotion back to the third tier of the English

League. (At this point it was actually Exeter that led the League by a point from Carlisle, Gillingham, Workington and Bradford City, all of whom had 54 points.)

The first of the three took place on Friday 17 April 1964 against Barrow. The rather critical reporter commented in the *Evening News* the following day that 'Carlisle made heavy weather of things in the early stages...' Such heavy weather, in fact, that they were only 3–0 up at half-time with a couple from Evans and one from Joe Livingston; with Joe adding a fourth in the second half, the faithful knew that victory the following Tuesday night against Rochdale would secure promotion and probably the club's first title.

Eleven and a half thousand people wound their way down Warwick Road on the night of the Rochdale game in eager anticipation of what was in store.

What *was* in store was perhaps an understandably tense first half, where Rochdale played their role as party-poopers to full effect – breaking up play, getting blocks in and generally getting on everyone's nerves. All of Carlisle's big players went close: an Evans shot, a McIlmoyle header from a Taylor corner; a lunging effort from Livingston, but all with no reward. Then, two minutes before the break came the seminal moment of the game – a four-man move involving the skipper, Ginger Thompson (in what was his final home game) and Taylor ended with Evans crashing in the all-important goal. It was like the cork popping from the bottle as the release of tension and anxiety exploded from the terraces.

Throughout the second half, it was McConnell who put in a 'Captain's knock' tirelessly bustling box-to-box and leading his men towards victory. When the victory was confirmed at the final whistle, the multitudes poured onto the field to mob their heroes, knowing they were almost there.

The players finally found their way back to the dressing room but in complete antithesis to the previous season, the fans chanted their delight and demanded their return; eventually the appearance of Alan Ashman and his charges – emerging in the Directors' Box – brought another giant roar into the Carlisle night. Hughie McIlmoyle still remembers the game and the scenes afterwards:

'It was a terrific atmosphere that night. We were understandably a bit edgy because the stakes were so high. It was a pretty close game. Johnny got the goal but I think the fans just about pushed us over the line – the atmosphere was great afterwards with all the fans on the pitch chanting away.'

Evans's goal was the Blues' 70th home goal of the season; a season that had welcomed almost a quarter of a million fans through the turnstiles. The final hurrah to see if Carlisle could clinch promotion *and* the title was to be played out away at Brighton.

Before that, however, Ashman was already thinking about the following season. Less than 24 hours after the Rochdale triumph, the manager moved quickly to secure the signing of a player who had been on his wanted list for some time. Right winger Jimmy Blain was – like Evans – a Liverpudlean who had started his career with Everton. Like McIlmoyle, Blain was plying his trade at Ashman's hometown club, Rotherham, as the Carlisle manager prepared to make his move.

Blain had been closely monitored by Ashman's man in Yorkshire Wally Ardron for some weeks. (Ardron was also a South Yorkshire lad who had – like Ashman – gone on to play for Nottingham Forest where the two became friends.) Ardron informed Ashman on the morning of the Rochdale game that other clubs were sniffing round the winger and suggested now was the time to play his hand.

The following morning Ashman rang up Rotherham and agreed a fee of £3,000. To make sure the deal was sealed, the Carlisle manager suggested that all parties meet as quickly as possible at a mutually convenient venue. Thus, Jimmy Blain signed for Carlisle United on 22 April 1964 in a hotel car park at Scotch Corner!

While Blain made arrangements to move north for the following season, his new teammates had unfinished business. On Saturday 25 April 1964, they travelled to the Goldstone Ground for their final League game of the season, knowing that nothing short of a win would do if they were to clinch the Championship.

Although Gillingham were playing that same day they still had a further two games to play afterwards, so regardless of the result at Brighton, the title would not be decided that afternoon.

Carlisle did not worry about any 'as it stands' tables, however, and set about their game as they had the previous 45. Marauding forward at every opportunity the Blues simply overran their hosts who resorted to kicking everything that moved; the problem was the opponent and ball were moving far too quickly and by half-time the game was already in the bag; who else but Evans (2) and McIlmoyle (his 39th League goal) had shot the visitors into an unassailable three goal lead.

Although he did not know it at the time, the game proved to be Ginger Thompson's 374th and final appearance for the club. The tough tackling midfielder was not particularly contemplating retirement as he left the field that day, but an Achilles tendon injury in the close season brought the curtain down on his outstanding service to the club. It was perhaps fitting that he finished his career on such a high.

The whole team were on a high when they got back into the dressing room to find out Gillingham had lost 2–1 to Rochdale; it meant the Blues were four points clear of the Kent side which, therefore, needed to win both their matches to snatch the title away.

The sad postscript for Carlisle is that that is exactly what happened; Gillingham won both their remaining games away to York and Newport by the same score of 1–0. It summed up Gillingham's season: miserly defence and sneaking victories by the odd goal. (I know what you are thinking – that's a bit rich coming from an Arsenal fan of long years standing!)

Runners up to Gillingham in 1964.

Whether you preferred to watch a free flowing Carlisle match with plenty of goals, or a more functional Gillingham performance was academic; the fact was that in those days, the game did not favour the teams that scored the most goals (as it does today) through a 'Goal Difference' system. Instead, it favoured those who conceded the least through a 'Goal Average' system.

It was an anarchic system that had been in existence since 1888 when two points for a win and one for a draw was introduced. The bizarre calculation was to divide the goals scored by the goals conceded to produce an average. In this case therefore, Gillingham scored 59 goals and conceded 30, giving them an average of 1.97; while Carlisle scored 113 and conceded 58, giving *them* an average of 1.95. Thus, Gillingham won the title by having a better goal average.

If Goal Difference had been in operation then, the Blues would have stormed away with the title with a difference of plus 55 to Gillingham's plus 29. Goal difference was actually introduced to the 1970 World Cup Finals, but it would not be adopted by the English Leagues until the 1976–77 season.

It took some of the gloss off the Cumbrians' achievement and the feeling of injustice was not lost on the Carlisle players as Peter McConnell recalls today:

> *'The race towards the top spot was nip and tuck all the way, and we won four of our last five games to make sure that we would be involved in the shake-up. We were eventually pipped at the finishing post by the Gills on goal average, and when you consider that we scored twice as many goals as they did that season, it brings home how ridiculous that method of deciding League positions was.'*

If the players of Brunton Park were a little bit miffed in the end, there was genuine reason for the whole of the footballing county to feel proud; a single point behind the Carlisle Blues were the Workington Reds, who pushed their neighbours and Gillingham all the way.

Alan Ashman and Ken Furphy exchanged congratulations as the season finished, as the local press noted that they had both achieved promotion in their first full season in charge of their respective clubs. (Furphy left Borough Park soon after to take up the manager's post at Watford).

Bradford City ended up as the big losers as this is how the table looked at the end of the season.

Fourth Division

| | P | | Home | | | | | Away | | | | GA | Pts |
		W	D	L	F	A	W	D	L	F	A		
Gillingham	46	16	7	0	37	10	7	7	9	22	20	1.97	60
Carlisle United	46	17	3	3	70	20	8	7	8	43	38	1.95	60
Workington	46	15	6	2	46	19	9	5	9	30	33	1.46	59
Exeter City	46	12	9	2	39	14	8	9	6	23	23	1.68	58
Bradford City	46	15	3	5	45	24	10	3	10	31	38	1.23	56

In the grand scheme of things the 1964–65 season can easily be overlooked given that it may appear to be a relatively modest runners'-up spot in the lowest League in the country. But whether historians choose to focus on it or not, it is certainly a season that sticks in the memory of those who took part. Hughie McIlmoyle scored an incredible 44 goals – the most by any player in the whole of the English League, 'I'm glad I got that record with Carlisle United,' recalls Hughie, 'it's something I'm proud of.' (The club presented Hughie with a clock to commemorate his achievement, with the inscription 'Football League Leading Goalscorer'.)

The rest of the team did not do too bad either, scoring 130 goals in all competitions, with no fewer than eight hat-tricks.

The skipper Peter McConnell, spoke later of his determination to put things right following the relegation in 1963–64. As we all know, talking a good game is easy, producing on the field is another matter. Like McIlmoyle, McConnell's record speaks for itself: 51 appearances (he only missed two games), scoring six goals and creating countless others. The classic leader who was always at the vanguard (and often the rearguard!), he would write in his autobiography:

'That season was at the time, the best the club had ever enjoyed, and it still sits proudly up there amongst the great achievements at Brunton Park. When I think about the players that we had in the squad, it is little wonder why we did so well.'

The sentiment was echoed by goalkeeper and future great Allan Ross. When reflecting on his career prior to retirement he said:

'Apart from the friendliness of the club, what struck me most was the immense individual skill of the players in my first ever year at Carlisle. As a team, we must have been fabulous to watch. We scored 113 goals and were every bit as entertaining as the one that went into the First Division 10 years later. That Fourth Division team was probably the best we have had – at least while I've been at Carlisle.'

Perhaps if the season *is* overlooked it is because it acted as a prelude for even greater achievements that were to follow.

ALL'S WELL
THAT ENDS WELL

T he 1964–65 season could easily be split into two memorable halves: the first for what happened off the pitch, the second for what happened on it.

The period between the end of the previous campaign and Christmas 1964 saw the most intense and controversial transfer activity the club was ever likely to see. Alan Ashman clearly was not going to rest on the laurels of the previous season's success, as he wasted no time in the summer months reshaping his team. Jimmy Blain, of course, was already on the books after his move to Brunton Park (via Scotch Corner) in April. Following Blain from Yorkshire shortly afterwards was a player who had personally enjoyed a terrific season with Bradford City.

As the Bantams themselves had just been pipped for promotion, Stan Harland obviously took the view that, if you cannot beat them, join them. He was signed by Ashman in June '64. Harland stood over six feet tall, and would form what the local press quickly dubbed 'the big three' – the formidable half-back line of Stan, captain Peter McConnell and Tommy Passmoor.

Another future fans' favourite joined in August, a week before the first game of the season. Twenty-four-year-old North East auto-electrician Peter Garbutt was the centre-half and captain of FA Amateur Cup winners Crook Town. Garbutt thought his chance of playing professionally had gone until a quiet drink one summer's afternoon with some mates changed his life forever:

'I had had lots of trials with clubs but unfortunately they came to nothing. I was in the pub one day when a local scout called Walter Myers came into the pub and said that Alan Ashman from Carlisle United was interested in me. He asked if I would go across and play in a couple of trial matches for them. I couldn't believe it – the chance of getting paid for playing football!'

Garbutt took his chance with both hands – the games were against Darlington and the centre-half commanded the central defensive position well and Ashman was convinced enough to offer him a contract. 'I got a £20 signing on fee,' recalls Garbutt today.

The season itself got under way with an away trip to Colchester. It was as though the close season had not occurred as Hughie McIlmoyle scored the only goal of the game after 12 minutes. The only blemish on the controlled performance was an injury to new signing Stan Harland. The injury was enough to keep him out of the first home game of the season against Port Vale. His place was taken by the popular David Oliphant who celebrated the appearance with Carlisle's goal in a 1–1 draw. Sadly it was to be Oliphant's last of 109 games in a Carlisle jersey and he made the short journey across the border (like many Carlisle players before and since) to Queen of the South.

Oliphant's departure followed that of Sammy Taylor (in July) and the retirement (through injury) of record appearance-holder Ginger Thompson. Others to follow in the months ahead would include inside-forward Reg Davies and wide-men Frank Kirkup and Eric Johnstone.

Ashman's intentions were obviously to build on the achievements of the previous campaign but the early weeks of the new season were not shaping up as planned. Strangely, given the abundance of goals scored in 1963–64, finding the net was proving difficult this time round.

The supporters and the local press were starting to get a bit twitchy as the dreaded 'team in transition' tag threatened to be the strap-line for the season ahead. It was not until the second week in September that the Blues recorded their first home victory – against Oldham 2–0. Even then, the *Evening News* was critical, as its report lamented, 'United again found goals difficult to get against a mediocre Oldham side'.

Consecutive home victories did nothing to assuage the paper as it reported on the tight 1–0 victory over Southport in a League Cup replay. 'Finishing was again United's weakness. The Eric Johnstone goal came as a relief to fans.'

Drab goalless draws against Watford and Exeter followed; Joe Livingston was dropped from the team altogether (and would feature little in the rest of the season) and news leaked out that Ashman was looking for a new inside-forward to complement McIlmoyle. Just as the natives were starting to get restless, United finally clicked into gear with a 4–1 hammering of Bristol City in the League Cup; equally good was the fact that Hughie helped himself to two – his first since the opening day.

Two days' later, the fans were perked up further when the news came through that Ashman had got his man. Well, that is not strictly true – his man was actually Harry Middleton of Shrewsbury Town – but Ashman quickly switched targets when he learned that Swindon Town's Frank Large was available. Ashman secured his services for £6,500. Like the manager – and quite a few Carlisle players from the period – he was a Yorkshireman. Two things distinguished Frank: first he had an inability to settle at a club for any length of time which led to multiple moves throughout his career; and second, he played every game as if his life depended on it and therefore gave everything for whichever jersey he happened to be wearing. It was almost as though he possessed a nervous energy that manifested itself through the chasing of lost causes for 90 minutes; this all meant the fans adored him. If ever anyone lived up to his name it was Large. Skipper Peter McConnell – who dubbed him 'The Human Bulldozer' – summed up what it was like to play with him:

'If you had the ball and you didn't have anywhere else to go, you simply hung it up and dropped it in to the box. Big Frank did the rest for you. Either the ball, the 'keeper, or both would end up in the back of the net!

It was thought that Large and McIlmoyle would be the perfect foil for one another: Frank's work-rate, coupled with Hughie's right-place-right-time instinct would pay great dividends for the Cumbrians. Large signed in time to make his debut against Bournemouth the following day. The match proved an epic and Carlisle did get a hat-full of goals – sadly the visitors scored more as the Blues suffered another defeat (4–3).

The following game proved to be one of those fateful events that changes the course of a season and a career. It took place on 1 October 1964 at Kenilworth Road, Luton, and it proved significant for two reasons. First, the magnificent Frank Large scored his first goal for the club; but it was his strike-partner McIlmoyle who – with his movement and positional play – shone that day and caught the eye of an interested spectator.

Wolverhampton Wanderers had been an outstanding team throughout the 1950s; although they still played in the top flight, they were now starting to look old and in need of new blood. The chief scout had actually watched McIlmoyle play at Barnsley the previous season when he was scoring goals for fun but the club decided to stick with what they had. The 18 months in the meantime had forced a change of mind, however, and the Molineux club were on the lookout for a new front-man.

Not that they were looking at Hughie! The scout had gone to Luton to watch the Hatters' John O'Roake but he played poorly on the day, while his opposite number-nine pulled the home defence this way and that. It was enough to put McIlmoyle back on the wanted list and – unknown to everyone – the club from the Black Country started to plan their approach.

A couple of games later saw the Blues at home to Gillingham. How ironic that it was almost a year to the day that Hughie had bagged his magnificent hat-trick against the Gills, that the Blues would repeat the 3–1 scoreline with their best performance of the season so far. Although McIlmoyle did not actually score on this occasion, he again tormented the visitors' defence setting up goals for Large, Johnny Evans and Peter McConnell.

His performance was good enough to convince the watching Wolves' party that this was their man. They made their representations to the Brunton Park club after the game and tabled a formal offer of £30,000 on Monday 19 October.

Knowing that sort of money was too good to turn down, the board accepted the offer pending the player's personal terms. Remarkably, it was the player himself who almost scuppered the deal – Hughie admitted years later that he never wanted to leave Carlisle and would have been happy to politely refuse Wolves' overtures.

Ivor Broadis's name crops up twice in the relation to the deal that took the Scot away from Cumbria. His transfer fee of £18,000 to Sunderland in 1948 was still a club record at the time; now in 1964 the journalist, fan and friend pointed out to McIlmoyle that it was a no-brainer for a player to be offered a move like this:

'Hughie was a terrific player – he could've played for Scotland. When he was wanted by Wolves he was reluctant to go but I told him he would be playing at a higher level and for more money. He was living in a club house at the time and I told him he could come back later in his career and he could buy the house!'

Ivor's words seem to get Hughie thinking and his about turn saw the striker agree to travel to Molineux with Alan Ashman and chairman E.G. Sheffield. The move was completed before the week was out.

The move sent shock waves around Cumbria; Hughie was the star man, how could anything ever be the same again? Today's chairman Andrew Jenkins recalls his own reservations:

'It was a very brave decision at the time. George Sheffield was a very quiet man. I always used to go down to the ground about 2:00pm and I remember him saying "they're not going to like it but they'd got to realise we can buy three players with this". It was all about strengthening the team. He had a great working relationship with Alan Ashman and Dick Young who understood what he was trying to do.'

Inside the club was one thing, outside the club was something else. One young supporter also remembers the event vividly. Ross Brewster was a Keswick schoolboy at the time who – like the rest of us at that age – was obsessed with the game and his team. Travelling by train to the city for every home game to watch his heroes play, he typically loved Hughie more than anyone else. (All schoolboys are the same – the strikers are always our favourite players!)

Ross came home from school on the day in question to find his mother was quite upset [on his behalf]. The youngster thought a favourite aunt had died or next door's dog had been tragically run over – it turned out to be much worse than either scenario:

'My mother said, "I've got some bad news, I don't want you to get too upset but it was on the news that Hughie McIlmoyle has left Carlisle." I remember I ran to my

room and was in tears, never coming out for the rest of the night. I believed it was the end of Carlisle United as I knew it! And they had signed Frank Large as the replacement – they were like chalk and cheese! Hughie was a player of sophisticated skills; he was an all-round player; Frank had this lock of blond hair – he was like a battering ram. Things would never be the same again. I thought we'd been sold down the river!'

Alan Ashman kept his counsel on the move. Instead he quickly demonstrated that the money would be reinvested in other areas of the team. A week after selling McIlmoyle for a club-record sale, Ashman broke the record buying-fee when he paid Halifax Town £10,000 for their midfield skipper Willie Carlin. Carlin had scored 21 goals for the Shaymen the previous season and Ashman hoped he could weigh in with his fair share at Brunton Park to assist Large and Evans up front. This coupled with his pace and creativity in the middle of the park made him a valuable addition to the team.

The Blues showed no ill-effects from the McIlmoyle sale as they went on a five game unbeaten run. The balance, however, did not seem quite right and Allan Ross was also going through a difficult spell in goal. The other goalkeeper in the squad meanwhile was becoming increasingly frustrated with his understudy role. Joe Dean could take no more and by mid-November he submitted a transfer request.

No sooner had his request gone in, he found himself back in the team – Rossy's poor spell had culminated in a mistake at Roots Hall that gave Southend United both points. Dean took over the jersey, therefore, for the home game with Barnsley on 28 November. It was an afternoon where everything clicked into gear and gave the crowd of just under 7,000 a reminder of what Ashman's men had produced last season. Dean was immaculate and Willie Carlin got his first goal for the club, along with others for Large, Evans, and a rare Hugh Neil strike. The win kept United in touch near the top in 7th place, five points behind the leaders Bristol Rovers.

Ronnie Simpson became the final piece of Ashman's jigsaw when he signed from Sheffield United in early December 1964. Simpson played on the left wing and it was hoped he would give balance to the team by complementing Jimmy Blain on the right. What also distinguished Ronnie from his new colleagues was that – as David Oliphant had moved on and Ginger Thompson had retired at the start of the season – he became the only local born regular in the side (although Barry Brayton remained a useful squad member).

Simpson made his debut at home to Colchester United on 12 December. Despite the visitors taking an early lead, Carlisle quickly got back into it and the new boy seemed at home from the start, setting up Frank Large on 22 minutes. Once parity was restored, the Blues ripped into their opponents and goals in the second half from Blain, McConnell and another from Large delivered one of the best victories of the season.

Peter McConnell on target against Workington in 1964.

Just as it looked as though Ashman had found the right formula, bizarrely, one of the best victories of the season was immediately followed by *the* worst defeat. The Cumbrians travelled down to Griffin Park and were mullered 6–1 by Brentford. Peter McConnell's theory: 'The result hurt and in a way I think it was a good thing because it gave us the slap in the face we needed'.

The captain's view appears to be confirmed by the winning of all four points against local rivals Workington Reds during the holiday period. The two 1–0 victories gave the team and the supporters confidence going into the second half of the season. The first came on Boxing Day when a Frank Large effort was good enough to take the two points, then two days' later skipper Peter McConnell hammered in the winner at Borough Park.

From that point on, the team remained virtually unchanged until the end of the season: Joe Dean, Hugh Neil, Terry Caldwell, Peter McConnell, Tommy Passmoor, Stan Harland, Willie Carlin, Johnny Evans, Jimmy Blain, Frank Large and Ronnie Simpson. They all developed an understanding and with it, a momentum that inched them towards the top two places as winter edged towards spring.

Carlisle had actually won five straight by the time promotion rivals Hull City arrived at Brunton Park in mid-February. As it was getting towards the business-end of the season, a lot hinged on the match with the Blues occupying second place among the jostling promotion chasers, while Hull occupied the top spot.

Over 17,000 witnessed an end-to-end, yet goalless, encounter where each side gave as good as they got. As the game moved into the last minute, Peter McConnell gave away a free kick deep in Carlisle territory. Instead of floating a customary ball into the box, City caught the defence on the hop by quickly slipping the ball short and wide to their winger Chris Chilton who took it to the dead-ball-line and clipped it across for Ken Wagstaff to volley in what appeared to be the winner. As the Hull players celebrated the victory, the Carlisle players raced over to the linesman to protest that the ball had gone out of play before Chilton got his cross in. Fortunately the linesman agreed and after some consultation with the referee, the goal was disallowed. Peter McConnell later wrote:

'It was a double relief for me because I actually shouted at Joe Dean to leave it because I was convinced it was going to be a goal kick. I can only imagine what Joe and the rest of the lads would have said if the goal had been given!'

After the Hull game, Carlisle won three out of the next four and topped the League for the first time on 12 March 1965 after beating QPR at Loftus Road.

It seemed that all of Alan Ashman's wheeling and dealing in the first half of the season had been vindicated, such was the team's cohesion. With Joe Dean playing with a new-found confidence, full-backs Hugh Neil and Terry Caldwell complemented each other perfectly – Neil, the ball playing defender, Caldwell, the staunch, ask-questions-later competitor. The half-back line of skipper Peter McConnell, Tommy Passmoor and Stan Harland had an almost telepathic understanding of where each other were, and (as far as McConnell and Harland were concerned) when to go forward and when to stay back. Willie Carlin and Johnny Evans linked up the play and chipped in with their fair share of goals, while wide men Jimmy Blain and Ronnie Simpson constantly provided for the one and only Frank Large up front. (Incredibly only Evans remained from the highly successful front five that won promotion the previous season.)

Large, in particular, was loved by the fans and revered by his teammates for his never-say-die attitude, and his constant chasing of lost causes for 90 minutes. The journeyman pro was destined to have a relatively short career at Brunton Park before his itchy feet prompted him to move on to his next mission, but the fact that he gave everything for each club he played for means he remains dear in the memories of all Carlisle fans (and Halifax Town fans; and QPR fans; and Swindon Fans; and Northampton Town fans – on three separate occasions; and Oldham Athletic fans. I've probably missed somebody out but you get the picture).

After the victory over QPR, another four wins out of the next five games set up what would prove to be a dramatic climax to the season; it would see the Blues play three games over the Easter weekend against two of their nearest rivals. First it would be Bristol City at home on Good Friday, and then two games against Mansfield Town on consecutive days: away on Easter Monday and then at home on Tuesday 20 April.

Going into the game against Bristol, Carlisle still occupied the top spot on 57 points – two ahead of Hull, four ahead of Mansfield and five ahead of Bristol – but

One of Dick Young's two-man team sessions.

significantly, the Cumbrians had the worst goal average of the four, so there was little margin for error.

On a rutted pitch, and in front of over 16,000 fans, it turned out to be a tense encounter with Carlisle having the best of the opening exchanges, most notably when Frank Large crashed the ball against the crossbar so hard it cannoned back to the halfway line! Increasingly Bristol 'keeper Mike Gibson was being tested but he responded on each occasion.

Then eight minutes into the second half nerves were frayed to breaking point when Brian Clark beat McConnell to the ball and fired in a shot just inside the post to give the visitors the lead. The game then swung the Cumbrians' way on the hour mark when first, City's right winger had to leave the field with a suspected broken leg, and then Johnny Evans slotted a ball through for the forward-charging Stan Harland who turned and hammered in the equaliser.

With Carlisle now fully in the driving seat and going for the two points, Gibson continued his heroics with outstanding saves from a McConnell shot and then an Evans header. Willie Carlin then thought he had won it but his goal was ruled out for offside. Clark then threatened to pull off an unlikely victory for the visitors but his late effort was blocked by the knees of Joe Dean. With the minutes ticking away, Hugh Neil sprinted down the right flank and fed Carlin inside; he pulled the ball back into the area where Jimmy Blain had drifted in unseen – from point blank Blain blazed over horribly.

The game finished with both sides wondering if a point was good enough: Bristol's chances of promotion now hung by a thread, while Carlisle worried about that inferior goal average as they prepared for the two decisive games against Mansfield.

The Derbyshire side meanwhile were now in third place, three points behind the leaders Carlisle. For their part, the Cumbrians knew that a victory would virtually put paid to the Stags' promotion chances and give them one less team to worry about.

Carlisle showed little signs of nerves as the first game got under way and they controlled it for most of the opening quarter. But the early season goal-scoring problems returned to haunt them as chance after chance came and went. By half-time, they were puzzled to find themselves a goal down, by full-time they were completely bewildered as to how they had lost a game they had otherwise dominated, 2–0. Now it was S.O.B. time.

The defeat left things in the balance as the two teams journeyed back to Brunton Park for the following day's encounter. Mansfield were now back in second place, a single point behind Carlisle, with a game in hand and a superior goal average.

The previous night's reversal did not dampen the expectancy of the *Evening News* as it hyped the return up for all it was worth 'United Confident of Making History' it's front page cried on the afternoon of the game. The stakes certainly could not have been any higher – Carlisle had been on top of the League since 12 March, now it could all come crashing down with a second successive defeat to their nearest rivals.

With the worst goal average of all the teams, anything but a win could see them miss out on promotion altogether. The local paper did not help:

The team prepare for the Mansfield title decider in 1965.

'*Never before in the history of Carlisle United has so much rested on the outcome of one game – their all-important top-of-the-table clash with Mansfield Town at Brunton Park tonight. This is the night of decision – a night when Carlisle United are a mere 90 minutes away from promotion, the Third Division Championship and the glamour of Second Division football next season.*'

No pressure there then.

As for the crowd, over 18,500 crammed in on the biggest night in the club's history. It was later reported that the gates were shut when the ground could not take anymore and around 2,000 stood outside in the car park from which you can see a tiny doorway marked 'Players and Officials'. Through it earlier in the evening had gone the same 11 players that played against Bristol at Mansfield the day before and for most of the second half of the season for that matter.

If you were one of those 11, now in that small Home dressing room on the night of 20 April 1965, you would be listening to the nervous chatter and banter among the players as you get changed. Then sitting alone with your thoughts in the enclosed space, the smell of perspiration and liniment fills your nostrils as nerves grab at the pit of your stomach. As the clock ticks nearer, the adrenalin pumps faster as the noise can be heard from the packed crowd above you: 'United…United…' they chant, punctuated by their staccato clapping ('The sound of the crowd made the hairs of your neck stand up,' later recalled Peter McConnell).

You have had the good-cop calmness of Alan Ashman; then the bad-cop gee-up from Dick Young; then the let's-give-'em-what-for-cop from skipper McConnell. You get the knock from the referee and the collective '*C'MON!*' goes up from your teammates. The door opens and the noise gets louder…'*UNITED!…UNITED!…*'

In the cramped tunnel the cacophony of chanting and clapping is bouncing off the concrete walls. You look over the shoulders of your blue-shirted colleagues to see the green pitch under the lights. The skipper turns round once more and gives you all the clenched fist sign. You finally run out and the ground explodes at the sight of the players.

Coiled springs, caged tigers, pick your metaphor – from the off, Carlisle overran their promotion rivals; it seemed as though there were 15 players on the field, such was their dominance. Again it was Large leading the line as though his very life depended on it. Hitting the bar after five minutes served as a precursor to what followed nine minutes later: McConnell won the ball in midfield and moved it forward to Willie Carlin, his first time pass sprayed it wide to Jimmy Blain who crossed without breaking stride, there was Frank Large to leap high and power a header in off the upright. If it were possible, the noise was cranked up a few more decibels.

Two minutes later and the bulldozer was at it again – this time Ronnie Simpson sent in a free kick and Large powered in before [the extremely brave!] 'keeper

Frank Large scores the opener against Mansfield.

smothered it at his feet. But he was only putting off the inevitable: on 20 minutes Carlin and Blain again combined to send a dangerous ball into the box. This time the mere presence of Large disconcerted the defenders to the point that one of them – John Gill – scuffed an effort towards his own goal and Johnny Evans nipped in to glance in the second.

Mansfield could not contain Blain down the Carlisle right and yet another ball to Large ended up in the back of the net but this time it was ruled out for an infringement by Evans. With 34 minutes on the clock, however, the hapless defenders were again left looking at one-another; this time it was left-back Terry Caldwell getting in on the act – he crossed a high ball and Gill completely missed what should have been an easy clearance. Large was loitering with intent as usual, and – although apparently taken by surprise at Gill's mistake – the big man lunged at the ball and got his left boot to it. Agonisingly for Mansfield, the ball trickled over the line for Carlisle's third. Game over.

The Blues had saved up their best display of the season for their final and most important game. They simply blew Mansfield away and the fans chants of 'United! United!' turned into 'Easy! Easy!' as they played keep-ball for most of the second half. The consensus was that – although Large scored two – man of the match was Jimmy Blain. It was some justice for the winger who had had an equally good game the day before, without the same rewards.

At the final whistle, the 12th man let loose the shackles and piled onto the pitch in a repeat of the scenes witnessed the season before after promotion was clinched against Rochdale. This time it was bigger and better: promotion to the Second Division for the first time and with it, the club's first ever title.

The players were carried shoulder-high by the jostling crowd towards the tunnel. Once there, the fans chanted their delight until their heroes reappeared – with Alan Ashman – in the Directors' Box; throwing their shirts into the hordes only heightened the excitement.

Manager Alan Ashman and skipper Peter McConnell lead the celebrations in the dressing room following the title victory.

Back downstairs and the celebrations continued with Dick Young being dumped, fully clothed, into the bath by Joe Dean and Willie Carlin, while the skipper and the manager cracked open the champagne and cigars provided by the chairman. Ashman told the press, 'It is a wonderful feeling. The boys gave everything they had in this match and they won it and the Championship very well. It was a great climax to the season.'

The chairman *himself* meanwhile suggested the achievement was of historic proportions. 'This is the greatest thing that has happened to Carlisle since the Roman occupation,' said E.G. Sheffield in his excitement, 'there has never been an event to match it'.

Peter McConnell was asked when he thought the team had a chance of promotion, 'When we won at QPR back in March – I said to myself this is it!' (Carlisle had reached the top of the League and led all the way thereafter.)

The skipper himself had had another outstanding season making 49 appearances and scoring a personal best eight goals. He still remembers the achievement of the team today:

'The proudest moment of all for me at Carlisle was when we won the title that night against Mansfield. We had been neck and neck for weeks and they had beaten us the day before 2–0. I couldn't believe that result – we were all really angry that we'd let them off the hook. I can't explain the following night – we were so sure we were going to win it. It wasn't arrogance, just pure confidence in what we were about – we knew we were a good team and we just knew we were going to do it. As a result

the club went up the Second Division for the first time in its 60-year Football League existence, and it felt wonderful to be part of it. To also be club captain through it all made me feel extremely proud.'

And the rest of the players soon join in.

(To rub Mansfield's noses in it, they failed to win their game in hand and were pipped for second place by Bristol City.)

Regardless of the fact that the club actually won the Championship, the 1964–65 season is an interesting season to analyse. Alan Ashman ignored the old adage 'if it isn't broke, don't fix it' by virtually breaking up the team that scored 130 and won promotion the previous campaign. Only five of the team that beat Mansfield were on duty 12 months earlier against Rochdale. Had this high-risk dismantling strategy not worked, who knows what the future would have held for the manager, or the club.

McConnell, who was originally bemused by Ashman's appointment, was now completely onside with what the boss was trying to achieve. He was also fulsome in his praise of his manager's decision-making:

'Looking back over the whole season, I think the outstanding event was the manager's decision to let McIlmoyle go to Wolves. Hughie was the hero, and the manager was taking a cool and very calculated gamble in letting him go and it paid off.'

The mild-mannered Ashman was now carving himself out a reputation as a manager with a shrewd eye for a player who would slot into a team which played attractive, free-flowing football. His tactical savvy and awareness of the opposition was also clearly developing as he had set a target at the start of the season for 60 points (exactly the total reached that delivered the title).

For some fans and press, the team had way exceeded all expectations, given the step up in class between the divisions. In 1962 Ivor Powell's side trod the same path believing that promotion to the second tier was a possibility – the reality was that the club could not hack it at this level and had ignominiously slipped back into the Fourth Division as a result. Why was it different this time?

By blending youth and experience, with camaraderie and desire, Ashman managed to turn the board's buy-small-sell-big philosophy into a stunning successful reality.

At the deserved civic reception that shortly followed the triumph, the skipper spoke of the confidence that already existed in the camp concerning prospects of survival in the Second Division. McConnell had experience of the second tier of the game through his time with Leeds United and now commented on how he thought the Third Division was actually *harder* '…because footballing teams like us often don't get time to play'.

Before the plates had been cleared away at the reception, the manager was planning for the next campaign by enhancing the footballing nature of the team, commented on by his captain. During the run-in, Ashman had watched Carlisle's reserves being taken apart by a bloke who appeared to just stand in the middle of the pitch, spraying passes to all points of the field; if a teammate made a run, he was found with a pin-point pass. As embarrassing as it was for the reserves, the watching Carlisle manager knew that this Huddersfield understudy would enhance his first team tremendously.

Chris Balderstone was originally signed by Bill Shankly for his home-town club Huddersfield Town in 1958 (Shankly always remained a great admirer of Baldy, and once described him as '...simply the best footballer I have seen outside the First Division'). After over 100 appearances – he lost his place in the Second Division side and Ashman pounced to secure his grace and skill for the Cumbrians at a bargain price of £7,000.

Balderstone was the first of three significant additions to the first team over the next few months. The second was the highly promising Nottingham Forest centre-forward David Wilson. Wilson came with quite a big reputation and carried the dreaded 'potential' tag. He turned out to be a good player, rather than a great one during his brief Carlisle career, although 23 goals in 54 appearances is pretty impressive in anyone's book.

If you were picking your all-time 11 Dave Wilson would not be in it, but Balderstone probably would, as would the young lad that finally got his Carlisle career under way shortly into the new season. There is always something special about a 'local lad made good', and – like Balderstone – Carlisle's own George McVitie was destined to wear the blue jersey with pride on over 300 occasions.

Unknown to George, Baldy and everyone else at the time, however, the club were preparing for what would be a 12-year spell in the top two divisions.

EARLIEST MEMORIES

Like all football fans, my earliest memories are firmly imprinted on my mind. But it was only many years later, in adulthood, that I realised my first seasons at Brunton Park were among the most successful in the club's history – the first would be 1970–71 when I was six years old. But even before then, my first recollections of the game came through watching television, and the very first was the FA Cup Final of 1970.

Today's namby-pamby players are often accused of feigning injury or 'simulation,' but if you were a nippy striker or an elegant midfield player in the early 1970s, there was no opportunity (or need!) for such histrionics.

In those days, the hard men of the game revelled in the forename-nickname-surname combo: if there was a rough-house player called Joe Bloggs, he would be Joe 'I'll-tear-your-head-off' Bloggs, or John 'I-know-where-you-live' Smith. Messrs Bloggs and Smith may well be fictional characters of course, but there was nothing fictional, or subtle, about Norman 'Bite-your-legs' Hunter, or Ron 'Chopper' Harris.

So here is how it went: you are the nippy striker or the elegant midfielder, the likes of Hunter or Harris get clattered into you early doors, you are now a moaning heap who is loaded onto a stretcher and carried off in excruciating pain, the last thing you remember is the deep-throated chortle of the lumpy Neanderthal who has put you out of action for two or three weeks. Job done.

In short, Hunter and Harris were not the type of characters who would wear gloves and a snood when they took to the field. So when the two lined up against one another for Leeds United and Chelsea respectively in the 1970 FA Cup Final, it could have been predicted that trouble was in store. When you mix in those other shrinking violets Jack Charlton, Billy Bremner and Johnny Giles of Leeds; and the delicate wall-flowers Peter Osgood, David Webb and Eddie McCreadie of Chelsea; and then add a dash of the two teams' legendary mutual loathing of one another, you are in for an X-Rated spectacle – and so it proved.

The original game, on an unusually awful Wembley pitch, passed off without major incident; it finished 2–2 and prompted a replay (remember those?) at Old Trafford a few days' later. It was this second game that erupted into an orgy of violence. At times the ball seemed incidental and appeared to be used as an excuse for kicking out at an opponent or somebody launching himself bodily towards the enemy: Harris with a kick to the back of the knee on Eddie Gray; Charlton with a head-butt on Osgood; Hunter and Ian Hutchinson trading punches, were just a few of the lowlights, and all worthy today of red cards and multi-game bans.

A record television audience of almost 30 million people watched the replay (or should that be stared in open-mouthed disbelief at what they were witnessing?). The game should have come with a health warning, that simply read, 'Welcome to the 1970s'. (For the record, Chelsea won the game 2–1 and both teams incredibly finished with 11 players on the field).

Later that summer came my second memory, and this time it really was of the 'beautiful game'. The World Cup was being held in Mexico, England were defending the trophy they had won four years earlier, but it was the Pele-inspired Brazilians who were expected to pose the greatest threat.

My brother Mark and I had religiously saved up our Esso World Cup coin collection (every time Dad filled the car up) in the weeks leading up to the competition and our excitement reached its peak when, during the early stages of the tournament, our parents allowed us to stay up late and watch England's group game against Romania at our grandparents' house. Due to the time difference, the game was not due to kick off until around 11:00pm. Suitably attired in jim-jams, slippers and dressing gowns, we climbed on Nana and Pop's sofa and waited for the witching hour.

Not only was there the small-boys' excitement about the occasion, looking back there was something different – even magical – about watching football from abroad in those days. Whereas today, with HD and surround sound, you do not know if they are playing on the surface of the moon or in your back garden, it all looks the same. In the '70s it was different; the satellite feed gave the picture a slightly fuzzy, mystical appearance, while the commentator sounded as though he was on the phone in an outside karsy. Even the foreign players had an aura about them, coming from clubs with exotic names like River Plate and Vasco de Gama (nowadays they all seem to play for Wigan Athletic or Man City reserves).

The scene was therefore set. This was it: the satellite buzz on the telly, the dodgy commentator, England at the World Cup…

The next thing I remember was waking up the next morning having missed everything (apparently I had fallen asleep as the teams were coming out)! Worse still – my older brother had seen it all: Geoff Hurst scored the only goal – it was great; England played in a strip of light blue – *it* was great; we now only need to get results against either Brazil or Czechoslovakia to qualify for the next round. *Great.*

The tournament progressed, of course, and became probably the most memorable World Cup of all time: England's great game with Brazil (including Gordon Banks's

Tim Ward signs Stan Ternent in 1968.

save); the epic quarter-final against Germany; and the great Brazilians' triumph in the Final against Italy. That game signalled the end for Pele and many of his incredible colleagues; four years later in Germany, even Brazil had resorted to trying to kick their way to success – fortunately, football won the day when Johann Cruyff's Dutch side beat them in the latter stages of the competition.

Meanwhile, back at Brunton Park, Carlisle United were preparing to welcome the new decade by bolstering their squad with some significant signings.

Much had changed since the Third Division title was clinched in 1965; Alan Ashman had moved on to West Brom after almost taking Carlisle all the way to the top flight in 1967 (more of that later). Ashman was replaced by 'Gentleman Tim' Ward who – despite having Dick Young by his side – could not continue where Ashman had left off. The team began to slide during his 18-month reign and his position became virtually untenable in September 1968 when some smart-arse scaled the Brunton Park

fence the night before a game with Norwich City, and daubed 'WARD MUST GO,' on the pitch with creosote. Norwich hammered Carlisle 4–0 and Ward characteristically did the gentlemanly thing a week later and resigned with his team sitting at the bottom of the League.

Bob Stokoe was appointed manager following Ward's departure and had steadily set about changing the squad. As the 1970–71 season approached, '60s greats like Peter McConnell, Terry Caldwell, Tommy Passmoor, Joe Dean and Hughie McIlmoyle (who had returned to the club under Ward) had all been moved on, and

George McVitie.

others like Peter Garbutt, Tommy Murray and George McVitie would soon follow. In had come the likes of midfielder Frank Barton, defender Graham 'Tot' Winstanley, full-backs Derek Hemstead and Joe Davis, and star striker Bob Hatton. (Graham Winstanley was given a family nickname as a child and to this day – within the football fraternity – he is known affectionately as Tot.)

In the close season of 1970, Stokoe continued the transition by adding Bobby Owen; he was a decent forward player who had been at Manchester City during the great Lee/Bell/Summerbee period. Unable to displace some of his illustrious colleagues, Owen moved on, and the United manager broke the club record transfer fee by parting with £22,000 in order for him to partner Bob Hatton in the Blues' attack.

Dennis Martin meanwhile had broken Carlisle hearts the previous season when he inspired West Brom to overcome a first-leg deficit against the Cumbrians in the semi-final of the League Cup. Although gutted by the defeat, Stokoe appreciated the Scottish winger's contribution and acted quickly to bring him to Brunton Park when he found out Martin was available. Mike Sutton was brought in from Chester and Tom Clarke was also added to the squad as reserve goalkeeper to Allan Ross. With the whole club buoyed by a solid mid-table finish and the League Cup run of the previous season, there was an air of expectancy around Brunton Park as the 1970–71 season approached.

Changes were also taking place around the ground itself and one was a proposed Juvenile's Pen for under-14s at the Warwick Road End of the ground. This enclosure (or the Boys' Pen as it was to become known) was to be mine and Mark's first experience of live football. The enclosure itself had been proposed for safety reasons, as the 1970s seemed to signal the event of crowd trouble (as well as the aforementioned problems on the field). The intention was that it would protect under-14s from any violence that broke out on the terraces. Looking back now, it is difficult to understand the logic of such a decision as it was actually the Warwick Road End – known colloquially as 'the Warwick' where any Brunton Park-trouble occurred! But the addition of the Boys' Pen would give me and Mark the opportunity of seeing our local team in the flesh.

Following the World Cup, we were football barmy. Mam had helped us fulfil another ritual for all small boys by taking us to buy our first football strips. If you were a small boy from Carlisle this meant visiting the best sports shop in town: Chivers's tiny hole-in-wall shop on Annettwell Street. You went in with all of the excitement of Mr Benn visiting the costume store.

Once inside the floor always seemed to be covered in training-shoe boxes around which wandered Colin Chivers's giant Alsatian dog. It did not matter how obscure your request was – whether you wanted a deep sea diver's helmet or a shinty stick – Colin would disappear into the back room like David Attenborough entering the

Amazon jungle. 'I know I've got one in here somewhere,' you would hear him mumbling to himself as the dog continued to eye you up and down, out front. Sure enough, 10 minutes later, as if by magic, the shopkeeper appeared with exactly what you wanted. As was his custom, Colin would then always knock a bit off the price and off you went – another satisfied customer.

So once we were togged out, we would be there in the back garden impersonating our favourite players while commentating on the particular game we were acting out. It was not long now until we were to see the real thing – but there was to be a sting in the tail for me. Most football fans remember their first ever match. But, as usual, I am slightly different – I do not remember the first game I *attended*, but I do remember the first game I *missed*!

Fresh from our summer's initiation into the televised game, and with the new juvenile's facility available at Brunton Park, Dad was preparing to carry out the age-old dad-ritual of taking his children (boys mainly in those days) to their first game. And what a game it promised to be.

Carlisle had secured a series of friendly matches against various Scottish teams: Hearts, Motherwell – and most prestigious of all – three games against the mighty Glasgow Celtic.

Today, it seems fanciful to believe that either of the Old Firm could get to the latter stages of the Champions League (the successor to the European Cup). But in the late '60s Celtic were then a true giant of European football, having actually *won* the European Cup against Inter Milan in 1967. Their victory in Portugal – the first by any British team – still ranks as probably the greatest British triumph, as it was achieved with a team of local boys, all born within a 30-mile radius of Celtic Park; the team became known as the Lisbon Lions. Their manager was Jock Stein: a giant bear of a man, who was understandably respected and revered throughout the game. Stein was friends with Stokoe and this friendship had helped secure the series of games between the Cumbrians and the European giants.

Sadly, the first Carlisle/Celtic game – which took place on 20 January 1969 – had to be abandoned after 55 minutes; it had rained torrentially in the city all day and by the time of the kick-off, there was surface water all over the pitch. The teams did their best and even scored a goal apiece but no amount of half-time-pitch-forking could keep the persistent rain at bay. By the time the referee blew to call it off, the players were literally ankle deep in water.

Undeterred from this false start, the two teams lined up again on the eve of the 1969–70 season. During the close season Carlisle had signed a member of the Lisbon Lions' squad: Willie O'Neill played in the first four European ties of the 1966–67 campaign but lost his place for the Final to Jim Craig. O'Neill was given the honour of captaining Carlisle – who took to the field in their new all-red away kit – for the game against his former club. Incredibly, Carlisle won 1–0 with a goal from Tommy

Carlisle and Celtic players leave the field after the abandoned game in 1969.

Murray, who latched on to Chris Balderstone's pass, turned on a sixpence and bent a beautiful shot around 'keeper Tommy Simpson. The result was incredible for two reasons: firstly, the Celtic team that played that day contained no fewer than eight Lisbon Lions.

The second reason is even more surreal: lifelong Blues' fan and historian David Steele attended the game and recalls today how it was the only match he had ever attended at Brunton Park when the winning goal scored by the home team was greeted with complete silence! It is not known how many of the large crowd were Carlisle supporters but we can only assume there were not many!

The mighty Jock Stein was a winner and extremely successful throughout his career (yet always wore an expression that suggested his finger had just gone through the toilet paper); he gave a post-match interview, in which a journalist – apparently wanting to curry favour with the great man – suggested that the result probably did not matter '…as it was only a friendly.' Stein snapped his giant head round and glared at the young man: 'Glasgow Celtic don't *play* friendlies,' he growled. (It is unknown as to whether the young hack was ever seen or heard of again.)

And if anyone out there thinks that the result was due to the Celtic side being slightly on the wane it should be noted that Celtic not only won the Scottish League Title again at the end of the 1969–70 season, they also reached their second European Cup Final (losing 2–1 to Feyenoord of Holland).

So, having competed in the European Cup Final only a couple of months earlier, the mighty Hoops were due in town for the third game in the series on Monday 3 August 1970 and this was it for me and Mark – we were going to our first game and we could not wait. *Just one more sleep!*

Then disaster struck on the morning of the game: I came down with mumps! I have never established if parrots suffer from mumps but be assured, I was as sick as one that day. And worse still (yes, you have guessed it), Mark was fit and raring to go with Dad on his own. (I cannot remember if there was a six-year-old's word for 'bollocks', but let's just go with *drat*.)

The next morning, while I was sitting there with a face like Marlon Brando's in *The Godfather,* I kopped the lot: the atmosphere was great; the floodlights were great; Celtic were great; Carlisle were playing in a new away strip – white shirts, red shorts and red socks – it was great. (Older brothers eh – you've got to love 'em haven't you?)

In fairness to Mark, he had just witnessed another Carlisle classic from the period in question. Whereas the Glasgow giants admittedly fielded a side picked from all areas of the squad, the team still included a couple of European heroes, plus the cream of the new generation, Danny McGrain, Kenny Dalglish and Lou Macari. Also playing for Celtic that night was a young left-back called John Gorman. Gorman had signed for Celtic as a schoolboy and worked his way through the ranks to be part of the 1970 European Cup Final squad. Carlisle meanwhile gave debuts to their three outfield summer signings, Sutton, Owen and Martin.

The game itself turned out to be a goal-fest with Celts winger Jimmy Quinn opening the scoring after nine minutes. The Blues (or should that be the Whites) came roaring back at their more illustrious opponents with two goals from new-boy Bobby Owen to give the home side a half-time lead.

The second half saw Celtic assert their authority on the game with an equaliser from Lou Macari and two more from Jimmy Quinn to complete a hat-trick before the hour mark. With a late goal from Vic Davidson for good measure the Glaswegians had run out 5–2 winners.

A few weeks later and not long into the season, left-back Willie O'Neill injured his ankle so severely that it signalled the end of his career and Willie's Carlisle stay was over after only 15 games. Jock Stein moved to help his friend Bob Stokoe out and offered him the services of his young 21-year-old reserve left-back John Gorman for a fee of £12,500 as cover for fellow Scot and former Hibs' full-back, Joe Davis.

Gorman would go on to become a Carlisle-great, getting in most fans' all-time XI but if the player himself had anything to do with it, the move would have never happened in the first place.

'I didn't want to leave Celtic. I was 21 and fancied my chances of breaking through into the first team. I had been part of the European Cup Final squad and was a member of the outstanding reserve team we had in those days that included Kenny Dalglish, Lou Macari, Danny McGrain, David Hay, and Jimmy Quinn. I didn't want leave but was virtually forced into it.'

Gorman's frustration was compounded when he arrived in September 1970: he did not play for three months, while full-backs Derek Hemstead and Joe Davis held down regular berths. Then in a game away to Bristol City, Hemstead got injured and was not fit to play in the home game with Portsmouth the following week.

Stokoe approached Gorman and asked if he wanted to deputise at right-back. Strangely, despite him being naturally right footed, Gorman told the manager he had been signed as a left-back and that is where he wanted to play. The mild-mannered Joe Davis shrugged and said he would switch sides to allow Gorman to play. It was a fateful decision as Gorman had a storming debut against Pompey; the Blues ran out 6–0 winners, with Gorman marauding down the left and winger Tommy Murray doing the same down the right to set up goal after goal. Bobby Owen scored two and Bob Hatton helped himself to four in the rout.

Once Hemstead regained his fitness, it was poor Joe Davis who had to sit things out as young Gorman went from strength to strength.

These internal manoeuvrings were way beyond my levels of understanding of course. As a six-year-old kid, I did not realise there was any difference between a prestigious friendly against one of the best teams in Europe and a bread and butter League game; it was simply 'the live game experience' that got me hooked. Like Alice experiencing her adventures in wonderland, my impressions of this alien, adult world – intriguing and exciting; humorous and surreal – have stayed with me ever since.

The Boys' Pen itself (these were the days before the equalities agenda) was an enclosed area at the front, left hand side of the Warwick Road End. There were large railings that protected the area from the Warwick itself, where older lads and many a wannabe yobbo took up their place.

Dad used to take us to the entrance to the enclosure and see us safely into the ground and then he would go round to the Scratching Pen to meet up with a few of his pals. At the end of the game, he would leave a few minutes early in time to meet us after the final whistle at the Warwick Road entrance to the ground. In the enclosure itself, we often met up with a friend whose dad, Mr Brown, normally stood behind us on the other side of the railings in the Warwick Road End itself.

The first impression you got when walking into the ground was the immaculate playing surface – I know it is a cliché but it really was like a billiard table. There were then two pre-game rituals that I remember vividly: the first involved a convoy of turquoise coloured three wheeler disabled vehicles that, at around 10-to-three, would drive slowly along the black cinder path and manoeuvre their way – via a 10-point turn – into position facing the pitch in front of the Paddock. Once they were safely in place, it was time for Carlisle United's warm-up man to do his thing. (I remember Dad telling us to '…look out for Twinkletoes' and not really knowing what he meant.)

Long, long, long before Foxy, Carlisle's current mascot, (sorry kids, but it is actually a bloke in a giant fox suit), there was George 'Twinkletoes' Baxter, who was guy who

George 'Twinkletoes' Baxter.

must have been well in his sixties when *we* started going to the games. He was Carlisle's Mad Hatter (literally); resplendent as he was in a red, white and blue top hat and tails. Carrying a stuffed fox called Olga, he would scamper onto the field at five-to-three as though it was he, and *not* the white rabbit that was late. With his distinctive staccato strides, and the odd hop and skip for good measure, he would reach the centre spot, lay down Olga and wait for the teams to come out.

The home crowd would cheer in anticipation of the arrival of the players. But after a while, I started to wonder what the away fans made of it all: they had made the 300 mile journey into this footballing no-man's-land to see some bloke in a top hat race onto the field with a stuffed fox, as if he was being chased by his rolling-pin wielding missus. What the hell was this place? Was it some version of *It's a Knockout* with Carlisle playing their Joker at the start? Their hoots of derision at the appearance of Twinkletoes seemed to fire up both sets of fans, and it was time for kick-off (I later learned that the away supporters were continually suggesting that the home fans expressed an unnatural fondness towards sheep). Once the game started, things then got curiouser and curiouser.

At the scoring of the first goal at every game, it was then time for another Carlisle tradition. A mulletted youth was dispatched from the tunnel to walk around the ground with a long pole, at the top of which was a blackboard with the time of the goal chalked on it. Now this sounds like a fairly innocent practice but it seemed to me from the get-go there were at least four reasons why such a custom should have been halted.

If it was a Carlisle goal the board was displaying, the crowd were so excited that nobody really *cared* what time it had been scored, they were just pleased it *had* been scored. What was the point? (Come to think of it, what was the point of the whole exercise anyway – it was long before the days of the 'first goal lottery'?)

If it were raining, by the time the lad got round to the Scratching Pen, on the opposite side from the tunnel, the damn chalk had been washed off and the idiot was walking round with a blank board.

If another goal was scored in quick succession (while he was still walking around the ground), he had to get a lick on and get back to the tunnel for an update.

Finally, and most importantly, if the poor guy was displaying a goal scored by the visitors, he was invariably showered with missiles and various bodily fluids from the home supporters as he trudged round the cinder track.

(I have just thought of a fifth: while concentrating on avoiding the abuse and projectiles from the terraces, the unfortunate youth would occasionally receive a ball to the back of the head after it had been cleared to touch – much to the cheering amusement of the whole crowd. I do not know what they were paying the kid but it was not enough!)

Again, I have to ask, what was the point of this practice?

At the opposite end of the ground (the Waterworks End) stood a black scoreboard with letters on it. At half-time, a guy would climb up and hang numbers under the letters – they were the half-time scores from games being played elsewhere; you had to buy a programme to see which letter corresponded with which game.

At half-time they would play records over the tannoy. I say records (plural); it seemed as though the club purchased three records each season and played them over and over throughout the campaign. The 1970s selection was *In the Summer Time* (despite it quickly being in the winter time); *Back Home* (despite the fact that England had been back home from the World Cup for many months); and perhaps appropriately *Two Little Boys*.

Another thing that amazed me in those early days was a publication called the *Sports Special*. Newspaper sellers would appear all around the ground at about half-past-four to distribute the yellow-coloured newspaper for 3p. What was so unusual about that, you might ask (apart from the fact that it was only 3p). Well, what blew me away was the fact that on the front cover of the newspaper was a report and a photograph on the game you were actually watching! How did they do that? And why did people buy a newspaper to read someone else's opinion of what was taking place in front of them?

Other curiosities for this inquisitive six-year-old included the ritual, tribal chants and songs directed at the opposing fans by the aforementioned wannabe yobbos behind us in the Warwick; I was intrigued as to how this large section of noisy, aggressive humanity knew exactly when to commence the chant. Who thought the chants up, and who directed proceedings, I would think to myself. The chants would regularly contain words and meanings that I had not heard before, which in turn prompted me to check with Mark, my worldlywise eight-year-old brother; but he would normally give me an impatient, 'just watch the game,' in response. (I remember trying some of the chants myself when I got home, believing them to be quite catchy. Mam apparently disagreed – I can still taste the Palmolive to this day.)

But probably the thing that left the biggest impression on me during those childhood visits to The Brunt were the 'toilets'. (Let's just say that Armitage Shanks and Twyfords had not been consulted when the amenities were thought of.) A square, roofless breeze-block construction had been erected at the corner of the Warwick Road End and the Paddock. Inside the construction, around the edges were, what could only be described as gullies that were supposed to run into an underground drain (the operative words in that sentence were 'supposed to'). There were no cubicles.

Men from the Warwick and the Paddock, along with youngsters from the Boys' Pen would troop into the area and do what needed to be done. As you can imagine the scent that filled the air was an acquired taste and on a cold day, the air temperature could be guessed at from outside the construction by the steam that was rising from the inside.

As if the practice of having to take your turn in this vile enclosed space was not bad enough, something happened one afternoon that has lived with me ever since. Steeling myself for the uncomfortable ritual, I entered: there it was, in the corner of the block, for everyone to see...a large, steaming turd.

I stood looking at the thing (I am sure it was looking at me). It was like one of those monster-beings off *Dr Who*: slightly comical but still scary enough to give you the heebie-jeebies. Men and boys took great care to give it a wide berth. I could not believe it, someone had actually dropped his keks and dumped in the corner of the pen – or as my dad used to say 'had a razzermattazer' (I do not know why, but you know what dads are like). I suppose when you have to go, you have to go, but from that day to this, I attempted to avoid the place by not having any fizzy drinks before the game.

Although I cannot remember much about the results on the field in my first season, the history books tell us that the pre-season expectancy around the place, proved justified in the early weeks, with the Blues getting off to a solid start and picking up some momentum as autumn turned to winter. Then disaster struck on 1 December when a story broke that top-flight Blackpool had approached the board and asked for permission to speak with Bob Stokoe about their vacant manager's position. Blackpool had been promoted to the First Division the previous season, and as good a start as Carlisle had made in *their* division, the Seasiders had stuttered, stumbled then sunk to the bottom in *theirs*. The result was the inevitable dismissal of manager Les Shannon.

Blackpool received 25 applicants for the vacant position but they chose to ignore them all and approached the Cumbrians about *their* manager. Rumour had it that they had approached Carlisle earlier in the season and had received short shrift. Now, in December, they were back again. On the 2nd the United board broke their silence and confirmed that an enquiry had been received. The ambitious Stokoe had obviously indicated to his employers that he would welcome the opportunity to speak

Mr Chairman E.G. Sheffield.

to Blackpool, but chairman E.G. Sheffield was unequivocal in his statement to the press: 'We regretfully have to refuse to allow Mr Stokoe to terminate his contract that still has two years to run.'

When tracked down by the press, Stokoe gave a curt, 'I have no comment,' and promptly went for a day's golf at Powfoot.

The local newspapers suggested that was an end to the matter, but it continued to rumble on as the days went by. Things came to a head on 15 December when the club offered Stokoe a new, improved contract, worth £7,000 a year plus bonuses if the team won promotion or trophies. Stokoe turned it down and George Sheffield reported Blackpool to the Football League for an illegal approach to his manager. Illegal approach or not, the rift between the club and the manager was widening and by the 20th Stokoe was publicly adamant about his desire to leave the club. Two days before Christmas he called a press conference and informed the journalists present that, 'I desperately want away'.

Finally, on 29 December, Sheffield informed Stokoe and the press that after a two hour meeting, the board had agreed to release him from his contract: he was free to go.

Within a week of the acrimonious parting of the ways, Carlisle offered Ian MacFarlane his first managerial position, following coaching roles at Middlesbrough and Manchester City. The board had interviewed MacFarlane along with Lawrie McMenemy before giving the job to Stokoe upon Tim Ward's dismissal two years earlier. Reasonably impressed with MacFarlane's credentials, they installed him as manager as the New Year dawned.

To suggest MacFarlane was brusque in his manner is like saying Hitler was a little bit naughty. The big Scot had a fearsome reputation and a conversational vocabulary that was peppered with expletives, his no-nonsense approach was destined to ruffle feathers on and off the field.

Then on 2 March 1971 the Blues played their last money-spinning friendly against Celtic. The Hoops fielded a side that included Lisbon Lions' Jim Craig and Stevie Chalmers, as well as Dalglish, Macari and McGrain. The Carlisle side included John Gorman, who had played for the opposition in the first game in August – he was to be one of many stars on the night.

Skipper Chris Balderstone opened the scoring in the second minute and the tone was set for the evening. With Tot Winstanley outstanding in defence, Baldy started to dictate the game from central midfield. A minute before the break he sent a defence splitting pass inside Celtic full-back Jim Craig for John Gorman (playing on the left of midfield that night) to run on to; Gorman did not break stride as he rifled the ball into the net from a narrow angle; thus his first goal for Carlisle was against his old club.

There was no let up after the break and goals from Bobby Owen and Stan Webb put the finishing touches to an outstanding performance; a last minute effort from Vic Davidson could not dull the Cumbrians' achievement and the 4–1 victory proved a suitable antidote to the August-reversal.

As I continued to go to more games in those early days, I grew to love the likes of Baldy, Tot, Dennis Martin, Bob Hatton etc., but one player joined the club later in the year and gradually stood out above the others. He had long hair and all the fans seemed to give an extra cheer every time he got the ball. I learned that his name was Stan Bowles.

Stan's career started at Manchester City but his fiery temper and various off-field incidents resulted in him being sacked. One of his coaches at City was none other than Ian MacFarlane and when the big Scot became manager of Carlisle, he made a point of looking Bowles up who, after a spell with Bury, was playing at Crewe Alexander. It was October 1971.

Bob Hatton.

At the same time, clubs were starting to take notice of Blues' star striker Bob Hatton. Although Hatton had signed a new contract in the summer of 1970, significantly it contained a release clause that allowed him to leave if a favourable offer from a bigger club came in. Fifteen games into the season and, unknown to everyone, an offer did come in for Hatton from Birmingham City.

Bob scored in what turned out to be his last game for Carlisle in a victory at Luton; it was a much needed win after five consecutive defeats. MacFarlane knew he had to act quickly because Chris Balderstone had been put on the transfer list after becoming embroiled in a dispute with the club over appearances and wages, and knowing Hatton's days were numbered at Brunton Park, MacFarlane moved to try and secure the signing of Bowles from Crewe. The Alex were asking for in excess of £20,000 but Carlisle asked their fellow small-town colleagues for some leeway as far as the fee was concerned. After much toing and froing Carlisle bartered Crewe down to a niggardly £12,000. Bowles signed on the morning of 27 October 1971; on the same afternoon Carlisle sold Bob Hatton to Birmingham for a club record £80,000. (It was good business for Carlisle who had signed Hatton from Northampton Town for £9,000 in 1969.) Crewe manager Ernie Tagg was understandably furious and vowed never to do business with Carlisle United again.

A few months earlier, Carlisle had had their own acrimonious dispute with Blackpool over the Stokoe affair. Carlisle hated Blackpool, Crewe hated Carlisle – I suppose all is fair in love, war and football transfers.

Pleased with the business, MacFarlane set about bringing Bowles up to speed with how things were going to work by threatening to do all manner of unpleasant things with Stan's testicles if he did not conform. The player was already known for his gambling habits, and legend has it that the manager had the names and telephone numbers of every Bookmaker in Carlisle in his desk draw; if his star player was not where he should have been, when he should have been there, Big Ian (as Dick Young used to call him) would be on the phone threatening both the Bookie and the player. And as we all know, nothing focuses the mind more than

Dick Young prepares for another training session.

some big hairy-backed Scotsman threatening to rip your knackers off, and Stan (for the most part) did as he was told.

Bowles was ostensibly a left sided midfielder when he arrived but MacFarlane decided to stick him up front, without ever trying the new system in training. The move proved inspirational and Stan was a revelation in the role. Within six weeks of his arrival at the club, Bowles put in a display against the League-leaders (and eventual Champions) Norwich City that had the home fans drooling in anticipation of what was to come from the future England International. He ended the game waving the match ball in the air, while the crowd stood cheered his stunning hat-trick (one of his goals consisting of a sensational dribble through a dense huddle of yellow shirts before firing high into the net from an acute angle).

By the time we started going to the games, Stan had given the mighty Tottenham Hotspur an even mightier scare in the FA Cup some weeks earlier, when he inspired the Blues to a 1–1 draw (he scored the goal) at White Hart Lane. He was as popular with his teammates as he was with the fans. A laughing Allan Ross later recalled:

'He was a bloody pain, talk about vain! He believed he was the new George Best and acted like a multi-millionaire, throwing his money around like it was loose change. We all really liked him. He brought something really special to the club,

and he was an inspiration in the dressing room and suffered a lot of friendly abuse from the rest of the players. He took it in his stride and always had a smile on his face. It always seemed that he got more fan mail than most of us, he liked that a lot I think. I think when he went, we were all a bit saddened. He was class and could turn on a sixpence.'

'Do you think Stan will be playing today Dad?' we would ask in our excitement as we went to every game. How could Dad possibly know, but he always gave us the reassurance we were looking for.

Stan once told Carlisle's greatest supporter, Geoff Thomlinson that he relied on pure, natural instinct when he was on the field, 'I can't see without my contact lenses, not that that matters because I never look where I'm passing anyway – I just know when to pass and where to pass it to.' This natural gift was evident throughout his brief United career; although he only ever played 33 games for the club, thousands of fans would also include him in their all-time 11.

The last time I saw Stan play was in the last knockings of his career, when he turned out for Brentford at Brunton Park during the early 1980s.

In adulthood, I had gravitated to the Paddock on the west side of the ground. Two or three steps down in front of me regularly stood a guy who was built like the proverbial outdoor facility; this guy had a voice to match his giant frame and he liked nothing better, each week, than to give the opposition the benefit of his wisdom and perhaps even point out certain deficiencies in their play.

During this particular game (and I stress this was *during* the game, while the ball was in play), Stan had the ball on the Brentford right, about halfway inside the Carlisle half (and therefore just a few yards from where I was standing). Bowles had the ball under his right foot by the touchline, shielding it from the Carlisle full-back.

Suddenly our friend, two steps down, shouts out, 'All right Stanley? Nice to see you back!'

Stan looks up – the ball still in play under his foot – and replies, 'All right mate, nice to be back!'

Bloke on the terrace: 'Will you be gan to the Pagoda wid the lads tonight?' (referring to a then Carlisle nightclub).

Stan: 'No I'll have to be back on the bus with these lot,' (jerking a thumb over his shoulder).

With this (mid 'conversation'), he performed a double drag-back with the sole and instep of his right foot and nutmegged the Carlisle defender in the process; scampering down the touchline he crossed a beautifully flighted ball to the far post that had the rest of the defenders and the 'keeper scrambling across the goal. Fortunately for Carlisle, his own Brentford teammates were not on the same wavelength either, and his excellent ball was scrambled away. Stan jogged back along the touchline to halfway with the whole of the Paddock and the West Stand giving him a standing ovation. He gave the big guy in front the thumbs up and a wink as he went past.

I suppose this episode was a sign that Stan was getting old – if it were any other time during his career he would have probably dumped his Brentford teammates and taken up the offer of going to the Pagoda.

Stan Bowles – the main man.

GIANT-KILLINGS . . .

During Carlisle's assent, one of the great characteristics of the side was their ability to raise themselves two or three levels when it came to being drawn against their elders and betters in the domestic Cup competitions.

First evidence of this came in January 1968, when the Blues were drawn away to their not-so-near neighbours Newcastle United in the third round of the FA Cup. Although they were becoming established in the second tier of the League, this was considered a big step up in class against a top-flight Magpies' side who boasted Bryan 'Pop' Robson, Bobby Moncur, Welsh international centre-forward Wyn Davies, and Northern Ireland goalkeeper Ian McFaul in their ranks.

From the fans' point of view, the tie offered a great day out; a taste of the big time at a top flight ground that (thankfully) was not too far away. Tickets were snapped up as the day drew nearer; the anticipated 10,000 Cumbrians soon became 12,000, and on the Thursday before the game, it was estimated that 15,000 were to make the journey east.

This boded well for the players as, from their point of view, it promised not only potential glory on the field, but a considerable pay day off it. The players' basic wage was £25 a week, with £5 appearance money and £6–8 win bonus; but in the FA Cup there were 'crowd bonuses': the bigger the crowd, the bigger the bonus. In reality it meant each player earned an extra 10 bob for every 1,000 spectators over a gate of 5,000, and an extra pound for every thousand over 10,000.

In the Blues' dressing room, full-back Hugh Neil was the figures-man who worked out his and his teammates' bonuses. According to skipper Peter McConnell, Neil could '…tell you to the exact penny what you were going to be paid that week.'

A Cup upset looked a long way off three weeks prior to the game; star striker Hughie McIlmoyle was injured and was definitely out, while 'keeper Allan Ross was recovering from a broken wrist and was doubtful. Manager Tim Ward was in the process of buying Scunthorpe's top scorer and former England Youth International Frank Barton (who would go on to prove popular with the fans during his successful stint with Carlisle) but he was also unavailable as he was Cup-tied.

Ivor Broadis

A fortnight before the big game, former Carlisle player-manager-turned-journalist Ivor Broadis was going across to Newcastle to cover their League game with Nottingham Forest, on which he would be reporting in the following day's *Sunday Sun*. As Allan Ross was injured and missing from the Carlisle line-up that travelled to Birmingham City on the same day, Broadis offered to take the 'keeper across to watch the Magpies' game.

Once there, Ross bought a programme for a shilling; inside were pictures of the epic 3–3 Tyne/Wear derby that had taken place two weeks' earlier. Two of the pictures showed Newcastle's full-back and penalty specialist Ollie Burton slotting two spot-kicks. The pictures appeared to be mirror images of one another as Burton fired in, towards Jim Montgomery's right hand side of the goal in each image. Ivor looked over Rossy's shoulder and said, 'If you play here in a fortnight's time and they get a penalty, you'll know which way to dive!' The two laughed and thought no more about it.

Finally the day came and the city packed onto scores of trains, buses and cars for the 60-mile trek east. 'Carlisle Empties Due To Cup Fever!' cried the *Evening News*.

In Geordie-land meanwhile, fans and local media certainly saw the novelty in hosting their Cumbrian neighbours but did not see any cause for alarm, regarding the outcome of the game. Newcastle's love affair with the FA Cup dated back to the previous decade when they won the competition on three occasions (the manager Joe Harvey captained the team in the first two victories). This third-round encounter was viewed by many as a nice warm up for the later stages.

Footballers pre-game rituals have changed little over the decades: arrive at the ground, walk onto the pitch to get a feel of the place and generally kill whatever time remains until kick off. Hugh Neil killed the time by totting up what he and his teammates were going to make from the game – at 1:30pm it was announced that there were already 15,000 fans in the ground. McConnell noted that Neil was feverishly scribbling down the numbers before giving the rest of the team the thumbs up.

Most of those 15,000 were the travelling Carlisle fans. Among their number were my dad and his mates: lads from the building trade, car mechanics and postal workers – in short, a group of blokes not renowned for their subtlety or discretion. These were the days before the crowd violence of the 1970s demanded segregation in the grounds. Dad's group, therefore, were one of hundreds of pockets of Carlisle fans surrounded by the incoming Geordie hordes. The home fans cottoned on to the diminutive figure of Carlisle forward Tommy Murray, who – at 5ft 7in – was dwarfed by his teammates and the opposition as they wandered round the stadium; Dad recalls today that they were giving him '…plenty of stick'. (Murray had signed for Carlisle from Airdrie in

March 1967 and was a popular figure with the fans who appreciated his busy style and high work rate.)

The players disappeared down the tunnel for the final hour's preparation. Allan Ross had had the plaster removed from his broken wrist only 48 hours earlier; incredibly he was passed fit to play and took his place in the corner of the away dressing room.

At last it was game time and the players ran out to the deafening strains of *The Blaydon Races*. Even my dad acknowledged that Tommy Murray looked like a schoolboy among the adults, 'If he was at the head of the line coming out, you would have mistaken him for the mascot!' The Newcastle fans took great delight in giving poor old Tommy, and his supporters, merciless stick about his size and appearance.

By now the crowd had risen to a massive 56,550. With pound signs in his eyes Hugh Neil gathered his teammates together. The Carlisle fans responded with a roar as they saw their team get together in the classic 'let's-give-'em-what-for' pre-game huddle; little did they know that it was not a pep-talk from skipper McConnell that was taking place, but it was Neil telling his mates they had all earned an extra 50 quid!

The referee's whistle got the game under way and from the off, it did not disappoint. The home side had the first attack with winger Jackie Sinclair who pulled the ball back for Burton to send in a dangerous cross, but Blues' centre-half Peter Garbutt was there to head away; Carlisle were then on the offensive with left-back Terry Caldwell replying in kind, but the Newcastle 'keeper McFaul smothered at the feet of John Rudge who was deputising for the injured McIlmoyle.

Much to the home fans amusement, Tommy Murray wasted a good chance after six minutes when he latched on to a through ball from Chris Balderstone but hit his shot well wide.

Meanwhile, at the other end, Allan Ross had to come out to block a Wyn Davies shot but he looked on helplessly as the loose ball rebounded to Bryan Robson who cleverly lobbed the ball towards the empty goal, but the excellent Garbutt was again on hand to scamper back and clear the ball from under his own bar.

All of this occurred in the first 10 minutes but acted as the prelude to one of the game's defining moments; back it went to the other end of the field courtesy of a beautiful diagonal ball from George McVitie to his wing twin Frank Sharp. He sent in a first-time cross that caused a moment's hesitation between full-back Burton and centre-half Bobby Moncur; who was the blue jersey ghosting into the box but Tommy Murray who rose and glanced a header across the front of McFaul and inside the far post. Explosions of blue and white erupted like tiny bush fires among a forest of black and white. 'When we saw it was la'al Tommy Murray that had scored,' recalls Dad, with some hilarity, 'take what we give 'em around us'.

Back on the field, the goal served to fire up the home side who came at the Cumbrians with everything they could muster, only to find Allan Ross in inspired

Tommy Murray scores the winner at Newcastle in 1968.

form: a shot by Robson, a header from Davies and a couple of crosses dealt with from Sinclair saw the visitors safely through to half-time.

The second half began as the first had ended, with the Magpies on the attack; this time it was Sinclair who hammered a shot just over the bar. Carlisle were themselves determined to attack whenever possible and an excellent cross by McVitie (*who else?*) was met sweetly by Balderstone on the half-volley but his shot went just wide.

The end-to-end epic finally swung the underdogs' way with two incidents in the final quarter of the game. First, on 73 minutes, the stadium erupted as Ross was finally beaten, only for the home fans to look across and see that the linesman's flag was raised for offside. Then with 10 minutes to go – from another high ball into the Carlisle box – central defenders Gordon Marsland and Peter Garbutt were harshly adjudged to have fouled Wyn Davies in the air: penalty kick.

Ivor Broadis watched from the press box as Allan Ross stood on his goalline preparing to face Ollie Burton. The journalist and the goalkeeper were clearly thinking the same thing.

The silence that always precedes such a kick descended across the stadium, the shrill whistle pierced the winter's afternoon; Burton ran up hammered his shot towards his favourite side, Rossy later recalled:

'I remember seeing the pictures [of Burton's penalties] and knew which way I was going to go; I took a chance.'

Burton's penalty was a good effort but Ross flung himself across his line to beat it out by the foot of his right post; the alert McConnell raced in to the box and hammered away the rebound to safety. More blue and white cheering and a knowing smile in the press box.

Newcastle's last hurrah came with a corner, a couple of minutes from time, but it was the imperious Ross who took the ball off the giant Davies's head. At the final whistle, the Carlisle fans could not contain themselves and invaded the pitch to mob man-of-the-match Ross. Of course, Daley and his colleagues were magnanimous and gracious in victory.....*Yeah, right!* How they were not lynched by the black and white hoards as they took great delight in rubbing their hosts' noses in their defeat remains one of the great mysteries from the period. (Among the Newcastle throng was a young, disappointed 18-year-old called Bill Green. Little did he know that a few years later he would be captaining the side he was cursing that day.)

Peter McConnell recalled how many of the Newcastle players had been dismissive of Carlisle before the game, which '…compounded that when they stormed off the pitch, without shaking hands when the full-time whistle was blown.' The only player McConnell had any time for was Wyn Davies; despite being well-policed by the outstanding Peter Garbutt throughout the game, the big Welshman made a point of congratulating every Carlisle player before they went down the tunnel.

Tommy Murray obviously took great delight in the triumph; when interviewed afterwards he said, 'It gave me a great kick to score that goal. All the talk [before the game] about Davies and it was the smallest player on the field who scores the winner with his head!'

The following day, in his *Sunday Sun* match report, Ivor Broadis referred to his and Ross's visit to St James' Park a fortnight earlier, and the price of the programme bought by Ross that inadvertently helped the 'keeper. His headline read: 'One Shilling Costs Newcastle Thousands!'

The Newcastle game proved to be the one high spot of manager Tim Ward's brief reign in charge – before the year was out, he would leave the manager's job. He had succeeded the popular Alan Ashman and made some good signings during his 15 months (including bringing Hughie McIlmoyle back to the club) but struggled to take the club to the next level.

He was known to everyone as 'Gentleman Tim' and was considered by many to be far too nice to be a manager in the cut-throat world of football. Captain Peter McConnell later expressed some sympathy for Ward:

'He inherited a side on the downturn, which is always going to be difficult, because many of us were edging towards the wrong side of 30, and I don't think he had a big enough personality to cope with a bunch of characters like that. He just didn't carry the authority, and I don't think he enjoyed the man management side of things.'

Bob Stokoe

McConnell's assessment is given credence when it is considered that Ward left the management game completely after his spell with Carlisle.

In his place came former Bury, Charlton and Rochdale manager Bob Stokoe. Stokoe was destined to be loved, loathed and tolerated in equal measure by players, supporters and board members alike. But love him or hate him, there is little doubt that he could get the best out of his teams. There was no better example of this than when his Carlisle team embarked on the League Cup campaign of 1969–70.

By this time Stokoe was part-way through rebuilding the team: out (and not without some controversy) had gone the likes of Hughie McIlmoyle, skipper Peter McConnell and full-back Hugh Neil (Neil became a key member of Carlisle's backroom staff after ending his playing days); in had come characters like striker Bob Hatton, midfielder-cum-centre-half Stan Ternent and defenders Derek Hemstead and Graham 'Tot' Winstanley.

On Tuesday 14 October 1969, the team in transition found themselves hosting the mighty Chelsea in the fourth round of the League Cup. The Londoners boasted household names such as Peter Bonetti, John Hollins, David Webb and Peter Osgood (not to mention our old friend Ron 'Chopper' Harris). They came to Brunton Park as favourites to lift the trophy having beaten League Champions Leeds United in the previous round. (The two would, of course, meet again later that season, with dire consequences, in the FA Cup Final).

Any indication of a Cup upset seemed unlikely when, during a League game at Watford the week before, Carlisle's main striker Bob Hatton was injured and became a major doubt for the big game. The Blues were also without defensive stalwart Peter Garbutt. None of this deterred a crowd of 18,500, who turned up ready to cheer their lads on in another David and Goliath contest on a damp Carlisle night.

Sure enough, the night got off to a bad start when it was confirmed that Hatton had failed his fitness test and would be replaced by Willie Brown

Once the game started, things did not seem to be getting any better for the hosts. Chelsea won a corner on the right and the in-swinger caused some confusion in the Blues' defence; Tot Winstanley misjudged his leap and the ball fell invitingly to Alan Hudson who – surprised by the opportunity – pulled his shot just wide.

Following the early scare, Carlisle then followed their usual pattern in such games, by slowly growing into it: stringing a few passes together, getting the ball out wide, and getting at the opposition full-backs. No one was better at this than George McVitie who set about tormenting Chelsea hard-man Ron Harris down the right (not sure if that was your wisest ever decision George). Bonetti was tested to his fullest with a succession of teasing crosses.

As the game became stretched, Charlie Cooke found John Hollins at the other end but Winstanley made up for his earlier misjudgement by blocking the midfielder's shot and deflecting it away for a corner.

There then occurred one of the most shameful incidents that Brunton Park had ever witnessed. In the 27th minute a stone was thrown from the Warwick Road End and hit Peter Bonetti on the head. The Chelsea 'keeper went down badly hurt and all hell threatened to break loose. Police waded into the crowd and the perpetrator was identified and arrested. After several minutes the game resumed and it seemed as though it was the home team that were more affected by the incident – surely our homely, welcoming footballing outpost was not threatening to become a hostile hotbed of football hooliganism?

It was Peter Osgood that stirred the home team from their dumbfounded torpor when he cleverly found space, turned and shot but the ball was just off target. Carlisle managed to get through to half-time all square.

Whatever Stokoe said to them did the trick as they immediately grabbed the initiative in the second half. Terry Caldwell floated in a cross that caused all manner of confusion and just drifted beyond everyone; Chris Balderstone then lifted a ball into the box for Frank Barton but the midfielder had it whipped off his toe. Then a Balderstone corner was met sweetly by Willie Brown but Bonetti showed no ill-effects from the first half incident, and reminded everyone why he was nicknamed The Cat, as he leaped across his goalline to keep the header out.

At the other end Winstanley and Tommy Passmoor were marshalling their illustrious opponents well and when they did get through, Allan Ross was in his usual immaculate form – good saves from Hollins, Osgood and Birchenall kept the score all square.

Finally, on 74 minutes – the breakthrough. Willie Brown received the ball on the D of Chelsea's penalty area; he was fouled from behind by Harris (I know – hard to believe isn't it?). Balderstone and Hemstead stood over the ball – the wall formed; Brown, Barton and Stan Ternent took up their positions in the box. It was the dead-ball specialist Baldy who took the kick, chipping it into the box; the rather feeble effort was cleared but only as far as Hemstead who hammered a left-foot drive towards goal on the volley from 25 yards; the ball skidded on the wet surface just in front of Bonetti and squirted through his legs. The whole ground erupted into a deafening roar as the films of water that had settled on the netting exploded into the night air. Blue jerseys mobbed the full-back and their opponents (playing in their change kit of yellow) stood around in abject disbelief. (It was one of only two goals Derek scored for the club – but it was one that many fans remember with some delight.)

Tommy Murray replaced George McVitie and nearly doubled the lead with a glancing header, the likes of which had proved so successful at St James' Park 18 months earlier. But one-nil it remained and at the final whistle The Brunt erupted as London blue-bloods came a cropper, like a few before, and many after.

The reward for beating Chelsea was a fifth round tie away to Oxford. A decent travelling support saw their team earn a goalless draw, with the reply taking place at Brunton Park a week later. The second game proved every bit as tense as the first; with extra-time looming Chris Balderstone sent a long ball down the right for the fit-again Bob Hatton to chase. The Oxford centre-half came across to intercept but stumbled as he did so, leaving the striker through on goal; the crowd held their breath as Hatton knocked the ball around the 'keeper only to be brought down in a sprawling heap. Sixteen thousand appealed simultaneously and the referee duly obliged with that distinctive elongated blast on the whistle that always signals the inevitable spot-kick. Appeals gave way to euphoria and then to excruciating tension as the skipper Chris Balderstone stepped up to take responsibility (there are never any atheists in the crowd when there is a last-minute penalty in a football match). Baldy calmly slotted in the winner and the Blues were in a semi-final of a major competition for the first time in their history. In the semi, they found they had to slay another giant in the form of top flight West Bromwich Albion.

The night of Wednesday 19 November 1969 is an historic date in anyone's book: Carlisle took to the field against the West Midlanders (oh yes, I knew there was something else: Apollo 12 landed on the moon and astronaut Charles Conrad performed the second ever moonwalk).

Meanwhile, back on planet earth, The Brunt was jumping, the crowd was in excess of 20,000 and they were crammed into the ground to witness probably the biggest game since the Championship decider against Mansfield five years earlier. The West Brom manager knew what to expect, saying beforehand, 'Make no mistake, we are the underdogs. Carlisle relish playing clubs like us. They dismiss the big club reputation. We will have our work cut out to get a result at Brunton Park.'

Carlisle started the game to-the-manor-born, completely uninhibited by either their illustrious opponents, or the size of the prize that awaited the winners. George McVitie in particular set the tone by roasting Albion's skipper Graham Williams on several occasions early on. It was through McVitie that Carlisle's first chance came; his long cross was met by Balderstone and his shot squirmed through the hands of 'keeper John Osborne; as it dribbled excruciatingly towards the line, Williams just got back in time to clear away.

West Brom's only effort of note was thwarted by Allan Ross when he came out to block a shot from Tony Brown.

At the other end meanwhile, headers from Willie Brown and Tot Winstanley brought more '*ooohs*' from the home crowd, as did Bob Hatton when he trapped a Hemstead cross, swivelled on a sixpence and shot just over.

Five minutes before the interval, Balderstone unleashed a 25-yarder with the outside of the foot which bent away from the 'keeper, leaving Osborne clutching at thin air; he was saved when the ball crashed against the inside of the post before

Allan Ross clears his lines in the West Brom semi-final of 1970.

rebounding across the goalmouth – Carlisle's misfortune was compounded when Hatton raced in and lunged at the ball but missed by inches.

It only served to fire up the crowd even more, who, by the time the players emerged for the second half, were making an almighty racket. Despite the visitors having the wind advantage on this gusty night, United picked up where they had left off, constantly pressing the Albion goal.

On 67 minutes, Hatton went down under a duel challenge from Williams – the whole ground erupted as one, much as they had against Oxford in the previous round; this time, however, the referee waved away the appeals.

Albion brought on a stylish winger to see if he could make the difference. His name was Dennis Martin and the following summer he was to sign for Carlisle United and start an outstanding seven-year period with the club.

But on this night, it was Carlisle's current winger who was starring: George McVitie jinked his way for the umpteenth time and stood up a teasing cross towards the back post from the byline; Osborne duly played the part of the scampering goalkeeper who knows he has to go for a ball he is unlikely to get; to his credit he got a hand to it but could only palm it into the path of the onrushing Frank Barton who lashed the ball into the unguarded net. It is unrecorded as to whether Charles Conrad heard the roar that went up, but residents of Warwick Road had seldom heard such a din. It was matched by the commotion that greeted the final whistle; Carlisle United had played one of the top sides in the country off the park and – with the second leg to follow – were now only 90 minutes from Wembley.

If the West Brom tie was a footballing feast, one short month later, Carlisle were at it again; this time in a real muck-n-nettles caper against Nottingham Forest in the FA Cup third round. Like West Brom, their Midlands neighbours were a top flight side and before the decade was out (admittedly with a different team and manager) they would be European Champions.

It was Saturday 3 January 1970, when the Cumbrians made the journey south for the away tie. The country was gripped in a severe winter and in these days before under-soil heating, the City Ground pitch was part-frozen, part-boggy, depending on whether or not the winter sun had managed to peep over the top of the grandstands and thaw it out.

By this time Carlisle's giant-killing reputation was catching the eye of the Fleet Street journalists who were starting to follow the exploits of the small club. The game finished goalless but there was no doubting who the *Sunday Express* correspondent felt deserved the spoils – he wrote the following day:

'*Carlisle carried on as if the FA Cup were merely a logical successor to their League Cup conquest. They ripped into Forest, made the midfield their own, through Frank Barton and skipper Chris Balderstone and carved out most of the worthwhile goal chances.*'

The Blues (and especially the frugal board) must surely have been happy with a replay, due to take place three days later at Brunton Park. Forest manager Matt Gills did not appear to be too phased by the prospect either when he said in his pre-replay press conference, 'Little clubs get just one chance in the Cup, Carlisle fought well on Saturday but we'll fight harder tonight'. (Hmmm.)

By game time on the Tuesday night, it had snowed heavily and the pitch was thick, almost covering the players' boots. Playing conditions like this are virtually unheard of today but in decades past – without the modern-day state-of-the-art facilities and equipment – they were commonplace. The other feature of this particular game that you seldom see today was the necessity to use an orange ball! (Remember those?)

So the Brunton Park crowd were ready for all the fun of the fair when their heroes took to the field; and they did not disappoint. From the off, Carlisle outplayed their top-flight opponents, picking up the momentum they had built a few days before at the City Ground.

It was United's forward workhorse Bob Hatton who again set the tone in the first quarter of the game; during one of his forays he weaved his way between two defenders and curled a shot that the 'keeper Peter Grummitt could only parry to the edge of the box; for once the normally accurate Balderstone misshit a shot that was going wide until Tommy Murray diverted it into the unguarded net.

From then on it was Blues wide man George McVitie who dictated the pace, again giving top-flight defenders a torrid time; a square ball from him to Balderstone resulted in the skipper's curling shot going just over.

Just before the break, disaster struck for the East Midlands outfit: defender Terry Hennessey, under no pressure just short of the half-way line, turned and attempted a 40-yard back-pass. Inevitably, the ball held up in the snow and who else but McVitie nipped in and calmly slotted the ball past the advancing Grummitt. The second half was more of the same with the home side dominating and Tommy Murray almost added a third on 63 minutes with a trademark header from a Balderstone free kick. Forest grabbed a consolation towards the end but it proved too little too late, as the perennial giant-slayers had struck again.

'United Cut Forest Down to Size in Arctic Cup Replay', rejoiced the *Evening News*, the following night. The scale of Carlisle's triumph is measured by the fact that the defeat for Forest came in the middle of a seven-game unbeaten run in the League above the Cumbrians. Incredibly, it was Carlisle's first Cup replay victory since the preliminary rounds of the 1919–20 competition.

Will the next contestant step forward please?

Today, Manchester City is lauded as the world's richest club due to a bottomless pit of money their Far East owners possess. As these words are written, the modern-day City have just started on their adventure to surpass the achievements of their predecessors from the period in question, by winning the FA Cup and sitting on top of the Premier League. But whereas Manchester United founded their success in the late '60s on Best, Law and Charlton, Manchester City had their own Holy Trinity of Francis Lee, Mike Summerbee and Colin Bell. When you complement these three with the likes of Neil Young, 'keeper Joe Corrigan and central defender Tony Book, the club from Maine Road were a formidable outfit – if any confirmation of this were necessary, the League Championship (1968), FA Cup (1969), and both the League Cup and European Cup Winners' Cup (1970) provided it.

On 9 September 1970, City embarked on the defence of their League Cup with an away tie to you-know-who in the second round. It proved to be another epic that United fans would not forget in a hurry.

Bob Hatton had been struggling with injury in the week before the game but passed a late fitness test and took his place in the team alongside former City reserve team striker Bobby Owen. Due to the clash of colours, both teams took to the field in their second kits (as was traditional at the time): Carlisle in their 1970 all-white away kit, and City in their red and black stripes.

Perhaps it was United's Real Madrid-type kit that inspired them but from the get-go it seemed as though Carlisle believed the game was there for the taking. The two strikers combined after three minutes and forced City skipper Tony Book into a hasty interception and this set the tone for the evening.

On 12 minutes, skipper Chris Balderstone sent a precise, trademark cross ball to the unmarked Frank Barton but the attacking midfielder sent his shot over the top. From Corrigan's clearance, another white wave ensued, this time resulting in one of Carlisle's summer-signings, Dennis Martin, firing in a shot that the City 'keeper did well to turn over. In came Baldy, only for his shot to be scrambled behind for a repeat. The second effort fell to the feet of Martin again and this time he made no mistake in slamming the ball past Corrigan.

Carlisle were constantly giving City the hurry-up, and the best they could conjure up was the odd snap shots on the edge of the box; but efforts from Mike Doyle and Colin Bell were both dealt with well by Allan Ross. In the 25th minute came the visitors' best move with all three of their stars involved: Mike Summerbee crossed for Francis Lee to cushion the ball into the path of the onrushing Bell who hammered a shot just wide.

On the half hour, it was the home side going close again: Bobby Owen latched on to a back pass from Tony Towers, only to be thwarted by Corrigan who dived bravely at the ex-City man's feet.

There was a crescendo of noise from the home fans as the half-time whistle blew and the players walked off to a standing ovation.

After the break it was more of the same, with Carlisle dictating the pace. A Stan Ternent cross was headed behind by Towers; Corrigan was at full stretch to deny Hatton from the resulting corner.

But they do say form is temporary and class is permanent, and City showed this on the hour; a move down the left saw Bell and Lee combine and the England man got the better of the magnificent Winstanley for the one and only time in the game: 1–1.

Not that this phased Tot or his teammates – they simply continued as though the set-back had never occurred and moving into the last quarter of an hour, they got their just reward. Frank Barton fed Bob Hatton in the inside left channel. Hatton raced through the defence and as Corrigan advanced to cut down the angle, Hatton coolly waltzed round him and slotted the ball into the empty net. The Brunt exploded.

Almost 18,000 witnessed a performance that was unquestionably one of the best in this stellar period of the club's history. Then, as now, City were one of the top two or three teams in the country, and yet Carlisle controlled the game throughout and played with an authority that belied their status as a mid-table team in the second tier of the Football League. When City equalised, there was no panic, United simply reasserted their command on the game, which resulted deservedly in Hatton's winner. And even then, there was no question of a shaky last 10 minutes; United simply played the game out to its inevitable conclusion.

Manchester City's manager was Joe Mercer who was a real gentleman of the game. He was his usual magnanimous self afterwards, commenting of his conquerors with a smile, 'They were excellent, they really were'. (I wonder if his mind was cast back 20 years as he said it. Mercer was the Arsenal captain when the Gunners were given a fright by the Cumbrians in the legendary Cup tie of 1951.)

Given that 1970 was the first season Dad took Mark and I to Brunton Park, I suppose there is a fair chance we were at the City game although neither of us could swear to it (every game is an adventure at that age – they do tend to blur). The first big Cup upset I can remember vividly, therefore, came in 1973.

By then, Alan Ashman was back in charge and the FA Cup saw the Cumbrians drawn against Yorkshire opposition in the opening rounds. Huddersfield Town may have been the top club in the country under Herbert Chapman in the 1920s but 50 years later they were (like Carlisle) just another provincial club trying to make the best of what they had. The best of what they had unfortunately was not enough to trouble the Cumbrians who found themselves with a much harder prospect in the next round: hosting Sheffield United.

The Blades were a good top-half-of-the-table First Division side and would prove a tough test for Carlisle; a test that was made harder with the [cup-tied] absence of right-back Peter Carr (Carr had signed in December 1972 from Darlington) and the suspended front-man, Joe Laidlaw. Laidlaw would be replaced by Kenny Wilson, which should have given the Yorkshiremen even greater confidence. Instead, John Harris appeared to be talking down his team's chances as they prepared to make the journey north actually commenting in one press conference that they 'feared' the away tie.

The Sheffield team contained 'keeper Tom McAllister and Alan Woodward, but their star man was Tony Currie. With his looks, his long blond hair and with a charisma to match, he was the archetypal glamour footballer of the early 1970s. This, of course, also made him the natural hate figure for the opposing fans, and the Carlisle fans duly played their part.

Carlisle wasted no time in getting stuck into their illustrious opponents. The classic Blues trio of Ray Train, Chris Balderstone and Les O'Neill immediately got hold of the midfield as the home team took the initiative. Sadly for the home team, their main striker on the day was the aforementioned Kenny Wilson and – much to the groans of the home supporters – the Scot contrived to waste no fewer than three good chances.

Against top flight opposition this should have proved fatal but Wilson's teammates were undeterred. Before the crowd began to fear the worst following the striker's profligacy, Balderstone received the ball out wide and dummied his full-back; the typical inch-perfect Baldy-cross was met by the head of Dennis Martin; Tom McAlister dived to his right and apparently shovelled the ball away but the explosion of noise from the excited crowd at the Waterworks' End and Martin's appeal to the linesman were rewarded when the officials confirmed the ball had gone over the line. The place erupted.

The Blades came back into the game and created a couple of good chances but they were wasted. Their frustration was compounded when Currie was booked for a foul on Ray Train; the football crowd duly played their part and turned into a pantomime audience, mercilessly berating the villain (the best I could come up with was '*Get your 'air cut!*' Be fair, I was only eight).

The Blues were bordering on 'comfortable' at half-time but all of the good work was undone in the 52nd minute when centre-half Brian Tiler under hit a back pass and Blades front-man Bill Deardon nipped in to equalise. Typical Carlisle of the period, the lads simply took the setback in their stride and took the game back to the favourites.

On 75 minutes Les O'Neill hammered in a shot from the edge of the box that was well tipped over by McAllister. From the resultant Balderstone corner, there developed the mother-and-father of all goalmouth scrambles. It seemed Allan Ross was the only player on the field not to be involved in the scram-ally (another Dadism by the way); the ball ping-ponged about: the defenders unable to clear, and the attackers unable to force it home. After what must have been 30 seconds of mayhem, O'Neill again managed to get a shot off, only for it to be blocked on the line; the ball skewed away between the far post and the six yard line; two Sheffield defenders lunged at it, as did Carlisle utility-man Bob Delgado; he not only got there first but his connection was sweet and the ball flew into the back of the net.

We all went bananas – it all took place in front of us at the Warwick Road End. I can still see Delgado leaping for joy with his arms in the air and his heels in the small of his back. At the final whistle the crowd spilled on to the pitch and mobbed the hero of the hour. *Another classic!*

. . . AND NEAR MISSES

When Carlisle were not actually *slaying* the giant, they were giving him a damn good run for his money. The first near miss that I choose to record, however, was not actually on the field of play but off it.

We know today that all of the big stadiums are all-seater. This is because of the tragedy that occurred at Hillsborough, Sheffield in an FA Cup semi-final in 1989 when a combination of overcrowding, bad decision-making and fans being fenced in (due to the hooliganism that was rife in the '70s and '80s) cost the lives of 96 Liverpool supporters. If the event was not tragic enough, what made it more so is that this sort of disaster (admittedly not on such a scale) had happened all over the world far too frequently in the decades prior (as far as Britain was concerned, most notably at Ibrox Park, Glasgow and Burnden Park, Bolton). Fortunately Carlisle United and Brunton Park were not part of that fateful list – but only just.

After beating Newcastle United in the third round of the FA Cup in 1968, they drew Everton at home in the next round; another big crowd shoe-horned itself inside Brunton Park in anticipation of another David and Goliath encounter.

There were so many fans in the Warwick Road End that some had hauled themselves out of the throng and clambered up the side of the covered end. Scores of supporters could be seen clinging on to the side of the corrugated structure as the game got under way.

The Toffees (containing World Cup winners Alan Ball and Ray Wilson) made a good start and took an early lead through Joe Royle; but as usual the home side came back into things, started to get into their stride and press their illustrious opponents.

As Carlisle worked a move down the right hand side, there was some excitement, and then confusion in the packed Warwick. The crowd surged forward and the rickety old fence that segregated the fans from the pitch collapsed. As those pressed up against the fence fell forward, hundreds behind lost their balance, causing a domino effect, with people – now helpless on the ground – in danger of being crushed.

The players closest to the incident instinctively stopped playing and the referee immediately responded by halting the game. As the police and ambulance-men raced

A packed Warwick Road End shorty before it collapse during the Everton game in 1968.

across to help the injured, players stood in horror at what was taking place before their eyes. Carlisle captain Peter McConnell gave an eye-witness account and described the heroics of one of his teammates:

> '*Suddenly there were people and falling bodies everywhere. There were lots of shouts and screams, and you could clearly see the fear and panic on some of the faces right at the front of the crowd. We all wanted to help, but there didn't seem to be much that we could do. Then I saw Tommy Passmoor pushing his way through some of those who were stumbling around at the front. There were some, who had managed to pick themselves up, and they were obviously trying their best to get clear, but Tommy was ignoring this as he seemed to have his eye on one particular area. He then bent down, and I was stunned when I saw him reappear with a tiny girl in his arms. The poor little thing was screaming, terrified, and I have absolutely no doubt that she would have been badly injured, or possibly worse, had Tommy not reacted as quickly as he did.*'

Many people were carried away on stretchers and taken to the Cumberland Infirmary but thankfully – due to the actions of the emergency services, Tommy and the players – there were no fatalities.

This all puts football into a certain perspective; Bill Shankly's '…more important than life and death' quote may have made good copy at the time but in reality it is somewhat different. It *is* only a game, albeit one that excites, depresses and generally drives us all nuts in equal measure.

But all of this is to digress; let's get the ball out again. No doubt readers are wondering what happened to the second leg of the League Cup semi-final against West Brom? Well the fact that it is covered in this chapter and not in the last rather gives the game away but for the record, here is how things panned out.

If you remember, the Blues were one-up after the first leg and the whole city was gearing up for a trip to Wembley. My dad and his mates – having been present, of course, for the first leg – got hold of a tranny van and set off on the 200 mile journey south, along with 5,000 other Carlisle fans to see if the lads could clinch the trip to the Twin Towers. They made up a crowd in excess of 30,000 on the night.

The first half began as the first leg had finished – with the underdogs on top; completely uninhibited by their opponents, their surroundings, or a gate that was three times bigger than the one they were used to, Carlisle took the game to West Brom in an effort to assert their authority on the tie.

The game – and the tie – turned on two incidents, either side of the interval, and both involved United striker Bob Hatton. First from a corner, through his terrific movement in the box, Hatton lost his marker and powered a header on target; fortunately for the home side, their full-back on the line managed to block the effort and scramble it away.

If that was not close enough, three minutes into the second half came the defining moment of the semi-final. Hatton, who had worked the channels superbly against such experienced defenders, received the ball, about 25 yards out; jinking inside he hammered a right foot shot that had 'keeper John Osborne beaten all ends up; the ball slapped against the inside of the post and agonisingly rolled back along the goalline before it was cleared to safety.

Then on 53 minutes, West Brom finally got the foothold they had been hoping for in the previous 142. Allan Ross came out to challenge for a high ball with Albion striker Geoff Astle; the ball broke to winger Bobby Hope, who hammered in the first goal of the evening, which tied the scores up on aggregate. Ten minutes later and the home side worked the ball down their right and the low cross was turned in by Colin Suggett at the near post. Four minutes later and the tie had gone: Ross was penalised for taking more than four steps in his area (another old rule that does not exist today). From the resultant indirect free kick – with the Carlisle players crammed on their own goalline – Astle touched the ball to Tony Brown who hammered it; sadly for Carlisle, it found its way through the blue wall. Suddenly, from nowhere, it was 3–1.

Both sides made substitutions: striker Tommy Murray came on for Stan Ternent, but it was the Albion substitute who would make the difference and take the game away from Carlisle with a fourth goal. Dennis Martin would sign for Carlisle months after this game but on this night, he put his future employers to the sword with the Baggies' final goal.

In the space of just 19 minutes, West Brom had completely turned things around. The 5,000 Cumbrians were now feeding off scraps and all they had to cheer was a late consolation from Frank Barton. They trudged away from the Hawthorns that night towards their cars, trains and tranny vans, dreaming of what might have been. 'Probably just as well,' bemoaned one of my dad's mates, 'we'd have probably got hammered in the Final anyway.' (You can't beat the spirit of your average football fan, can you?)

So the favourites went through after all, as expected. Oh, and by the way, there was another thing: West Brom's manager who knew a thing or two about his opponents – which is why he was so complimentary and wary about them – was none other than Carlisle-legend Alan Ashman.

The following season saw the Blues make a solid start to the League campaign but by Christmas the manager Bob Stokoe had departed for Blackpool. Less than a month into his reign, therefore, the new manager Ian MacFarlane found himself with a plumb of a FA Cup third-round tie at home to Tottenham Hotspur.

Twenty-six minutes into another epic, the Carlisle fans erupted as their heroes threatened to punch above their weight once more. Bob Hatton won the ball in the air and controlled his header for his forward-running striking partner; Bobby Owen delayed his pass beautifully for Dennis Martin, who slipped through on the goal side of Spurs full-back Joe Kinnear and slotted the ball past the great Pat Jennings.

The game then exploded in controversy five minutes before the break. With the Blues looking as though they were going in at half-time with a deserved lead, the visitors mounted an attack through a diagonal ball from winger Jimmy Neighbour. Both Martin Peters and Allan Gilzean seemed well offside but to the home team's (and their fans') incredulity, Gilzean headed the ball in with Allan Ross (and everybody else) waiting for the referee's whistle. It blew alright but to signal the goal and not the expected free kick. The Carlisle players mobbed the referee and he was persuaded to consult his linesman; one of those classic breath-holding silent conversations took place that every football fan is familiar with. The goal stood – *there was uproar!*

From the restart, Spurs won the ball in midfield and again played the ball forward quickly. Peters went in and appeared to impede Ross; the ball broke and the World Cup winner bundled it into the empty net. Ross appealed that he had been fouled, but again the referee allowed the goal. The place went mad – from being 1–0 up and cruising, Carlisle went in at half-time 2–1 down after conceding two questionable goals within the space of 60 seconds. The ref got dog's abuse as he left the field.

Undeterred, Carlisle cleared their heads during the break and came out determined to pick up the pace they had shown for the first 40 minutes. Within two minutes Dennis Martin chipped the ball into the opposition area and there was Bobby Owen to calmly control the ball and slam it past Jennings.

United were superb for 75 minutes until the top flight side finally seemed to get to grips with the game. Their stamina ended up winning the day when, in the last quarter

Tottenham Cup tie at Brunton Park in 1971.

of the game, Jimmy Neighbour converted one of a succession of chances – it proved to be the winner.

One year on. Same competition, same round, same opposition; the only difference was that this time it was away at White Hart Lane. This provided an excuse to treat everyone at the club to a mini-break in London. For good measure, it was decided to invite descendants of John Peel's family to accompany the party, and if that was not enough, the Blencathra Hounds were loaded into the back of a land rover and off they all went down the M6.

A photographer from the *London Evening Standard* caught up with the 'hicks from the sticks' at the Alexandra National Hotel at Finsbury Park. Fascinated by the hounds, he spent two hours trying to get the perfect picture of them and the team in the car park of the hotel while bemused guests looked on.

When it came to the game the following day, the hounds were paraded around the pitch as 'D'ye Ken John Peel' rang out over the tannoy from our magnanimous hosts. (What the home fans made of it all is a mystery – perhaps they were inwardly musing over Cumbrians' affection towards animals again. *Can't see it myself.*)

Once the game started the players did not disappoint – even topping the performance against their illustrious opponents 12 months earlier.

Tot Winstanley was magnificent against the likes of Martin Chivers and Allan Gilzean; due to a couple of injuries, his central defensive partner that day was striker Bobby Owen, while at the other end Stan Bowles was in his element. Tot recalls the game vividly:

> *'Bobby was absolutely great [in the makeshift role]. He was calmer in our box as a defender than he usually was in the opposition box as a striker! Bowlesy was unbelievable that day – they couldn't get the ball off him. He ran the show from start to finish.'*

One of the great characteristics of United from this period was their self belief and a determination never to be knocked off their stride. They had displayed it in the game with Spurs the previous season; they were now displaying it again in this tie. Allan Gilzean had bundled the ball in, against the run of play, after a goalmouth scramble in the first half. Undeterred, the Blues fought back and Jennings was called upon to leap full stretch to tip over from a Martin header after Bowles had beautifully flighted a ball perfectly onto the forward's head. The same two then combined only to see the latter's shot go just wide.

At the other end, Blues' full-backs were snuffing out the danger from Spurs wide men Jimmy Neighbour and Ralph Coates.

Let me digress a moment to say a few words about the latter of these two. It has to be stated up front that Ralph was a terrific player (you did not play for teams like Burnley and Tottenham without being one) and he duly received a couple of well-earned England caps before his career was over. But he was distinctive character for two other reasons: first, he was probably the only top flight player before or since called Ralph; and second – and more importantly – he had the mother and father of all comb-overs, which sadly often distracted you from his considerable talent. It was never established whether he invariably got the better of his opposing full-back through his fleet-footedness and trickery, or whether the poor guy could not play for laughing at Ralph's dodgy barnet.

As far as hairdos go, the period covered in this book starts with the good old fashioned, post-national service, short back and sides. Once the sixties started swinging, however, the Beatles-inspired Mop-head came into being; then it was the turn of the Mullet which signalled the start of the seventies, before the daring, androgynous Perm took hold. But for pure, unadulterated comedic value, nothing could quite match... *The Coates.*

I concede fully that when the players lined up in late July for their pre-season photos, Ralph invariably looked okay; if you got your hands on a Ralph Coates Soccer Stars sticker, you would see his well-groomed auburn locks making him look every bit the self-assured elite sportsman. Alas, it was all an elaborate ruse – it turns out that Ralph had done a wrap-around job that any Sikh male would have been proud of. Twenty minutes into every game – once Ralph has sweated up a bit – the auburn locks would unravel and morph into something that resembled an unsightly lasso that dangled ungainly from the side of his head. If the full-back entered into a foot race with the Spurs winger, he risked being clothes-lined by the offending accessory.

On this occasion thankfully, Carlisle full-backs John Gorman (who would eventually sign for Spurs in 1976) and Derek Hemstead managed to control the player, his secret weapon, and their wing-twin neighbour throughout the first period. As the half wore on, Carlisle became stronger and their growing confidence culminated in a superb equaliser.

The players and the Blencathra Hounds prepare to take on Spurs in 1972.

Martin threaded an inch-perfect pass through to the skipper Balderstone who delivered a signature chip forward to the magnificent Bowles who pivoted with an amazing balance and shot inside the post while defenders and 'keeper were rooted to the spot.

The second half was more of the same with Carlisle dominating and earning a well-deserved replay. Spurs boss Bill Nicholson described Bowles as '…a great player' after his display.

The third game with Tottenham in the space of a year did much for the coffers at Brunton Park. By the end of the '72 replay, Spurs must have been hoping to avoid the Cumbrians in any future Cup competitions. They got through it – but only just.

Carlisle picked up on the Tuesday, where they had left off on the Saturday. Balderstone and Martin both worked Jennings hard in the first half before Stan the man struck again, turning in a half-cleared corner from Balderstone. Bowles was again outstanding throughout and, after Chivers had equalised, went on a mazy dribble, beating Mike England and the sprawling Joe Kinnear in the process; his curling shot left Jennings clutching mid air but cruelly hit the bar and bounced clear.

With echoes of their previous encounters, Spurs again scored against the run of play with the Scottish centre-forward Gilzean again converting, just before half-time.

After the break, the home side could not convert their intense pressure into goals. Camped in the Spurs area with corner after corner, the team of internationals

God knows what they made of it all!

resorted to pushing and obstructing the blue waves. This only resulted in corners being turned into free kicks around the box.

There was definitely another goal in the game: unfortunately for Carlisle – as with the game a year earlier – it was the stronger team that got it. Martin Chivers scored the clincher 20 minutes from time to finally put the Cumbrians in their place, although the 3–1 scoreline did scant justice to the underdogs' efforts over the two matches.

This tie catapulted Stan Bowles into the national spotlight and subsequent League performances during the latter half of the 1971–72 season raised his stock still further; by season's end, many top flight clubs were rumoured to be watching Bowles. When his mentor and advisor (not to mention testicle rearranger) Ian MacFarlane was dismissed as manager and replaced with Alan Ashman, Bowles's exit from the club came a step nearer. Carlisle turned down a £100,000 bid from Crystal Palace for his services but it was now only a matter of time. Ashman later confided that, 'I never really liked footballers like Stan Bowles. He was a maverick and didn't conform well to discipline. They are fantastic entertainers, but lack consistency and aren't really the team players we need.'

Ian MacFarlane.

Stan's last game for the club was another giant-killing attempt: six games into the 1972–73 season, the Blues were drawn at home in the second round of the League Cup against Liverpool. The Merseysiders boasted the awesome strike partnership of Kevin Keegan and John Toshack. No surprises then, in the first half, when Liverpool turned defence into attack and their front line combined to set up Toshack who shot at goal; Rossy could only parry and there was Keegan nipping in with what my dad would call 'a snibber's goal'.

Typical of Carlisle as back they came: Bowles and Dennis Martin forced top class saves from the reserve 'keeper Frank Lane, before the break. *At* the break, Ashman withdrew Bowles, who had a slight hamstring, and replaced him with Les O'Neill. It was a significant substitution as it confirmed Ashman's later admission that he was more likely to trust the combative team play of the likes of an O'Neill over the mercurial talents of a Bowles. Although both players would ultimately be remembered quite rightly as Carlisle greats, they were very different in their approach.

Les O'Neill had been tracked by former manager Ian MacFarlane for a couple of years before the big Scot captured his signature for Carlisle shortly before he was sacked. (Les recalls with irony, that he never played a game for the manager who signed him. Even today, whenever he sees MacFarlane in their footballing circles, the big man still shouts across the room – much to his own amusement and Les's embarrassment – '*Hey wee-man! You got the fucking sack at Carlisle!*')

As he had failed to sign O'Neill on previous occasions, and little knowing that he was to get the opportunity again, MacFarlane signed a similar type of player in 1971. Ray Train had started his career at Walsall and came further north for £5,000.

Allan Ross saves Tommy Smith's penalty at Anfield in 1972.

On the occasion of the Liverpool game, O'Neill was sent on to buttress the midfield further, *alongside* his fellow workhorse Train and give greater protection to the outstanding Stan Ternent at the back.

The tactical change worked perfectly and Ashman's decision was vindicated when, 20 minutes from time, O'Neill stormed through the Liverpool defence, drew the 'keeper and delicately chipped the ball over the advancing Lane (maybe not so different from Bowles after all!) to earn a draw and a replay at Anfield. As the old saying goes, 'the crowd went wild.' Les remembers the game as being quite significant:

'Bowles was a fantastic player. There was a different style of play – MacFarlane was happy for guys like Bowlesy and Baldy to express themselves but Alan wanted the team to be solid with a couple of players holding things together (me and Ray). Having said that it sort of happened by accident with Stan's injury.'

The crowd also went wild a few days later when it was announced that the club had accepted a bid of £110,000 from Queen's Park Rangers for Stan Bowles. His short, 10-month spell at Carlisle was over – but what a spell it was! (Bowles inspired QPR to promotion at the end of the 1972–73 season. One of their many victories came at Brunton Park and, yes, you have guessed it, Stan was on the score sheet in their 3–1 win.)

The replay with Liverpool was probably the only time during this period that Carlisle United were firmly put in their place: the Blues skulked away from Anfield having been hammered 5–1, but even then, Allan Ross enhanced his reputation by saving Tommy Smith's penalty on 70 minutes.

Undaunted by the Liverpool defeat, the Blues were soon to pick themselves up as the New Year brought the FA Cup and more contestants who were forced to attempt the Total Wipeout course that was Brunton Park.

In the fourth round, Carlisle overcame top flight Sheffield United to reach the last 16 for only the third time in their history. Their reward for beating the Blades was (for this youngster at least) the biggest prize of all: a home tie against First Division League-leaders Arsenal. My everyday team were about to play my glamour/fantasy team (I did well not to wet myself when the draw was made).

Less than two seasons earlier, Arsenal had become only the second team in the 20th century to complete the League and FA Cup double. I remember the Cup Final against Liverpool vividly – when Steve Heighway scored the first goal of the game I burst into tears (some things never change!). But fortunately for me the Gunners came back to win 2–1 and I was out in the back garden again ('…John Radford…to Charlie George…it's there! …what a goal!' *Again* – some things never change!).

Eighteen months on and if anything Arsenal were a better team with World Cup winner Alan Ball replacing George Graham in midfield, after his move from Everton the previous year.

A typical Arsenal/Old Etonian quote came from manager Bertie Mee when he said ahead of the game, 'Obviously one would prefer a home draw. I understand they are a hard team to beat on their ground, but we shall do our best.' They would need to – by this time Carlisle United did not respect reputations and frankly, fancied their chances against anyone.

Because the game would naturally be all-ticket, clubs like Carlisle had a 'voucher scheme' that drew fans into as many games as possible before the big one: if you had voucher(s) from attending these games, you got the first opportunity to buy a ticket for the big game. (Sneaky, eh?)

It did not matter to us much because Dad took us to every game anyway. For the record, on this occasion, there was only one home game between the Sheffield and Arsenal ties; it was against Burnley. We turned up and I duly got my voucher. Oblivious to those around me I wandered into the ground holding it; staring at it. I felt like Charlie Bucket when he discovered he had a golden ticket for Willie Wonker's Chocolate Factory. (And remember, this was not a *ticket*, it was just the voucher that enabled you to *get* a ticket.)

Ordinarily, this would have been (and actually *was*) a big, exciting game in its own right. Burnley were top of the League and would eventually go up as champions, but I stood there for most of the game like a glazed imbecile, wondering what the ticket would look like, and then what the game would be like. But wait a minute! What if something goes wrong? What if the match is postponed? What if I get mumps again on the morning of the game? What happens if someone decides they made a mistake at the draw and it's actually Accrington Stanley we are playing? What happens if aliens invade?

With mumps, Accrington Stanley, aliens, and various other reasons for postponement all jostling like impatient queue-jumpers for attention in my twisted mind, I was lurched from my near panic attack by Dennis Martin who equalised for Carlisle four minutes from time, after the Blues had fallen behind to an early Martin Dobson goal (not that I had taken much notice). Normally, a gate of under 10,000 would have cheered the equaliser; but on this occasion, almost 18,000 waved their vouchers in the air. The game finished 1–1 (if I am honest, on this occasion, it could have been 10–0 either way, I do not think I would have minded).

The day arrived – no mumps, no aliens, no Accrington Stanley. It was real and it was about to happen. In a way, it was as though history was repeating itself: as a 12-year-old boy, my dad had made the trip down to Highbury with *his* dad when Bill Shankly's Carlisle were drawn away to the Gunners in 1951. I cannot remember how many times since I have asked him to retell the story of his great adventure and the subsequent replay, but on 24 February 1973, it was my turn to get a bit of the Carlisle/Arsenal magic.

The task facing Carlisle in 1951 was enormous; in 1973 it was not much easier: Arsenal were not only top of the League, but they had only lost one of their last 21 Cup ties – and even that was in the FA Cup Final of the previous season to Leeds. They were bidding to become the first team in the 20th century to reach three consecutive Finals.

That did not deter the upset-hunters however: the *Daily Mail* correspondent was virtually licking his lips in anticipation as he wrote:

'Cup giant-killers Carlisle, skilful and sure-footed, showed last week that they are ready to add the First Division leaders' head to those already buried in their now famous graveyard.'

To put the icing on the cake, BBC's *Match of the Day* obviously fancied an upset as their cameras were sent to Brunton Park for the first time ever to cover the game (*Yey!*).

Pre-game the atmosphere was electric – 24,000 fans crammed in to The Brunt. The teams took to the field – I was mesmerised. Arsenal's red and white jerseys looked redder and whiter than on the telly; I was completely star-struck and their players (my favourite was John Radford) looked enormous in real life. How could these little blokes from Carlisle possibly cope?

Almost immediately, there was hesitation in the Blues' defence and Pat Rice and Peter Storey combined to set up Alan Ball, who duly scored for Arsenal at the Waterworks End. The history books state that the goal came after six minutes; I swear to this day, I have no idea what happened to the first five minutes, 30 seconds – it seemed to me like their first attack. This was juggernauts versus hedgehogs – *it is going to be a massacre!*

But typical Carlisle – the hedgehogs started to dodge the oncoming convoy, string a few passes together, get a bit of confidence, even create a couple of chances.

As the half went on the United midfield of Chris Balderstone, Les O'Neill and Ray Train gradually got a grip of the game, while front-man Joe Laidlaw (who had signed from Middlesbrough during the close season) started to cause Frank McLintock and Peter Simpson all sorts of problems. Left-back John Gorman was his usual outstanding self and one of the highlights of the half was when – facing his own goal – he dropped his shoulder and did a Cruyff turn to leave Alan Ball stumbling the other way

Then the moment of the game arrived just before half-time. Carlisle worked the ball neatly through midfield and forward to the overlapping Gorman; he crossed first time and Dennis Martin, who had drifted in from the other side, leapt high and twisted in mid air to power a header into the bottom right-hand corner of Geoff Barnett's net. *The ground erupted!*

It did not get any better than this for one wide-eyed eight-year-old at the Warwick Road End: Blues and Gunners – my everyday team and my glamour/fantasy team – giving each other as good as they got. By this point I was like a cheering idiot – I could barely contain myself every time either side won a throw-in. People were starting to look at me with pity ('poor la'al lad: must be special needs').

By the interval, it was difficult to see how there was a division between the two teams. It was Gorman who had caused most of the problems for the Arsenal defence and he was the subject of a row that broke out in the away dressing room at half-time. Skipper Frank McLintock recalls the heated discussion:

'John Gorman had a particularly good first half and caused a lot of problems. I found that George Armstrong, our winger, was almost behind me at times, chasing John, so I told George to let him go and that we would push our midfield over to the right when John Gorman had the ball and when we won it back to immediately give it to George in the more advanced position. Thank God this worked and we gradually got back into the game.'

It certainly did work out as the skipper had hoped and as the second half progressed, Arsenal gradually asserted a little authority with Ball, Storey and Eddie Kelly gaining some control of midfield. On 70 minutes, they won a corner while attacking the Warwick Road End. The box was crowded with players from both sides and for some reason, I was watching Frank McLintock on the corner of the area, as if anticipating what was about to happen. The ref blew the whistle and George Armstrong sent the ball in; I followed McLintock as he darted forward towards the penalty spot; unfortunately for Carlisle, his marker did not follow Frank's run as closely as I did, and the Arsenal skipper bulleted a header into Allan Ross's top right hand corner. (Tot Winstanley reckons that this was the start of blocking at set pieces that is so common place today. Tot's theory is that somebody probably blocked Dennis Martin – McLintock's marker – giving the impression that Frank had slipped his shadow altogether.)

Allan Ross thwarts one Arsenal attack in the Cup tie of 1973…

....but can't prevent Frank McLintock (obscured) scoring the winner.

The Arsenal skipper did not score too many throughout his career, so he remembers the game and his goal fondly today: 'I remember the header well – it was well timed and landed right in the back of the net. Happy days!'

With 10 minutes to go it was nearly three: John Radford rounded Bob Delgado but the magnificent Gorman was across to cover and snuff out the danger (Gorman remembers this game today as one of his best ever). The sensational game finished 2–1 and yet again, Carlisle had been far from disgraced against one of the country's top sides. The special day ended when Mam and Dad allowed us to stay up and watch the highlights on *Match of the Day*. (I don't think I got much sleep that night.)

The following day, former Carlisle-great-turned-journalist Ivor Broadis gave his assessment of his old club's latest tale of what might have been in his *Sunday Sun* column:

> *'In the end, Carlisle learned the hard way a sort of lesson that you can't budget for in the endless hours of 'homework' preparing for the tie. You can get away with the odd moment of mental aberration in the lower class bread and butter stuff – at this level you are punished for your mistakes. United made two – and that was too many. It is no consolation that they played the best football of the match.'*

Twelve months later it was Liverpool again who must have looked skyward as they drew the Blues in the FA Cup fourth round. This time, the game was at Anfield and given the last time the teams played there, Liverpool ran out easy winners and, given further that Liverpool had not failed to score all 1973–74 season, only one result was expected. For their part, Carlisle had already put the cat among the pigeons by despatching Cup holders Sunderland in the previous round. (Technically, this was not a giant-killing in itself, as Sunderland were in the second tier alongside the Blues. They themselves had caused a major shock in the previous season's Final when they beat Leeds 1–0.)

With sizable and vocal away support that had travelled to Liverpool, Carlisle settled in for a busy defensive afternoon. Ashman had signed forward Frank Clarke from Ipswich and central defender Bill Green (who assumed the captaincy) from Hartlepool during the previous close-season. Clarke was the only man up front on the January afternoon – not that he got much of a look-in as the home side pressurised the upstarts from up north as the half went on. Green and his defensive colleagues played at full stretch throughout and Allan Ross was, as usual, magnificent, saving well from both Keegan and Toshack.

The one outfield player who looked completely at home for Carlisle was the ever-elegant Chris Balderstone who played as a sweeper (by the end of his Carlisle career, Baldy had filled in – and mastered – virtually all positions). Described by many as one of the most stylish players ever to play for Carlisle, Bill Shankly himself praised Baldy after the match claiming he was probably the best player to be playing outside the top flight (Shankly actually signed Balderstone when he was the manager of Huddersfield Town in 1958).

The home fans sportingly applauded Carlisle off the field at the end of the goalless draw.

The reward, of course, was a money spinning replay at The Brunt. It turned out to be more of a money spinner than would be normally expected, as it was it was destined to be played during the day.

In the '50s and '60s, afternoon football was commonplace (in Carlisle's case, it usually took place on Thursdays – half day closing), but with the advent of floodlights, midweek *afternoon* football was a thing of the past as the 1970s dawned. But in the winter of 1973–74, Britain was in the grip of a political and industrial crisis. We were all suffering power cuts and Prime Minister Edward Heath declared a three-day working week. As floodlights were banned as a result to save on the lecky, the big replay took place on the afternoon of Tuesday 29 January 1974.

We all got the afternoon off school (not bad these strikes, if you ask me!) and took our places among the 21,000 strong crowd. Good crowd, two good teams, but I remember a slightly surreal atmosphere (let's be fair: a January, Tuesday afternoon in Carlisle does not exactly conjure up images of the Nou Camp does it?).

Liverpool were big box office, and Kevin Keegan was the jewel in their crown (probably the most high-profile player in England at the time). The Warwick Road end, however, did not respect reputations and gave the diminutive striker plenty of stick throughout the game. Being one of the top sides with a large squad, Shankly had the luxury of bringing in one or two other internationals who sat out the previous

Saturday's game. Alan Ashman on the other hand, retained the same 11, partly through loyalty to their good performance, partly through expediency as no one else was available.

Carlisle put in another good performance that afternoon, showing greater adventure than in the original game. Early on, a high ball from Les O'Neill finally put the wind up the Liverpool defence who had been virtual spectators three days earlier; panic ensued before it was scrambled behind for a corner. A good ball in from Dennis Martin then found Frank Clarke who got a decent header in that was saved on the line by Clemence. Clarke then turned provider as he teed up a shooting chance for O'Neill who fired in a trademark effort that went just wide.

The move of the first half also came from Carlisle when they swept from one end of the field to the other: Balderstone to Martin who plays the ball out left for Laidlaw; he crosses only for Liverpool full-back Alec Lindsay to stretch and turn it behind for another corner.

The crowd started to pump up the volume and Laidlaw fires in the resultant corner; skipper Bill Green out-leaps Larry Lloyd, and Lindsay and Clemence get in a terrible tangle before the ball is shovelled behind again.

You always know when the big team are rattled because they invariably resort to roughhouse tactics. Shortly before half-time, Bobby Owen got the ball on the right and dribbled past a couple defenders before Larry Lloyd clattered into him, much to the outrage of the home fans. (These Tuesday afternoons maybe were not too sedate after all!)

So often, tales of what-might-have-been, *become* tales-of-what-might-have-been because the more experienced, stronger team exert a greater pressure in the second half, as the underdogs' performance and fitness levels drop a little after giving so much in the opening period.

So it was on this occasion when Liverpool came out and managed to keep Carlisle at arm's length following a goal five minutes after the restart by Phil Boersma.

A mark was left on Ray Train in the 65th minute for good measure and the midfielder had to limp off; with nine minutes to go Keegan set up his strike partner John Toshack to seal a reasonably controlled, if a little flattering 2–0 victory.

Never mind – in the glass-half-full world of Cup football, getting knocked out always allows you to concentrate on the League.

"WE'RE GAN TO THE STADIO OLYMPICO, EH!"

So then, another question to start a heated debate: which is Carlisle United's greatest ever result? Perhaps two games against Chelsea spring to mind – the League Cup fourth round tie in 1969 or the first top flight game in 1974 – or perhaps the Manchester City game in 1970? Maybe you would plump for the Championship-winning game against Mansfield in 1965; or one of the great tales of what-might-have-been – against Arsenal (1951), Birmingham (1958), or Tottenham (1971)? You may even go for one of the lower League triumphs like the Wembley victories over Colchester (1997), Brentford (2011) or the Jimmy Glass game against Plymouth (2002).

In typical controversial fashion, I would go for none of these, but would instead make a play for a much overlooked triumph on 1 June 1972. It came in the famous Olympic Stadium in the Italian capital and the opponents were the Serie A giants AS Roma. The occasion was Carlisle's one and only European campaign – the Anglo-Italian Cup.

Carlisle had none other than Arsenal to thank for their one and only venture into European football. (Well, I had to get one in somewhere didn't I?) In relating the tale, it strikes me that a football fan's lot is, at times, not a happy one; just when you think your team has exhausted every possible way of letting you down, they invariably find another one when you least expect it. This not only results in you being gutted at another defeat, but you end up hating yourself for caring about these wasters so much.

So it was with Arsenal in 1969. They had fought their way to the Football League Cup Final at Wembley in March of that year in an attempt to win a trophy they had never won before. Once there, they somehow contrived to lose 3–1 to Swindon Town, who were in the third tier of the Football League! (The Swindon team was actually captained by former Carlisle favourite Stan Harland.)

'Hooray for the underdogs!' some might cheer.

'Yeah, whatever!' others might respond.

The upshot was that the humiliated Gunners had to skulk off back to Highbury with their tales firmly between their legs, while the Robins of Swindon bob, bob, bobbed their way back to Wiltshire with the three-handled Mickey Mouse Cup (they are all Mickey Mouse Cups when you don't win them). But there proved to be a sting in the tail for the men from the County Ground; whereas a triumph in the League Cup qualified the winners for Europe competition the following season, continental officialdom decreed that a team from the Third Division would not be allowed to compete with Europe's elite. Even the most hardened (or bitter) Arsenal fan must surely have sympathised with Swindon's predicament but whatever the Italian is for 'them's-the-rules-matey' was relayed to the West Country and that was that.

In Italy meanwhile, the Coppa Italia may well have been the primary Cup competition (unlike the League Cup in England which has always played second fiddle to the FA Cup), but it was considered the poor relation to the Seri A title. It was therefore decided to invite the winners of the Coppa Italia to play Swindon Town as a way of assuaging the Robins for losing out on entry into the Inter-Cities Fairs Cup (the forerunner of the UEFA Cup).

All credit to Swindon: they promptly added Roma (who had a certain Fabio Capello playing for them) to the list of high-profile casualties in the two-legged tie that proved popular with fans and press alike.

Contributing to the organisation of the tie was Luigi 'Gigi' Peronace, who was, in effect, one of the first football agents. (It was Peronace who organised the first transfers of players from England to Italy: Gerry Hitchins, John Charles, Denis Law and Jimmy Greaves being the first.) Gigi was living in London at the time and he knew

a good thing when he saw it. Acting quickly on Swindon's success, Gigi introduced a competition and invited six teams from each country to take part. The Anglo-Italian Inter-League Clubs' Competition – or the Anglo-Italian Cup, as it became known – was born. And for good measure, Swindon also won the inaugural event, beating Napoli 3–0 in the Final. (So maybe it was *actually* Peronace who we have to thank for Carlisle's venture into Europe, but I prefer to go with the Arsenal theory.)

Critics viewed the competition as another version of the popular European *It's a Knockout*

Gigi Peronace – founder of the Anglo Italian Cup.

without the laughs, but to clubs from the lower half of the top flight, and the top half of the second tier of English football – who were thereafter invited to submit an application to compete – it proved an enticing prospect.

It was always Peronace's intention to invite clubs from all over the country to take part. Therefore, two years after its inception, with Carlisle having both finished fourth in the Second Division in the 1970–71 season, and having made an audacious bid to take part, Peronace invited the club representing the city that was once the North West frontier of the Roman Empire to join the European football wannabees.

The Blues *had* played the odd game against foreign opposition in the past (most notably when they played friendly matches against Sparta Prague and Maastricht at Brunton Park in 1967 and 1970 respectively) but had never competed against continental opposition in an organised format.

In March 1972, a little press release came out of Brunton Park, stating that the club was '…likely to retain a one team system for next season, due to the geographical isolation of the club and the wage structure'. The statement would prove significant by the season's end, but at the time it virtually went unnoticed as incredibly, confirmation came through that Carlisle had been accepted into the Anglo-Italian Cup to be played during June of that year.

The excitement was tempered somewhat by the complex rules. (Be warned – you really have to pay attention at this point.)

In those days, the classic Italian system was to play *Catenaccio,* which roughly translated meant playing with a flat back-nine and a sweeper (it actually means 'door-bolt' but you get the picture). As a consequence Italian football was not renowned for being the most open. In an effort to negate this negativity, the organisers decreed that two points would be awarded for a win, one point would be awarded for a draw, and a further point would be awarded for each goal scored. Moreover, the offside law would only come into play from the line of the penalty area to the touchline.

Carlisle prepared for their Italian job, determined to win the hearts and minds of the locals by throwing souvenirs (rosettes and pennants) into the crowd before the games. (Leeds United had actually pioneered this approach, although their critics would probably accuse them of lulling the opposition into a false sense of security before kicking the crap out of them during the game.)

There would be three groups consisting of two English teams and two Italian teams. The English teams would play the Italian teams home and away but would not play the other English team in their group; likewise with the Italian teams (in reverse, of course. I am sorry but I *did* warn you!). Joining Carlisle from England in 1972 (not that it mattered as they would not be playing them) were Birmingham City, Blackpool, Leicester City, Stoke City and Sunderland. Having said that, the best English team and the best Italian team (regardless of the group they were in) qualified for the Final.

So, to summarise, although English teams never played each other, they were competing against each other by trying to get the best record of wins and goals scored. Paradoxically, they actually played the Italian teams but did not actually compete against them as far as overall standings are concerned. (Even I am confused now and trust me, I have *researched* this!)

Club officials Andrew Jenkins and David Dent, and manager Ian MacFarlane travelled down to a hotel in Mayfair for the draw. It could not have worked out better: the Blues were drawn in Group 1 along with the glamour club of the competition, AS Roma. Also in the group were a small club from the south of Italy called Catanzaro, and Stoke City (not that *they* mattered of course).

I have this priceless image in my mind of a group of tanned, sophisticated Roman officials in the glamorous Mayfair setting, with their coats stylishly draped over their shoulders, looking quizzically at the draw; I am not sure what the Italian is for '*Where the fucking hell's Carlisle?*' but I would wager that that's what they were thinking as they exchanged puzzled looks. (Don't worry fellas – half of Britain doesn't know where it is either!)

As the domestic season drew to a close, MacFarlane and his charges moved towards securing a solid 10th place in the League. A little modest perhaps, having finished fourth the previous season, but there was still the Italian adventure to look forward to and preparations throughout the club picked up pace.

Then, a surreal week in early May, threatened to destabilise everything. It began with MacFarlane parading his two latest signings – Welsh International full-back Steve Derrett from Cardiff City, and midfield box-to-box man Les O'Neill from Bradford City. They seemed the perfect complement to an ever improving squad; something that promised much in the European campaign ahead and the following season when MacFarlane was determined to win promotion into the top flight. 'I am delighted with the new signings,' said the boss in his press conference, 'but I am continuing to look for another striker.' Even the news that defender Stan Ternent had been banned for the first month of the 1972–73 season (for receiving three cautions over the season!) could not dampen the spirits of the Carlisle faithful.

MacFarlane had been tracking Les O'Neill for some time so it was the perfect end to the season as far as he was concerned. The two exchanged phone calls over the following week, as O'Neill was keen to make arrangements to move to the city as quickly as possible. On the morning of 8 May, the player called his new manager again to find out which hotel he would be staying at when he came up. 'He didn't sound like the same Ian MacFarlane,' recalls Les, 'but I didn't really think anything about it'.

The reason for MacFarlane's subdued manner became clear at lunchtime on the same day. A brief statement from the club sent shock waves around the city:

'The directors have decided with great regret to give Mr MacFarlane six months' notice of termination of his contract as manager of the club, the reason for this being

he has not shown enough experience to manage a club operating a one team system and that insufficient progress has been made.'

To say the decision was harsh is an understatement. In his season-and-a-half, MacFarlane had carried on Bob Stokoe's good work in 1970–71 to finish fourth in the League (qualifying for the Texaco Cup in the process); he had then followed that up with a respectable 10th place in 1971–72. The Cup games against Tottenham Hotspur had propelled the club into the national limelight, and some of his signings were among the best from the period in question: Stan Bowles, Ray Train and Les O'Neill. All this had been topped off with the successful application to play in the forthcoming Anglo-Italian Cup. The players were as shocked as the supporters and Bowles later lamented on the club's decision to part company with MacFarlane:

'The big man was tough, too tough for me. There was no way I would get into any kind of confrontation with him. He was on my case from day one. I was terrified of him really. The thing being he made me into the footballer I became, skill and responsibility wise.'

The truth was never fully articulated about MacFarlane's sacking but rumours abound that the loud, straight-talking Scot (whose conversation was frequently peppered with expletives) had made as many enemies as friends in the boardroom. Whatever the reason, the fans were in uproar – the popular figure was considered by many to be one of the best coaches outside the top flight. Undaunted the club announced that the managerial reigns would be placed in the safe hands of Dick Young for the forthcoming Italian tournament, and that they '…were in no hurry to replace Mr MacFarlane'.

The piece in the *Evening News* suggested that, 'From the wording on the statement, the club will be looking for someone in the Bob Stokoe mould'. The dejected MacFarlane's only comment as he left the ground was, 'I am shattered'.

The rumour-mill quickly had it that it was not in fact Stokoe that was to return to Brunton Park but another fans' favourite, Alan Ashman. These stories were firmly denied by the board and they appealed to fans and press alike to get behind Dick Young and the team. After 16 years at the club as the perennial number two to no fewer than seven different managers, Young was about to be thrust into one of the biggest challenges the club had ever known.

With a break of a couple of weeks in May, the squad reassembled for a couple of warm-up matches against Workington and Kendal before flying out to Italy on 30 May 1972. With the Carlisle party of players and officials was the young Keswick lad and lifelong Blue, Ross Brewster, who had landed the perfect job in adulthood: reporter with the local paper covering Carlisle United. Now he was travelling with the team on the footballing trip of a lifetime.

Whereas it could be argued that AS Roma have never quite had the kudos of, say, Juventus or AC Milan, they did boast (as they do today) a rich history of domestic and European success. Although Fabio Capello had moved on, their playing staff still included Spaniard Luis Del Sol who was a former European Cup winner with Real Madrid, Italian international and prolific Serie A goalscorer Renato Cappellini, and Brazilian Tavers de Silveira Amarildo who scored in his country's victorious World Cup Final of 1962.

Their coach was the famous Helenio Herrera (who became the world's highest paid manager when Roma employed him on £100,000 a year plus £40,000 bonuses). Herrera's assessment of his forthcoming opponents was translated as, 'We have similar sides in the lower levels of our Leagues'. Herrera would have done well not to underestimate United – as the manager of many-a-favourite who had come a cropper against the legendary giant-killers could have warned him.

The Cumbrian party arrived in the Italian capital two days before the game and transferred to their hotel in the Roman seaside resort of Ostia. Gigi Peronace met the party the following day; Ross Brewster takes up the story:

'Peronace was a balding man with a very round face – he was the man who was the Mr Fix-it of his day. The day before the match he organised a trip to the stadium so we could have a look round and I remember you went through this tunnel into the ground because we were told that the home fans could turn a bit nasty after a defeat. Peronace then took the party to a very posh restaurant on one of the hills overlooking Rome. Bear in mind this was the early '70s and it was the first time some of us got to eat some of the exotic food that is taken for granted today. I had swordfish!'

Although the players had been shocked by the sacking of MacFarlane, Dick Young was a popular figure among them, and spirits were high in the Carlisle camp. The players were determined to play well for Dick, believing he had a chance of being retained in the top job. They were unaware of negotiations behind the scenes regarding the next manager.

Travelling independently of the team was the prototype Blue Army: life-long fan and local joiner Geoff Thomlinson and a couple of his mates. The three flew to Sorrento, calculating that it was about equal distance between the venues for Carlisle's two games: of Rome in the north and Catanzaro in the south.

The following day, Thursday 1 June 1972, was the day of the game. Strangely it did not kick off until 11.30pm local time; the best reason offered is that it was to avoid the oppressive summer heat of Rome, although it didn't do much for the preparation of Ross Brewster, who wished to file a report of the game afterwards, or the three fans who travelled north to Rome on the train knowing full well they could never get back to Sorrento in the middle of the night.

For the players, they had a light training session in the morning and a mid-afternoon nap as they prepared for what lay ahead.

The Italian season was still going on at the time of the tournament and Roma were in some good form having beaten Verona 1–0 the previous weekend. Estimates of the crowd vary between 20 and 30,000, the Romans filed in – perhaps in curiosity – to watch *i Giallorossi* take on the obscure team from the north of England.

Tot Winstanley described his feelings and that of his colleagues as they stood in the concrete underbelly of the stadium, waiting to walk up the steps and onto the pitch:

'To be honest we didn't take much notice of their reputation – they didn't frighten us. It didn't really matter who we were playing because we knew we were okay from what we'd done against the likes of Man City and Chelsea. We had a good team with Stan Ternent and Stan Bowles in the side along with Chris Balderstone who could certainly play a bit.'

The teams walked up and out onto the pitch – with the home fans' flares, red and yellow banners and horns filling the night air – and lined up facing the main stand, Roma in their deep red jerseys and white shorts, Carlisle in their change kit of yellow jerseys and blue shorts.

With the preliminaries over, the dignitaries introduced, and the pennants exchanged, the game got under way. The home side started quickly and as early as the second minute, some neat work down the Roma right resulted in Walter Franzot shooting from the edge of the box; Allan Ross hurled himself upward to claw the ball away from his top right-hand corner.

As the game settled down, United started to characteristically stroke the ball around with, who else, but Chris Balderstone pulling the strings. But just as things were taking shape, Roma struck shortly before the quarter hour mark: Franzot was again involved, this time as provider – his defence splitting pass found its way to Renato Cappellini just inside the area; the Italian hit-man's right-foot shot went low, just inside Rossy's right hand post. The inter-change between the Roma forwards was causing Carlisle problems and almost immediately after the opener, it was Cappellini who drifted wide left and fizzed in a cross that the onrushing Francesco Morini just failed to connect with.

The home side's tactic was to invite Carlisle on and then break with quick precise passing though the midfield. Undeterred, United pressed forward with Stan Bowles getting in behind the disciplined defence a couple of times. Then in the 30th minute, Dennis Martin sent a beautiful diagonal pass to Balderstone who went to jink past Franzot just inside the box; knowing he was beaten, the Italian thrust out an arm in desperation and the referee pointed to the spot. It was Baldy himself – the penalty specialist – who stepped up. He strode up and side-footed the ball to Alberto Ginulfi's right; the 'keeper leaped across and kept it out but could not control the rebound and the skipper kept his head to slot home the equaliser. There was virtual silence in the stadium, apart from the noise coming from the Carlisle bench and the handful of spectators who had made the trip (including Geoff Thomlinson, of course).

Before the visitors could build on the confidence the goal gave them, disaster struck in their own box within five minutes. In attempting to hook away a cross from the right, full-back Derek Hemstead only succeeded in slicing the ball in the air; Cappellini was onto it in a flash and slotted the dropping ball into the net.

As the half-time whistle blew, the Roma fans roared their approval and waved their red and yellow banners in anticipated triumph. Carlisle certainly had not disgraced themselves but they left the field wondering if they had missed their chance.

Tot Winstanley recalls today how when the Italian attacks broke down, they simply retreated into their zonal defence behind the ball, 'They would actually run past you and almost ignore you, even when you had the ball!' Dick Young had noted this too and encouraged his charges to keep passing and playing their normal game during his half-time talk.

Young's instructions almost paid instant dividends, with Bobby Owen forcing two good saves from Ginulfi. A corner kick caused panic in the Roma defence and was hacked behind for a repeat. A Hemstead cross was then met by Owen who headed just over. The Cumbrians were growing in confidence while the Romans were starting to look ragged. (This was typified by Stan Bowles who at one point was juggling the ball on the halfway line.)

In an effort to reassert the home side's authority, Herrera introduced striker Roberto Vieri and immediately he drew a fantastic save from Ross. It was arguably the turning point of the match. Full-back Aldo Bet hammered the ball anywhere as Owen's shot could only be parried by Ginulfi.

With 12 minutes left, and just as Roma probably felt they had ridden the storm, United got their just reward. Another slick move through midfield and a chip forward saw Bowles win a header and the supporting Dennis Martin hammered in a first-time shot for the second equaliser.

By now the game was being played deep into the early hours of 2 June and the Roma players were looking at each other – their confidence knocked – for inspiration and leadership. United meanwhile sensed an unlikely victory and poured forward, looking to press home their advantage. Four minutes after the equaliser, Carlisle won a free kick in the inside right position. Winstanley and Ternent both went up for the set piece. Balderstone sent the ball in that was headed half clear; Baldy collected the loose ball and a couple of quick passes found Frank Barton who was darting towards the byline, Barton wrapped his foot round the ball and sent a low cross diagonally back towards the edge of the box. Winstanley meanwhile had turned to go back when the original clearance was made, but once he saw his teammates regain possession, he turned again and jogged back towards the edge of the box, where he met Barton's cross

Hero of Rome – Tot Winstanley

without breaking stride. Tot recalls today what he still regards as the standout moment of his career: *'Frank's got it as near as damn it on the dead ball line and he pulled it back along the deck and I've caught it absolutely perfectly, as sweet as a nut with my right foot and it went about a foot off the ground right into the far corner. The goalie was well licked…and I just took off!'*

As the players jogged back to their positions, their tiny contingent of supporters were in ecstasy. Director Andrew Jenkins recalls how the big electronic scoreboard at the end of the stadium flashed WINSTANLEY…WINSTANLEY! Carlisle United were on the brink of a famous victory.

There was a late scare when Stefano Pellegrini broke through the square defence but the magnificent Ross stood up to him and deflected what proved to be the final chance away. In an effort to wind down the clock, Young sent on the two new signings Steve Derrett and Les O'Neill for Barton and Martin respectively. It worked. As the final whistle blew, the bench cleared and the yellow jerseys around field leaped for joy. Dick Young afterwards summed up the feelings of the whole camp, 'Absolutely bloody marvellous, who could have believed this scoreline?'

Geoff Thomlinson remembers, 'Their fans didn't half give the manager some stick – he had to run off down the tunnel!'

Ross Brewster, who filed his report for the late edition of the *Cumberland News* at around 4:00am local time described the feelings of everyone as a mixture of 'euphoria and bemusement'.

In the quick-fire format of the competition, Carlisle had little time to savour their historic victory. The following day they flew to the deep south of the country for the second game against Italian minnows Catanzaro. The provincial side were not so dissimilar to Carlisle in that they had spent years punching above their weight to try and achieve promotion to the top flight of Italian football. They had finally achieved their ambition two years earlier by winning a play-off against the better-known Bari to become the first club from the south of the country to win promotion to Serie A. Unfortunately, the small club were unable to maintain the level of achievement and were duly relegated on the eve of the competition they were now playing in. Like Carlisle it was their first venture into European competition.

The north/south divide in Italy was the reverse of what we know in England: the northern cities of Rome, Milan and Florence had style, wealth and sophistication in abundance, while the southern provinces experienced abject poverty, which in turn allowed organised crime to flourish.

While the official party from Cumbria arrived at a military air strip in Calabria and were transferred to a seaside country club just outside the main citadel of Catanzaro. Their three supporters meanwhile, travelled down through the night by train, arriving at around six in the morning. Geoff Thomlinson recalls it as one of those what-am-I-doing-here moments:

'There was bright sunshine but not a soul about – they dropped us off in the middle of nowhere. We were walking along the road with no one about. All of a sudden this rickety old bus comes along. We stopped the bus – we couldn't talk Italian and they couldn't understand us so we just jumped on and hoped for the best. So we came to this place that looked like a bit of a town and we got off; we found this grotty old shop – like a café place – and I said to the other two 'there's no way I am eating anything here.' It put me off going abroad for a long time!'

For the players meanwhile, things were a little more comfortable. Upon their arrival at their hotel they found a wedding being celebrated. Apparently the Italians in those days were obsessed with their goalkeepers so Allan Ross was given special treatment by all, as photographs were taken with the wedding party!

The day before the game, there was a lunch arranged for the visitors and it was decided that club secretary David Dent and Ross Brewster would represent the party. The two were picked up by…well…let's just say they were 'local dignitaries'. Now I know what you are thinking – local dignitaries are usually elderly councillors in robes, and one is normally wearing a ceremonial chain and a fancy tricorne hat. These 'local dignitaries', however, all wore white suits, dark glasses and sported menacing toothless grins.

When I was interviewing Ross Brewster about the trip, I naively asked him, 'Were they from the club?' 'They *were* the club,' replied Ross, darkly.

The motorcade drove into the city over a deep gorge that was spanned by the enormous, one-arched Viaduct Morandi-Bisantis; one of the tallest in Europe. They arrived at the best restaurant in the town's main piazza and as the 'local dignitaries' walked in with their guests, everyone else – whether they had finished their meal or not – quickly vacated the establishment. A regiment of obsequious waiters then showed the party to the best tables in the house and proceeded to serve them course after course.

Much to their relief, the Carlisle duo thought after about seven courses – when the ice cream was served – that the meal was coming to an end; but then more pasta came out. No doubt remembering that they had to make the return journey over that deep gorge, Dent and Brewster tucked in and said nothing. The surreal experience finally came to an end and the two were driven back to their hotel where the team were preparing for the match the following day. 'They were very hospitable,' recalls Ross. (He was hardly likely to say anything else was he?)

On Sunday 4 June 1972 Carlisle United lined up against Catanzaro in their run-down ground which had open banked terracing all around; there were only a couple of hundred spectators to start with. The three-strong Blue Army were not too impressed by their surroundings and their mood wasn't helped any after they learned that a spectator had been shot in the ground the previous week! (Another bizarre occurrence was to take place at half-time: they opened the gates for free, and thousands streamed in to watch the second half!)

United carried their form and confidence into the game from their sensational result 72 hours earlier and dominated from the off. With Ray Train this time bossing the midfield, Chris Balderstone and Stan Bowles were both freed up to display their sublime skills in the final third. The two combined to score what appeared to be the opening goal but Bowles's effort was ruled out for offside. Then Dennis Martin was brought down in the box and Balderstone had a chance to open the scoring from the spot.

Prior to the game, Baldy had asked Andrew Jenkins to film some of the game on Chris's new (state of the art) cine-camera. When the penalty was awarded, Andrew saw this as a great chance to capture one of Balderstone's finest hours on film. Incredibly – perhaps thinking about his near-miss the other night – the skipper fluffed his effort and the home side took the game past the hour mark still level. (So much for posterity!)

But on the day, Carlisle were too good not to take all the points and in the 65th minute, Balderstone and Bowles combined again for what proved to be the seminal moment of the game. Frank Barton fed the skipper on the left hand corner of the box and one of his trademark chipped passes was met perfectly by Stan who headed in past the sprawling Flavio Pozzani.

The only slight disappointment was that United never made it more convincing but could they ever have believed that they would be coming away from Italy with a record of played two, won two?

Everyone woke up safely the next morning without a horse's head in sight and the party headed for home.

Everything was now set up for the return matches at Brunton Park the following week; matches that would hopefully see Carlisle qualify for the Final as the best English team, and a return trip to Rome.

Upon their return, Ross Brewster was sent up to the Hilltop Hotel on London Road to interview the visiting manager from Rome, Helenio Herrera. With Brewster unable to speak Italian and the continental footballing guru in possession of only limited English, the interview consisted of the journalist asking several questions to which the coach repeatedly answered, 'Carlisla is-a better thana Stoka.' (Roma had beaten Stoke

2–0 in their second game). Ross gave the interview up as a bad job and went home and prepared for the game the following day.

Dick Young retained charge of team affairs as we witnessed Carlisle United and AS Roma take to the field. The two teams turned to face the main stand in one long line, forming their version of that iconic image of European football. This really was something special – and we were about to witness a real humdinger!

The game began and Carlisle picked up where they had left off a week earlier in Rome. Their domination of possession in the first quarter of the game, however, was stifled somewhat by *i Giallorossi*, who, presumably fearing a repeat of the upset seven days earlier, resorted to their more familiar, packed defence. Just as the home team were in danger of becoming frustrated, Ray Train took matters into his own hands on 26 minutes. Winning a 50–50 in the centre circle, Train quickly advanced 10 yards and feigned to pass through to Balderstone, who had created an opening with a clever run; in doing so, Baldy had taken one of the central defenders out of the game and Ray saw his opportunity to flash in a shot from 30 yards, that flew like a bullet into the top corner. Naturally, we all went mad and the game just opened up before us.

Within five minutes the Romans had put a breathtaking move together that resulted in Claudio Mannelli squaring things up. Four minutes after that, Baldy got the ball and cut in from the right, skipped through a couple of challenges and slotted the ball in at the near post.

The quality of football was amazing. Even as a kid, when every game is an adventure, I could not remember a game where both sides showed such skill at such pace. One of those sides was a top team from the Italian First Division; the other was Carlisle United.

After the break, the Blues continued to match – and outdo – their illustrious opponents. Stan Bowles headed just wide and then forced a scrambled goalline clearance. Then the skipper curled another superb ball in and Bobby Owen met it beautifully to glance his header in and make the score 3–1.

While Helenio Herrera sat in the opposition dug-out presumably confirming his belief that Carlisla was-a better thana Stoka, his team stood on the brink of elimination. His players realised this too and stirred themselves for one last effort as the game moved into the final quarter. Their cause was aided when Francesco Scaratti fired in a speculative low ball from the right; cruelly, the hero of last week, Tot Winstanley, turned the ball into his own net to make it 3–2. Game well and truly on!

With the visitors pressing for the equaliser, and Carlisle increasingly watching the clock, the Blues broke away in a – by now – rare attack; with three-on-two, incredibly it was Stan Bowles who blew the chance to seal the victory.

The miss proved costly as, with 10 minutes left, the ball broke to the prolific Cappellini, who hammered the ball low and hard past Allan Ross. The man, who thought at one point, a week earlier, that he had secured a victory with his goals in the

Carlisle line-up against AS Roma at Brunton Park in June 1972.

Olympic Stadium, had now secured a point for *i Giallorossi* in the return leg. The epic finished 3–3 and Carlisle had to win their last game to qualify for the Final.

Having lost all three of their previous games without scoring a goal, Catanzaro – presumably low on confidence after being relegated from Serie A – had already assumed the role of the group's whipping boys by the time they visited The Brunt on Saturday 10 June 1972. Knowing that a big win was required to reach the Final, United were in no mood to show the Italians any mercy.

Stan Bowles again spearheaded the Carlisle offence, as the visitors were systematically ripped apart. Some of his antics bordered on a breach of that unwritten footballing commandment 'thou shalt not take the Mick,' as a back heel through the legs of a defender here, or a step-over dummy there had us all in ecstasy. His mesmeric skill set up an early goal for Dennis Martin; he then decided to take on the whole of the Catanzaro defence single-handedly – dribbling past five defenders, he curled the ball round the 'keeper only to see it hit the joint of crossbar and post.

Stan Bowles terrorises the Catanzaro defence in 1972.

After good efforts from Train and Balderstone, Bowles made it two shortly before the break. Two more in the last 20 minutes (Bowles again, and Frank Barton) were sandwiched by a Catanzaro strike but the 4–1 victory was really something to see.

Unknown to us at the time, Blackpool were sticking 10 on some no-marks and with this ridiculous scoreline, Carlisle's chances of qualification evaporated. The outstanding Bowles could not contain his disappointment afterwards:

Manager Dick Young and Secretary David Dent with all they have to show from their Italian adventure.

'We were unbeaten and have been the best English team in the tournament. It's not right that we don't qualify for the Final. We have come through a very strong group. This club deserves to be there, not Blackpool who beat an unheard of village team.'

Just in case you still don't understand the rules (and I, in no way, would criticise you for that), here are the full list of fixtures and standings.

Anglo-Italian Cup 1972
Participants
Atalanta Bergamo – Italy
Birmingham City – England
Blackpool – England
Cagliari – Italy
Carlisle United – England
Catanzaro US – Italy
Lanerossi Vicenza – Italy
Leicester City – England
AS Roma – Italy
Sampdoria Genoa – Italy
Stoke City – England
Sunderland – England

First round (1 and 2 June in Italy)
Group 1
Catanzaro 0–3 Stoke City
AS Roma 2–3 **Carlisle United**
Group 2
Cagliari   1–0 Leicester City
Atalanta   3–2 Sunderland
Group 3
Sampdoria 1–4 Blackpool
LR Vicenza 0–0 Birmingham City

Second round (4 and 5 June in Italy)
Group 1
Catanzaro 0–1 **Carlisle United**
AS Roma 2–0 Stoke City
Group 2
Cagliari 1–3 Sunderland
Atalanta 5–3 Leicester City
Group 3
Sampdoria 2–1 Birmingham City
LR Vicenza 0–2 Blackpool

Third round (7 June in England)
Group 1
Stoke City 2–0 Catanzaro
Carlisle United 3–3 AS Roma
Group 2
Leicester City 2–1 Cagliari
Sunderland 0–0 Atalanta
Group 3
Blackpool 2–0 Sampdoria
Birmingham City 5–3 LR Vicenza

Fourth round (10 June in England)
Group 1
Carlisle United 4–1 Catanzaro
Stoke City 1–2 AS Roma
Group 2
Sunderland 3–3 Cagliari
Leicester City 6–0 Atalanta
Group 3
Birmingham City 2–0 Sampdoria
Blackpool 10–0 LR Vicenza

Final Standings
Group 1

	P	W	D	L	F	A	P	Total
Carlisle United	**4**	**3**	**1**	**0**	**11**	**6**	**7**	**18**
AS Roma	4	2	1	1	9	7	5	14
Stoke City	4	2	0	2	6	4	4	10
Catanzaro	4	0	0	4	1	10	0	1

Group 2

	P	W	D	L	F	A	P	Total
Leicester City	4	2	0	2	11	7	4	15
Atalanta	4	2	1	1	8	11	5	13
Sunderland	4	1	2	1	8	7	4	12
Cagliari	4	1	1	2	6	8	3	9

Group 3

	P	W	D	L	F	A	P	Total
Blackpool	4	4	0	0	18	1	8	26
Birmingham City	4	2	1	1	8	5	5	13
Sampdoria	4	1	0	3	3	9	2	5
Lanerossi Vicenza	4	0	1	3	3	17	1	4

Italian Ranking:

	P	W	D	L	F	A	P	Total
1. AS ROMA	4	2	1	1	9	7	5	14
2. Atalanta	4	2	1	1	8	11	5	13
3. Cagliari	4	1	1	2	6	8	3	9
4. Sampdoria	4	1	0	3	3	9	2	5
5. Lanerossi Vicenza	4	0	1	3	3	17	1	4
6. Catanzaro	4	0	0	4	1	10	0	1

English Ranking:

	P	W	D	L	F	A	P	Total
1. BLACKPOOL	4	4	0	0	18	1	8	26
2. Carlisle United	**4**	**3**	**1**	**0**	**11**	**6**	**7**	**18**
3. Leicester City	4	2	0	2	11	7	4	15
4. Birmingham City	4	2	1	1	8	5	5	13
5. Sunderland	4	1	2	1	8	7	4	12
6. Stoke City	4	2	0	2	6	4	4	10

NB: teams classified according to sum of points and goals scored.

Final – Rome, 24 June 1972
AS Roma 3–1 Blackpool

Conclusion: we woz robbed!

STRIVING FOR THE PROMISED LAND

O kay then, we've done managers, we've done games, now what about goals – what is the most important goal in the club's history? After a bit of debate and a few left field suggestions, I am pretty sure that a good 95 per cent of Blues' fans would probably put Jimmy Glass's lifesaver at the top of the list. After a little thought, I wonder how many would agree that second on the list should go to Ray Graydon. (What do you mean, Ray who? Ray Graydon, *that's who*).

If Jimmy's was unusual because he was our goalie, Ray's was unique because he never actually played for Carlisle ('Ah, it must have been an own-goal' I hear you cry – *wrong again!*) Ray Graydon was the right winger for Aston Villa and his penalty in a match against Leyton Orient on Friday 3 May 1974 at Brisbane Road created a moment of history for Carlisle United.

By the end of the game, Gaydon's goal proved enough to deny Orient the two points that would have given *them* promotion; instead at around 13 minutes past nine in the evening, about 300 miles north of the capital, Cumbria erupted as his goal, and the point it denied the home side, meant Carlisle United were going to the big time for the first time.

The two back-to-back seasons of 1973–74 and 1974–75 are probably the most famous in the club's history because they obviously represent the promotion to the top flight and then *the* season itself. But the incredible achievement of the promotion season often hides that it was third time lucky as far as the club was concerned. In terms of points accumulated and goals scored 1973–74 was the poor relation of seasons 1966–67 and 1970–71 when United just missed out on promotion to the promised land.

As the first of these was about to get under way, the country was buzzing with excitement. The '60s were swinging, England had just won the World Cup during the summer and the feel-good factor around the country was tangible.

It was that man Alan Ashman again who was at the helm of Carlisle United and who had guided his team to promotion from the Fourth Division, and then to the Third Division title. Their first season in the second tier was a respectable effort, finishing just one point and two places below halfway. The team's relative success was recognised by the supporters and season ticket sales for the following campaign exceeded 1,500 as opening day drew nearer.

Inevitably during the close season, the manager assessed his squad and made the necessary changes. Notable changes to the squad during the *previous* year had included the arrival of half-back Gordon Marsland from Blackpool and a swap deal involving Carlisle and Exeter City that saw Blues' winger Jimmy Blain going south and Eric Welsh arriving at Brunton Park in his place.

Welsh was a Belfast lad and he settled into his new club well after playing over 100 games for Exeter. As the 1965–66 season moved into its final third, he realised his (and arguably Carlisle United's) finest achievement. As the Home International matches loomed, Manchester City forward John Crossan had to drop out of the Northern Ireland squad due to injury. Manager Bertie Peacock selected Welsh to replace him for the upcoming game against Wales in Cardiff in late March.

Eric Welsh was picked to start in the game and thus became Carlisle's first [current] international player. The winger did not disappoint either as he put in a man-of-the-match performance, which included a goal in the 4–1 victory. As the season ended, Welsh deservedly retained his place in the squad and played in two glamorous pre-World Cup friendlies against Mexico and West Germany.

Gordon Marsland meanwhile had actually displaced Stan Harland from the team during the run-in and the Liverpudlian asked for a transfer as the season ended. Harland's reputation went before him which meant that there were no lack of suitors vying for his attention; as it was, Swindon Town's manager and chief scout camped out in the Brunton Park car park overnight to grab their man on the day before England were due to take on West Germany in the World Cup Final. As Harland left, Ashman brought in winger Barry Hartle from Sheffield United.

The season got off to a fairly inauspicious start with a measly two victories being returned from the first seven games. The final game of the sequence was at home to Wolves on 10 September 1966. Wolves had made a good start to their campaign and brushed Carlisle aside with a couple of early goals that led to a comfortable 3–1 victory. Peter McConnell recalls the significant defeat:

'It was particularly annoying, because we knew that they were one of the big boys. Whether they overawed us or not, I don't know, but we didn't get out of first gear and it was all over when they took an early two-goal lead. We just couldn't get going.'

Maybe the Blues could not get going in that game, but the defeat appeared to rouse them from their early season funk and they went on a sequence of five consecutive wins that included victories over East Anglian duo Ipswich and Norwich, and the much-fancied Coventry City.

The team were playing the typical Ashman/Young brand of open, attractive football and it was leading to end-to-end games with plenty of goals. This in turn, led to five-figure crowds at Brunton Park every week as the home fans lapped up their team mixing it at the higher level, with their death-or-glory approach.

On the last day of 1966 United drew with Huddersfield Town – it was only their second drawn game of the season. Carlisle's goal was inevitably scored by John Rudge who had moved *from* Huddersfield earlier in the month. Their 13 wins by the halfway mark saw them sitting in eighth place but only three points behind the leaders Wolves in the congested dog-fight for the top two promotion spots.

Everyone was contributing with David Wilson particularly troubling the scorers on regular occasions, while young George McVitie and the consistent Eric Welsh were both enjoying good seasons. The all-round contribution was typified by the 5–1 demolition of Portsmouth at Brunton Park on 4 March, when five different players got on the score sheet (McConnell, Balderstone, Welsh, Rudge and McVitie). The victory saw the Blues up to fifth, four points off second place with 10 games remaining.

Before long, the diminutive Tommy Murray joined from Airdrie and gave the forward line another dimension; with his low centre of gravity and bobbing-and-weaving running style, he was quickly causing defences all kinds of difficulties. Another spring arrival came in the shape of left winger Frank Sharpe as United prepared for the final push.

That final push consisted of eight unbeaten games that included five victories, but sadly for Carlisle the consistent Wolves and Coventry kept them at arm's length throughout. Carlisle ended up as the best of the rest, but their third place was six points from a promotion berth.

(The final game of the season was an emphatic 6–1 victory over Bolton. John Rudge scored a hat-trick and one of his goals – an effort from the halfway line – was marked down by many, as one of the best ever goals seen at Brunton Park.)

Personally it was another good season for skipper Peter McConnell (who played 45 games in all and contributed four goals) but the season remains one of his few footballing regrets:

'We were a force to be reckoned with and we could beat anyone on our day. It didn't matter that players came and went, there was a fantastic team spirit around the place – as there was all the time I was there to be honest – a lot of that has to go down to Alan Ashman and Dick Young. I think what hurt us was that we only managed three points from eight against Coventry and Wolves. I am not sure if that was the only reason but it certainly didn't help our cause. It turned out to be Alan's last season with us and it came as no great surprise when bigger clubs started looking at him.'

It turned out to be the team captain and midfield kernel's last tilt at the big time, as the next serious attempt the club made on the summit was in another post-World Cup season – that of 1970–71 – when McConnell and the majority of his colleagues had left the club.

Bob Stokoe had succeeded Tim Ward (who had taken over from Alan Ashman) and, over the previous 18 months, set about changing the team to the point where – on the eve of the campaign – only Allan Ross, Tommy Murray, George McVitie, Chris Balderstone and Peter Garbutt remained from the squad of 1967. New players included full-backs Derek Hemstead and Joe Davis (and John Gorman before long), central-defenders Stan Ternent and Tot Winstanley, and midfielders Frank Barton and Dennis Martin.

At the start of the previous season Stokoe had made Hughie McIlmoyle captain and then asked him about his opinion of a young striker who was with Northampton Town. McIlmoyle had been at Wolves when Bob Hatton had started his career and was excited about forming a partnership with him at Carlisle – he did not hesitate in recommending him to the boss. Stokoe later recalled the deal:

'One of the best deals I did at Carlisle was bringing Bobby Hatton from Northampton. I knew the Cobblers were always looking for money, so I offered them a silly price for the player. He was then regarded as being a hard-working and industrious striker with real finishing prowess. I couldn't believe it when they came back accepting my offer. I knew we could make money on him, but also that he would score goals for me. It was a good deal all round.'

Hatton came in and hit it off with McIlmoyle straight away; but no sooner were the two getting into their stride when Stokoe sold his skipper to Middlesbrough for £55,000. A year on and Bobby Owen was brought in to partner Hatton up front.

The eventful season was destined to be marked down as a successful one for the club but, like in 1966, it got off to a fairly inauspicious start. Although another debutant, Mike Sutton, scored on the opening day, the Blues went down 2–1 at Middlesbrough, and with a difficult home game against Birmingham City to come, the best the home fans could hope for was a slow burner of a season.

Birmingham came to town with a big reputation and a good opening day victory against QPR behind them. One of their star men was big striker Bob Latchford, who usually attracted the attention, and abuse, from the opposing fans. His dark hair and thick black beard made him look like Cut Throat Jake, the fearsome arch enemy of Captain Pugwash (admittedly, without the eye patch). Right on cue, after 10 minutes, it was the big number nine who went in on our own shrinking violet, Stan Ternent. The fans erupted and this instantaneous outraged roar from over 15,000 adults was enough to both frighten and excite a little lad like me who was attending one of his first games.

The bad feeling on the field simmered before exploding on 37 minutes – the two clashed again and the place went mad. Egged on by the noisy onlookers, the two players seemed unable to back down and it seemed to me that Latchford was goading the Carlisle man with the grown-up equivalent of the terrifying double-dog-dare. The two fronted up and buffeted one another almost comically with their chests. Then – in complete contravention of handbags etiquette – Latchford collapsed to the floor holding his face.

The referee raced across and started writing things down in a book he was carrying (which I thought was quite a clever idea). Much to the crowd's increasing outrage, he seemed to be noting down Bob's version of events which Ternent was strangely objecting to. Latchford wore a smug expression on his face, as he was being wiped down with the magic sponge; and as the referee chastised Stan like a naughty schoolboy with his back to the centre-forward, I half expected the Birmingham player to put his thumb to his nose, wiggle his fingers in the air and antagonise Ternent further, with that classic taunt of the skilled provocateur: *ner-ner-ne-ner-ner*. To the fans deafening incredulity the ref gave Stan his marching orders.

With a gaping hole in the Carlisle defence, Birmingham had little trouble breaching the rear-guard, and Latchford made a dramatic recovery to help himself to two out of their three goals. Despite the controversy and excitement, Carlisle ended the day played two, lost two.

A respectable draw at much-fancied Leicester a week later signalled an upturn in form and fortune – the Blues only lost two more games in the next 19. But it was a glass half-full, half-empty question as the run included nine draws and no away victories.

As the run developed rumours abound that the manager Bob Stokoe was on the brink of leaving the club. He had been linked with the vacant manager's job at Blackpool and by December 1970 – with Carlisle having turned down two approaches from the Seasiders – relations between the ambitious Stokoe and the club had deteriorated to the point where they both appeared to be communicating through the press.

Remember that Birmingham game earlier? Stan Ternent did, and when the two teams lined up for the return on 19 December at St Andrew's, legend has it that he reminded Bob Latchford of their difference of opinions at Brunton Park with a flailing elbow, which landed the defender with an invitation to a Football League hearing. As far as the game was concerned, Birmingham completed the double over Carlisle with a 1–0 win.

By this point manager Bob Stokoe's mind was elsewhere and he was openly engineering a move to Blackpool who had been quite brazen in their courting of the Carlisle manager for a month or more. Before long Carlisle were not only without an away win, they were without a manager as well: the club finally acquiesced to Stokoe's wishes and he was gone by the end of the month.

His replacement was an unusual choice: Ian MacFarlane had been interviewed when Stokoe had succeeded Tim Ward in 1968 – now the directors took a chance and gave the big Scot his first managerial post.

The two parties would make uncomfortable bedfellows but for the time being, the new manager set about building on the solid foundation put in place by the previous one. That solid foundation soon became a serious promotion challenge when the team won five straight, starting with a home win over Bristol City on 30 January 1971, which was followed by the first away victory of the season at Portsmouth.

The final victory of the sequence saw the Blues beat League-leaders Sheffield United with a Bobby Owen goal and suddenly, they found themselves catapulted into third place, only a single point behind the Blades.

MacFarlane added Stan Webb to his squad from Middlesbrough but his arrival coincided with a slight drop-off in form that would prove significant by the season's end. A heavy 4–0 reversal at Cardiff brought Carlisle's win streak to an abrupt halt, and a single victory from the next five games dented their promotion ambitions still further. Upon reflection, it was probably the final two games of the five that did for the club in the end: consecutive defeats within three days, first to eventual champions Leicester and then away to Millwall, left United six points adrift in fifth place.

If only...If only the first half of the season could have delivered a couple of away wins...If only the in-fighting at the club hadn't distracted the players during December...If only Stan hadn't elbowed Bob Latchford in the mush in the Birmingham return match and got banned...If only they hadn't had that little stutter towards the end of the season. If only...

MacFarlane's charges played some scintillating stuff during the last six games of the season, winning five and drawing one. But alas, it was to no avail – despite amassing their best ever points total in the Second Division (53) they finished three points behind Sheffield United who went up with Leicester.

The next tilt at the big time came two years later in 1973, although there was no suggestion before the season started that Carlisle United were going to attempt anything other than another season of consolidation in the second tier of the English League.

Notwithstanding his fourth place finish in '71, and respectable top-half finish the following season, Ian MacFarlane had been relieved of his duties in May 1972. Although the fans were initially bemused and angry at the sacking, they were somewhat assuaged when it was announced on the eve of the home game with AS Roma, the following month, that he was to be replaced with Alan Ashman.

Ashman had left the club in 1967 after believing he had taken the club as far as he could. He was lured away by top flight West Bromwich Albion, where, in his first year, he won the FA Cup. Two years later, of course, his Albion side broke many a United heart when they knocked Carlisle out of the League Cup at the semi-final stage. Ashman later recalled his mixed feelings about facing the club he loved:

'I didn't really want us to face Carlisle in the semi-final, but it was always going to happen. They had been having a good run, beating some quality First Division sides

on the way. I watched them beat Oxford United in the quarter-final and felt ill at the thought of coming up against them, not because I feared them, but because I knew it would be emotional for me. At Carlisle they should have beaten us by three or four goals. I told my players afterwards 'You lot have got out of jail here, take the initiatives and let's beat them at our place.' Thankfully we did, but only just. The final score (4–1) didn't tell the true story.'

Ashman was bizarrely dismissed as West Brom manager in May 1971 when on holiday in Greece. He openly admitted that the manner of his sacking had soured him against the English game, and when the Greek club Olympiakos offered him a position as Head Coach, he accepted. (Ashman was also known on the continent, having taken West Brom to the quarter-finals of the European Cup Winners' Cup in 1969.) Success followed in Athens as Ashman took his new side from mid-table obscurity to runners-up spot in his first season.

Carlisle had never wanted to lose 'their' man five years earlier and moved quickly to entice him back. The truth appeared to be that the board were looking for an excuse to replace MacFarlane and were brokering a deal with Ashman behind the scenes. The players may have wanted Dick Young in the role but he was destined to continue as coach. When Carlisle approached Ashman, he didn't hesitate – despite his success on the continent, the lure of 'his' club proved too much and the [re] match made in heaven was confirmed.

It must have seemed like a homecoming in more ways than one: as well as knowing the club and the city inside out, there were plenty of familiar faces to welcome him back after his five-year absence. E.G. Sheffield was still the chairman, Herbert Nicholson was still the physio and Dick Young was still very much the trainer. Added to those were former player Hugh Neil who was now the chief scout, winger Dennis Martin had been signed from Ashman's West Brom in 1971, and Allan Ross remained the Blues' number one.

Strangely, despite having a talented squad, Ashman's first season back in charge was modest at best – 34 points was only good enough for 19th place, only one point above the relegation births (although that didn't stop them putting the wind up Sheffield United, Arsenal and Liverpool in the Cup competitions).

The manager knew he needed to strengthen his team if they were to do better in 1973–74. 'Not many people have mentioned Carlisle in next season's top 10 but we must get into that position,' he told the local press. His first transfer activity of the summer saw him bolster the squad with utility men Mike McCartney from West Brom and Mick Barry from Huddersfield Town.

Next on his list were a centre-half and a centre-forward. The defender Ashman had his eye on was 22-year-old Hartlepool captain Bill Green. Green was actually having a medical at Swindon Town when Pool manager Len Ashurst rang him to tell him

Carlisle had matched Swindon's offer and had invited him over to meet the manager. Bill recalls a typical Carlisle transfer 'negotiation':

'I drove over to Carlisle to meet with Alan Ashman at the ground. He then drove me up to meet Dick Young on his allotment near Border Television where he kept his pigeon loft. I didn't know what to make of Dick at first but the whole thing felt right. We then went for a meal at the Crown Hotel at Wetheral and I signed almost right away. I knew a bit about Carlisle as I had come over to see them play quite a few times. They played good football and it was close to home so it was the perfect move for me.'

With a top central defender on board, Ashman turned his attentions to the other end of the field. Billy Rafferty had started his career at Coventry City before being signed by Bob Stokoe for Blackpool in 1972. By the middle of 1973 he appeared to be surplus to requirements with the Seasiders and remembers there were one or two clubs interested in him:

'I actually came up [to Carlisle] and had talks in the summer before the promotion. I remember I went to Alan Ashman's house at Wetheral. He brought the old chairman up Mr Sheffield. I was speaking to Alan for about an hour and he was telling me what he wanted. Then George Sheffield came up and his words to me were, "If you want to make money, don't bother coming here, but if you want to play in a good football team this is the place to be".'

While Rafferty was mulling over the move, one of his old coaches from Coventry City, Tony Waiters – who had taken over at Plymouth – made him an offer and Billy decided to move south instead of north.

Ashman instead captured the signature of Frank Clarke from Ipswich Town; one of five footballing brothers who all played professionally during the period.

While the fans were concentrating on the manager's wheeling and dealing in the transfer market, the authorities were proposing changes to the game that would prove significant to him and his team by the season's end. On 1 June 1973 Ashman and vice chairman Harry Sherrard attended the Football League's AGM. At the meeting the majority of clubs voted in favour of introducing a three up and three down system as far as promotion and relegation was concerned between the top divisions, the first such change since 1898 (well, you can't rush these things can you?).

Mindful of Carlisle's struggles the previous season, Ashman voiced his ambivalence regarding the decision; his team had come perilously close to the drop a few months earlier, the last thing he needed was an extra relegation birth that may threaten the club still further.

With the season only three weeks away, skipper and county cricketer Chris Balderstone was excused pre-season training to play for Leicestershire on 1 August on the condition he reported to Brunton Park the following day. Balderstone was conspicuous by his absence on the 2nd and the furious Ashman suspended him and stripped him of the captaincy. He was replaced in the role by Stan Ternent who 'wore the armband' (not that they wore armbands in those days) for the final pre-season friendly matches – one of which was a 2–0 defeat at Workington that proved anything but friendly as numerous arrests were made as rival fans clashed inside and outside the ground.

The opening League game of the season was at home to Cardiff City on 25 August 1973. It wasn't great, but it wasn't disastrous either – the 1–1 draw at least saw the new striker Frank Clarke get off the mark.

The opening midweek game saw the Blues meet Workington again, this time at home in the first round of the League Cup. The Reds picked up where they had left off in the friendly game a couple of weeks earlier and raced into a 2–0 half-time lead – much to the displeasure of the restless home fans. The second half proved a little better for Carlisle who managed to scrape a draw with two Bobby Owen goals, although a replay at Borough Park, due for the following week, did not seem like a particularly attractive prospect.

Before that Carlisle had to travel to Kenilworth Road for their first away game of the season against Luton Town – it would prove to be a bizarre turning point. Bill Green remembers the game vividly; during the very early stages he found himself standing in the middle of the field as the ball was being respotted. He looked up at the clock which sat over the main stand: it read 18 minutes past three and Carlisle were 6–0 down:

'We somehow managed to scramble through to half-time without conceding further and trouped into the dressing room. Alan Ashman was quite calm and said we had to clear our heads and try and win the second half, which we did 1–0 with a Bobby Owen goal. It seems strange but the second half of that 6–1 defeat seemed to give us confidence.'

Ashman took the decision to make Green the skipper for the replay at Workington, and a Les O'Neill goal clinched a much-needed victory. The game, along with the first League win against Notts County a few days later seemed to steady the ship but then – despite the experienced Balderstone being back in the team – three straight defeats saw the Blues slump to second from bottom.

The clocks went back on 27 October 1973 and that afternoon Carlisle produced one of the high spots of the season to date with a 3–0 defeat of Fulham. Much to the amusement of the home fans, the Cottagers' goalkeeper Peter Mellor fumbled the ball into his own net for one of the goals. (Remember that name.)

A win, loss, draw sequence saw the team sneak out of the bottom places but as Christmas approached it still seemed to be shaping up as a fairly modest campaign and Ashman's fears about that third relegation spot appeared to have some substance.

But then an eight-match unbeaten run during December and January (which significantly included two wins over Leyton Orient and the return fixture against second placed Luton) saw the club reach the dizzy heights of the top half of the table. Les O'Neill remembers one of the games in that sequence in particular:

'It was the Notts County game when I got a couple of goals, and all of a sudden, we seemed to start playing football. John Gorman wanted the ball all the time – he was like a left winger – he was probably the first overlapping full-back.'

Gorman's full-back partner by 1973 was Peter Carr. He had replaced the classy Derek Hemstead who received a – what turned out to be a career ending – cruciate knee ligament injury in a game against Nottingham Forest in September 1972 the previous year. Carr arrived at the club three months later having played over 100 games for Darlington, despite him only being 21.

Carr proved successful and popular in the right-back role but he was little like the man from whom he took over; whereas Hemstead was a nice footballer in the mould of Hugh Neil (the player *he* succeeded in 1969), Carr was a robust no-nonsense character, more akin to Neil's full-back twin Terry Caldwell during the '60s. Later in his United career, Alan Ashman once said to Carr, 'You would kick your grandmother, wouldn't you?' 'Aye, I would if she had the ba'!' replied Carr.

Gorman and Carr were joined in the back four by the new skipper Green, whose central defensive partner differed throughout the season: Brian Tiler (who had been signed from Aston Villa a year earlier), Stan Ternent, Bob Delgado and Tot Winstanley all played at one time or another.

By the time the clocks went forward again in March, the Cumbrians had somehow clawed their way up to fourth place in the close-knit League and confidence was boosted still further with a 5–1 thumping of Swindon Town, in which Frank Clarke scored four. Middlesbrough were the class of the field and appeared to have the title wrapped up by this point but Luton, Blackpool, Orient, Sunderland and – from nowhere – Carlisle now fancied their chances of going up with them. (By this time Alan Ashman appeared to have drawn back from his position of disagreeing with the three-up rule.)

On Easter Tuesday 1974 a crowd of almost 20,000 crammed into The Brunt for the visit of Sunderland, who were now the outsiders in the promotion race. The corresponding fixture the previous season was a real hair 'em scare 'em affair, with the Blues coming out on top in a seven-goal thriller. A year on and the two teams were taking part in a far more cagey encounter. For the most part, they cancelled each other out – Sunderland hitting the woodwork being the only highlight of the first half. The game's seminal moment came early in the second half and favoured the home team. Joe Laidlaw went on a surging run past a couple of defenders before being clattered on the edge of the box; a glance between referee and linesman resulted in the unmistakable elongated blast on the whistle that always signals a spot kick. The crowd erupted, fell silent, and then resumed their delirium as Chris Balderstone's effort bulged the net for what proved to be the only goal of the game.

The defeat signalled the end of the Black Cats' promotion ambitions but for Carlisle, it put them in dreamland: fifth, but on the same number of points as Blackpool and Orient above them and two behind second placed Luton (Middlesbrough were out of sight by this time in the top spot).

The fixture list played its part in the drama too as the Blues' next game was away at Blackpool, four days after the victory over Sunderland. The large Carlisle support travelled with some expectancy as an unchanged team took the game to the Seasiders but their two best efforts from Bobby Owen and Joe Laidlaw came back off the frame of the goal, while at the other end, the home side were ruthless in their finishing; the optimism generated from the victory over Sunderland was completely dissipated after United skulked away from Bloomfield Road after suffering a 4–0 defeat.

Blackpool were now third, two points ahead of Carlisle and Orient with a better goal average but having played one game more. The Blues' position was quite clear – they had to win their final two games and hope that Orient and Blackpool fail to win their matches. What's more, they were going to have to do it without their inspirational captain Bill Green who was handed a two-match ban after picking up his third booking of the season.

The first of the two games was a rearranged fixture at Oxford's Manor Ground (it had been postponed from February). The stakes could not have been higher as Oxford needed points to avoid relegation and they started stronger before the visitors gradually took control. The tension was unbearable as the game went into the final five minutes still goalless and the Blues' dream fading. Then with three minutes to go, Carlisle won a free kick halfway inside the Oxford half on the right. Balderstone floated in a trademark effort towards the far post, where the ball broke for Bobby Owen to crash in the winner – cue mayhem in the away end of the ground…

Carlisle had nibbled and chipped away at the teams above them throughout the season and now – going into the final game – they actually had a chance of winning promotion, despite the fact they had never occupied any of the top three spots at any point of the season.

Coincidentally, the final match of the season was a repeat of the previous season-ending fixture – a home game against Aston Villa, a team Carlisle had never beaten in any of their previous 10 League and Cup encounters. In April 1973 the teams played out a 2–2 draw, with ex-Villa man Brian Tiler getting his only goal for the Blues. At the heart of the Carlisle defence for the '74 game, was the ever dependable Tot Winstanley filling in for the suspended Bill Green.

With Blackpool away at Sunderland and Orient away at Cardiff, United had to put everything out of their minds and concentrate on trying to topple the Midlands' giants – what happened elsewhere was in the lap of the Footballing Gods.

Naturally for me, as a kid, it was one of the stand-out games of the period and had echoes of the title-decider against Mansfield nine years earlier (not that I was at that one you understand!). The second highest League attendance of the season turned up on 27 April 1974 to see if dreams really could come true.

Like their predecessors of April 1965, Carlisle started the game confidently, and when Bobby Owen flicked on for Joe Laidlaw to bullet in the opener before the first quarter was up, expectations were cranked up a notch further. Two mulletted loons could not contain themselves any longer and ran onto the pitch in celebration (I remember thinking the one with the blue and white scarf tied round his head looked particularly intelligent). They were both led away to help the police with their enquiries.

Although not in contention themselves, Villa's proud history and good record against the Cumbrians spurred them on and back into the game, and for a 10 minute period, they peppered the Carlisle goal, hitting the frame of the goal and drawing the best out of Allan Ross.

Half-time came and confused messages rumbled round the ground about how Orient and Blackpool were doing in their respective games.

The break seemed to do Carlisle the world of good and the second half started in the same vein as the first, with the home side playing with skill and assurance. *The* moment then occurred halfway through the second half when Dennis Martin picked up the ball on the Carlisle left. Harried by a couple of defenders, Martin actually went to ground at one point but then managed to get back to his feet, retain possession, wriggle free of his markers and get a cross in for Frank Clarke to power in the Blues' second – the ground erupted once more. The goal had an effect on both teams: Carlisle suddenly adopted an invincible air, while Villa knew the game was up and subconsciously defaulted into end-of-season mode.

The whistle went and – like the great triumphs of the '60s – the crowd started to scale the walls and pile onto the pitch to share the moment with their heroes. Mark and I gave each other a quick should-we-or-shouldn't-we look before deciding the police could not possibly pick us out of over 10,000 people. As we ran as far as we could – amid the thousands of fans – towards the tunnel; a group of fans further on were in an even greater sense of delirium than the rest of us. Mark turned round and said, 'Bill Green's just run on the pitch and said Orient and Blackpool have both lost!'

We were up! Well… not quite…

We got home to find that Blackpool *had* lost but Orient had actually drawn, and crucially, the O's still had one game left to play. For the first time all season, and having completed their fixtures, Carlisle United were lying third and in one of the promotion positions. Middlesbrough and Luton were up, Blackpool were out of it and the third spot came down to the final game of the season between Orient and none other than Aston Villa.

Orient needed to win to leapfrog Carlisle – a draw would see the Blues go up by one point. After the defeat at Carlisle, Villa manager Ron Saunders assured his opposite number Alan Ashman he would be doing everything he could to get a result at Brisbane Road.

News of the Orient-Villa result reaches the **Cumberland News'** *offices on 3 May 1974 and the* *promotion party begins.*

It seemed like the whole of the county held its breath for a week before a game that was to take place 300 miles away between two teams no one had a particular affiliation to. Having said that, everyone became Aston Villa fans on the night of Friday 3 May 1974.

While the majority of the Carlisle players gathered round the radio at the *Cumberland News'* offices on Dalston Road, where they were being treated to a reception, three of their number actually travelled to London to watch the agony unfold. Bill Green, Joe Laidlaw and Allan Ross were travelling down to watch [Bill's beloved] Newcastle United play in the Cup Final the following day against Liverpool. They, therefore, took the opportunity to watch the Orient/Villa game scheduled for the night before.

The atmosphere was electric as just under 30,000 fans squeezed into Brisbane Road to see if Orient could regain their top-flight status after an 11 year absence. The nerves of the tiny Carlisle contingent were eased somewhat when Ray Graydon slotted Villa's penalty in midway through the first half (the second most important goal in Carlisle's history, remember?).

But then when Micky Bullock equalised for Orient in the final quarter of the game, the tension became unbearable for all concerned. Allan Ross later recalled his mood as he acted as summariser for Radio Carlisle in the press box:

'I have never been so excited watching a game of football in my life. The last 10 *minutes, when Orient looked as though they might snatch something, were sheer* *hell. I thought the game was never going to end. The worst thing about it all was I* *didn't have any cigarettes and by God, I needed them in those final moments!'*

The final whistle put Rossy and his mates out of their misery and sparked celebrations in Cumbria that could probably be heard at a silent Brisbane Road.

Bill Green remembers going into the players' lounge after the game, 'As you can imagine, we weren't given a good reception by the wives and those who were there'. Not that that put the Carlisle contingent off – Allan Ross bought the whole Villa side a thank you drink.

Back in Carlisle meanwhile, the promotion party began as players, officials and press gathered at the Newspaper House. Alan Ashman was asked about his previous achievements, not only with Carlisle but his FA Cup triumph with West Brom.

'Achieving promotion to the First Division with Carlisle is definitely my best achievement. I am delighted for the all the lads. The lads down at Orient I really feel for them. I wish they were here. I wish I was there. It's fantastic.'

As the champagne flowed and the noise levels rose in the background, Dick Young was more considered in responding to his how-do-you-feel question:

'I think it's a great achievement for everyone concerned with the club. I never dreamed when I first came to Carlisle – which is 19 years in July – that Carlisle would bypass Manchester United. I always looked at Carlisle as a Third Division side, and when we got to the Second Division I thought we might struggle but we've stayed in the Second Division for quite some time and now we've made the First Division. What's going to happen in the future I don't know but whatever happens it's a great achievement for everyone at the club: the groundsman, the man who sweeps the terraces, the manager, the staff, the players – a great achievement.'

(Manchester United were relegated as Carlisle were promoted.)

What is interesting in analysing the three seasons when Carlisle flirted with the big time, the ultimately *successful* season was actually the least productive in terms of points won and goals scored.

1966–67 Second Division	third (52 points)	Six points off promotion. Won 23, scored 71
1970–71 Second Division	fourth (53 points)	Three points off promotion. Won 20, scored 65
1973–74 Second Division	third (49 points)	Promoted. Won 20, scored 61

And so it was: there we all were in the summer of 1974, looking forward to our shot at the big time. But that's just the thing isn't it? I don't know about you but I always think the excited anticipation of Christmas Eve is always better than the anti-climactic reality of Christmas Day…

THE BIG TIME

F riday 22 November 1963. Normal people of a certain age remember where they were when Kennedy was shot; Carlisle United fans of a certain age, however, are more likely to remember where they were on Saturday 24 August 1974. That was the date when the Blues found themselves sitting proudly in first place of the top division in the country.

Before then, of course, was a summer full of expectation and excitement. Season ticket sales were naturally up as the whole of Cumbria waited with eager anticipation at our shot at the big time. Small crowds perhaps, small squad certainly, small chance some would say – but we were all getting ready for the trip of a lifetime.

Before a ball was kicked, however, Alan Ashman knew his squad needed strengthening for the tough campaign ahead. Veterans Brian Tiler (player-manager at Wigan) Stan Ternent (coach at Sunderland) and Bob Delgado (transferred to Rotherham) had all moved on. Ashman was, therefore, racing against time as he trawled round during the summer months to see if he could bolster his small squad of players, most of whom had limited top flight experience. In the end he settled for what he believed was quality as opposed to quantity.

First, and unsurprisingly, given Carlisle United's legendary acumen for a bargain, was free-transfer Eddie Spearritt from Brighton. If Spearritt would prove to be a good squad man, Ashman knew he needed a quality first-teamer to replace the central defenders who had left the club. He approached Coventry City about one of their young stars.

The Sky Blues had a reputation for having outstanding training facilities and a youth system that was the envy of clubs up and down the country. The problem they had was that their first team appeared to be continually fighting against relegation. When a new management team of Gordon Milne and Joe Mercer came in, therefore, they subscribed to the old adage that 'you don't win anything with kids'.

While they were scouring the market for experience, they allowed Ashman to speak with the highly rated Bobby Parker, who had played over 80 games in the top division for the club.

The First Division squad.

Ashman talked Parker into the move north with a guarantee of first team football every week and a suggestion that there would be other signings to follow. 'I was in and out of the Coventry side,' explains Bobby. 'I didn't know anything about Carlisle or the players up there; I only knew Alan Ashman and Ray Train from Walsall.' Ashman broke the club's transfer record to secure his services for £52,000. Parker would go on to become a Carlisle-great.

Already in possession of such status was another of Ashman's summer signings. Incredibly he approached Hughie McIlmoyle and offered him the opportunity to rejoin (for the third time!) the club that meant so much to him. McIlmoyle, who was in the autumn of his career, was still living locally and had been training with the team in order to keep fit, while he considered his future. He recalls what happened next:

'I was living in Scotby at the time and I had had a couple of offers that didn't interest me. Alan Ashman called me up and asked me to come down for a meeting with him and [secretary] David Dent. Alan said he had seen enough in training and asked if I fancied signing for the season. I couldn't believe it and jumped at the chance – I never wanted to leave the club on either of the two previous occasions. David said they couldn't give me a signing on fee – I told them I would give them a signing on fee!'

The fixture list was then issued and the countdown began in earnest.

On the eve of the new season, and in an effort to manage expectation, the manager mused philosophically, 'It's going to be hard and our First Division future may be uncertain, but then whose isn't?'

One of Ashman's peers and former Carlisle manager (now ensconced as Liverpool's revered demigod) Bill Shankly described United's achievement as:

'...*the greatest feat in the history of the game, Carlisle United getting into the First Division of the English League. It is an unbelievable achievement. Alan Ashman has done a great job, and so too has Dick Young. Dick has been with the club for a long time and I am delighted for him. I knew him as a player, and we are still very good friends. I wish them and the club well in the future.*'

Genuine praise for a team that could expect a difficult season ahead. But on the eve of a new campaign, when everybody is on the same footing, no football fan wants their expectations managed; everyone dreams of success, and getting giddy on the highs; the lows can be suffered by other clubs, while we all choose to ignore that well-known sporting cliché that 'getting to the top is one thing, staying there is quite another'.

On a bright August day, the Carlisle United party left to travel south for their opening match against Chelsea, one of the glamour clubs of the division. Chelsea themselves were on a high as they prepared to unveil their enormous new grandstand; on the pitch meanwhile they were looking forward to parading their big summer signing David Hay from Celtic.

By coincidence, Hay was staying in the same hotel as the Carlisle party the night before the game. This afforded former Celt John Gorman the opportunity to catch up with his ex-teammate, and the two – along with Gorman's roommate Les O'Neill – spent a pleasant evening chatting about what was in store for the following day.

Similarly, Hughie McIlmoyle spent some time chatting to his childhood pal Charlie Cooke. The two both hailed from Port Glasgow, had played in the same youth teams together, and had both been invited down for trials with Leicester City. Hughie moved south to Leicester while Charlie preferred to stay in Scotland and secured a contract with Aberdeen before eventually ending up at Chelsea via Dundee.

Game day arrived and ubiquitous local reporter Ross Brewster, who was, as ever, travelling with the team, described the scene on the coach as it travelled towards the ground:

'*We were driving down and people were looking at us a bit bemused. The Chelsea fans must have thought, "what a lot of country bumpkins". It was one of those occasions where – normally players are really cool beforehand. They go on the bus and the cards come out and they don't stop playing until they come off the bus – you normally have to drag them off. But that game they were all looking out of the window – as bemused as the Chelsea fans.*'

Carlisle's skipper Bill Green confirmed Brewster's summary when he said, 'I'd seen nothing like it, having been used to going to the likes of Barrow and Darlington on opening day, to go to Chelsea and Stamford Bridge was incredible.'

In those days, the pitch at Stamford Bridge had a track around the outside which rather distanced the fans from the players, and could, therefore, detrimentally affect the atmosphere. Sadly, the Chelsea fans also had a terrible reputation for hooliganism; but neither of these drawbacks deterred 2,000 travelling Blues' fans who followed their heroes to the capital to take their curtain call.

As the players sat in the changing room at Stamford Bridge waiting to take to the field, veteran Chris Balderstone later described his feelings:

'It was the proudest moment of my career in all sport. We were quiet, contemplating what might be. I turned to Rossy and asked him how he felt about it all. He said he

Chelsea players applaud Carlisle on to the field as they make their entrance in the top flight in 1974.

felt sick and felt uneasy in an excited sort of way. He looked a bit pale to be truthful and I really thought he was going to be sick. I never said anything to the others, but he was putting himself under immense pressure.'

For Allan Ross it was the culmination of 11 years of service to the club, having represented them in the three lower divisions. Like, Balderstone, he later said, 'Just to step out on to the field at Stamford Bridge that was unbelievable and the highlight of my career'.

The Chelsea players formed a guard of honour for the division's newcomers who took to the field in their change kit of yellow jerseys and white (normally blue) shorts. The game kicked off and Carlisle's adventure was under way. After a minute-and-a-half, Carlisle won a free kick down the inside left channel about halfway inside the Chelsea half.

Balderstone curled in a trademark left footed cross that drifted tantalisingly across the box. Frank Clarke made a darting run to the near post that had Peter Bonetti indecisively stepping forward and then back; as the ball floated towards the far post, United skipper Bill Green, who had gone forward for the early set piece, got between two defenders. Although he didn't make a clean contact with his header, his challenge was enough to cause further confusion between defenders and goalkeeper; the second ball fell kindly for Green in all the mayhem, and with only 106 seconds on the clock, the captain crashed the ball into the Chelsea net to put Carlisle ahead. Bill modestly comments on his goal today:

'I received a letter from a fan some weeks after the game and he had complimented me on my finish saying Jimmy Greaves couldn't have finished it better, with that

Bill Green repays them by scoring after 106 seconds.

Les O'Neill makes it 2 -0 to secure the famous victory.

dummy. He couldn't have been more wrong in truth, I took a swipe at it with my right foot and missed and then connected with my left – it was a fluke really.'

The travelling fans didn't care – they went berserk. Among the throng of Carlisle fans that afternoon was lifelong supporter David Steele: 'The noise was deafening – it was just an incredible start. The Carlisle fans were continually chanting throughout the game. It was fantastic – unbelievable really'.

Completing the trio of Carlisle veterans, of course, was Hughie McIlmoyle who actually started in place of the injured Joe Laidlaw and his composure and hold up play worked perfectly on the day. (Taking into account all of McIlmoyle's achievements throughout his career, he also later described running out onto the pitch behind Bill Green that afternoon as his most treasured memory.)

Full-backs Peter Carr and John Gorman were exceptional both in attack and defence, continually disrupting the Chelsea game-plan, while behind them Allan Ross commanded his penalty area superbly. The Londoners had their visitors under the cosh for long periods but even then, lady luck appeared to help out the minnows: Chelsea hit the woodwork twice (once from a mistimed clearance from Green!) and saw a couple of efforts cleared off the line.

Then, with 15 minutes to go, the game opened up completely, Carlisle moved the ball through midfield and Dennis Martin sent a beautiful pass through to the industrious Les O'Neill who was running through the inside right position. O'Neill's first touch took him slightly wider than intended and as he tried to wrap his foot round the ball in an attempted cross, he rather skewed his effort and it sailed over the head of Bonetti and into the far corner. O'Neill's intentions have always been the subject of some debate but; like his skipper on the day, Les is honest today about what happened:

> 'My goal was a fluke! I'd made a run across Dennis Martin to the inside right position where there was a massive hole and Dennis played the ball in front of me; as I am running towards the ball, I can see Hughie Mac making a run towards the near post, and all I wanted to do was clip it in there for Hughie to run on to. Peter Bonetti read what I was trying to do, so he had come across towards the near post to anticipate the cross and instead of bending the ball in with my instep I cut across it and it sailed over his head and inside the far post.'

The Cumbrians' day was complete; if the Chelsea players had applauded United on to the field, then the Chelsea spectators sportingly applauded them off it. Incredibly, Carlisle had opened their First Division campaign with a stellar victory away from home. Ross Brewster said there was a strange atmosphere on the coach of the way home, '...I don't know whether it really hit home. We made such a great start. The players were almost in suspended animation, wondering how long it was to continue'.

It was destined to continue a little longer as the first midweek game saw the Blues travel east to face their fellow newcomers Middlesbrough at Ayresome Park. Carlisle were brimming with confidence, not only from the Chelsea victory but also from the fact that they had made the same journey across to Boro three weeks earlier in the pre-season Texaco Cup (another invitational tournament, this time involving clubs from England, Ireland and Scotland that had not qualified for European competitions) and come away with a 1–0 victory. Boro themselves were high on confidence after a terrific 3–0 win away at Birmingham City on the opening day.

When the game got under way, United picked up where they had left off at Stamford Bridge – taking the game to their hosts. Before the quarter hour mark, their endeavour was rewarded when former Boro player and fit-again Joe Laidlaw found a yard and laid a neat pass into the path of O'Neill; with Les's confidence sky-high after his goal at Chelsea, he didn't hesitate and hammered it first time into the back of the net.

Carlisle played well throughout, with their slick passing and movement constantly causing problems for the defence. The victory was sealed as early as seven minutes into the second half when a stunning five-man move from the defence through midfield, to the overlapping full-back Peter Carr, resulted in his cross being met by the tireless O'Neill who glanced in his third goal of the season. Even the Middlesbrough fans applauded the Cumbrians off the field that night after a near-perfect away performance. At the time, Carlisle were the only team to have played two, won two, although the following night Manchester City won their game to sneak ahead on goal average.

The team City beat were another giant of the division, Tottenham Hotspur, and it was the Londoners who were to be the first visitors to Brunton Park, as the whole county now prepared for its first taste of the big time. Spurs had won twice in recent seasons at The Brunt in FA Cup ties, but with their hosts having won both of their opening League games, and they having lost both of theirs, it promised to be challenging contest.

Thousands of spectators streamed down Warwick Road all morning in anticipation of what promised to be the proudest day in the club's history. With two hours to kick off and the area around the ground packed, programme sellers shouted above the din to make themselves heard; the Spurs bus picked its way through the masses as the Carlisle fans howled their derision.

When the team sheets were submitted, it was discovered that Ashman had made a change to his winning line up. John Gorman had picked up an ankle knock and Tot Winstanley was brought in for what turned out to be his only League appearance of the season.

By the time the game got under way the place was jumping and, once again, the Blues settled in to their neat passing game. The home crowd were witnessing what the lucky few had seen at Chelsea and Middlesbrough earlier in the week.

As if things could not get any more exciting, Ray Train hit a shot that struck the underside of the bar, hit the goalline and came out. The blue jerseys and home supporters rose as one to cheer the goal (those close to the incident swear the ball crossed the line, but you wouldn't expect anything else would you?). Strangely, the incident had echoes of one of the Cup ties played between the two teams three years earlier when Spurs got the benefit of two controversial decisions. History repeated itself as the referee consulted linesman, and Spurs got the benefit of this decision – the 'goal' was disallowed.

Completely undeterred, Carlisle piled forward again and on 20 minutes, Joe Laidlaw was clattered in the box by Mike England and referee Capey pointed to the spot. The crowd went wild and then hushed as Balderstone stood up to take the kick. Baldy stroked the ball goal-ward, and Northern Ireland great Pat Jennings – who had a reputation as being a great saver of penalties – flung himself across his goal to keep it out. Groans turned to cheers as the referee blew again and judged that Jennings had moved before the ball was kicked (not allowed in those days). With pressure well and truly on, Balderstone reset himself. The twice taken penalty was later described by the man himself, 'As for my penalty, well, I had to retake it, but wasn't fazed by Pat Jennings's antics and I just belted it past him'.

Carlisle controlled the remainder of the game, with Winstanley imperious at the back while dealing with Martin Peters, Neil McNab and Ralph Coates (as well as the hair of Ralph Coates).

As far as we were concerned, Dad, Mark and I were on a family holiday in Yorkshire. On the day in question we were on a day trip to York, and were completely oblivious to the events at Brunton Park. As luck would have it, around 4:30pm, we found a television shop on the High Street that had the statutory half-a-dozen TV sets in the window. We were glued to the one that was showing *Grandstand.*

In those days they had what was called a 'Teleprinter' which was the forerunner of the digital as-it-happens vide-printer we are familiar with today on most sports channels. The Teleprinter was like a giant black thumb that bobbed up and down leaving typewriter-like text on what looked like rolling fax paper. The trouble was that the damn thing would invariably stick at the most inappropriate times; so it was on that fateful afternoon. With three expectant faces pressed up against Radio Rentals' front window, the results started to tick though. When it came to Carlisle's result, the inevitable happened: *Carlisle United 1 Tottenham Hotspur* (at this point the Teleprinter stuck and the giant black thumb flickered up and down infuriatingly – then finally) *0*. The three of us leaped up and down like idiots in York High Street.

We made the short distance back to the car and put on the radio, just in time for *Sports Report* with James Alexander Gordon.

Two asides at this point: first – my dad is one of these blokes who is always whistling and singing, whatever the circumstances (no doubt a legacy of him being an excellent semi-pro musician in his day); and secondly, *Sports Report* has the best theme tune in the history of radio and television (if you don't believe me, tune into Radio Five Live this Saturday at 5:00pm – they still use the same tune. You won't be able to resist doing some sort of Okey-Kokey-cum-knees-up as soon as it comes on).

So, when we got back to the car and put the radio on to hear the classic words: 'It's five o'clock and time for *Sports Report…*' we were off! As the music faded, there was the dulcet tones of James Alexander Gordon reading out the headlines (I always pictured James in full evening suit speaking into one of those microphones that looked like a giant throat lozenge): 'Carlisle United beat Tottenham Hotspur to go top of the First Division…'

(The famous 24 August 1974 Division One League table – top half – which shows Carlisle United as the best team in England.)

First Division

	P	W	D	L	F	A	W	D	L	F	A	Pts
		Home					Away					
Carlisle United	3	1	0	0	1	0	2	0	0	4	0	6
Ipswich Town	3	1	0	0	2	0	2	0	0	2	0	6
Liverpool	3	1	0	0	2	1	1	1	0	2	1	5
Wolverhampton W	3	1	1	0	4	2	1	0	0	2	1	5
Everton	3	1	1	0	2	1	1	1	0	3	2	5
Arsenal	3	1	0	1	4	1	1	0	0	1	0	4
Derby County	3	1	1	0	3	1	0	1	0	0	0	4
Stoke City	3	1	0	0	3	0	1	0	1	2	2	4
Manchester City	3	2	0	0	5	0	0	0	1	0	4	4
Middlesbrough	3	0	1	1	1	3	1	0	0	3	0	3
Chelsea	3	0	1	1	3	5	1	0	0	3	1	3

It did not get any better than this. No, seriously, it really did not get any better than this. The Blues' first reality tablet was uncomfortably swallowed on the following Tuesday night. In a strange fixture quirk, the teams who played less than a week earlier were scheduled for the return match; so it was Middlesbrough who were the second visitors to Brunton Park. On paper, Carlisle had nothing to fear – they had not only won at Middlesbrough less than a week earlier, but they had also beaten the Teesiders at Ayresome Park in the pre-season Texaco Cup.

But on the night, Carlisle seemed strangely subdued, almost as though they suddenly realised what they were achieving and developed a crisis of confidence as a result. For their part, Middlesbrough were more than a decent team; although they had been promoted along with Carlisle, they won the Second Division Championship by some margin (16 points ahead of Carlisle in third place) and were confident they could hold their own in the top flight.

Completely undeterred by United's success a week earlier, Boro came out the blocks confidently and David Armstrong scored after just two minutes. The Blues huffed and puffed after that but Middlesbrough kept them at arms' length throughout and held on for a fairly comfortable 1–0 victory. On the same night, Ipswich beat Arsenal and Carlisle's 15 minutes of fame at the top of the League was over.

The following game saw the Blues travel to Leicester. They went to Filbert Street in good spirits – despite the reversal against Boro, no one could have hoped for three wins from the first four games. The clash of the Foxes started well for the Cumbrians when Chris Balderstone and Joe Laidlaw combined to set up Hughie McIlmoyle for his first goal of the season. It was a significant goal for Hughie as it was his first after

Alan Ashman wins the dreaded Manger of the Month award for August 1974.

returning to the club (for his third spell) and it was against the team he started his professional career with, south of the border, in 1961. Things were looking even better for United when Graham Cross brought down Laidlaw in the box and the referee pointed to the spot. It proved the turning point of the game as the normally reliable Chris Balderstone missed the penalty. (Baldy was another with Leicester connections, as he played County Cricket at Grace Road for them for many years.)

A missed spot-kick always seems to put doubts into the minds of the team that misses it and this was a classic example. Carlisle gradually fell back and tried to hang on to what they had. On 85 minutes, the inevitable happened: a Leicester attack resulted in Peter Carr bringing down Leicester winger Len Glover. Frank Worthington made no mistake with *his* penalty.

The Blues held on for a creditable draw but the game would prove significant, as it would be the first of many involving missed opportunities and late goals that would ultimately shape United's season.

When Stoke City visited Brunton Park on 7 September, United sat fifth in the League. However, disaster had struck on the eve of the game when Alan Ashman was named Manager of the Month for August! The award had carried a curse for many a long year and so it was to prove for the Carlisle manager. Any self-doubt that may have been creeping in after the Middlesbrough and Leicester games was exploited to the full by the Potters who systematically dismantled the home side. Their display was typified by their striker John Ritchie of whom the generous Bill Green recalls '[Ritchie] took me apart. He scored and at no time in the match did I solve how to either stop him getting the ball or getting it off him'.

Stoke won 2–0 and this was followed by another defeat to a last minute goal at Newcastle. The ship was steadied somewhat with a couple of decent home performances (and clean sheets) against Birmingham and Manchester City, but then three quick defeats against fellow promotion-achievers Luton Town, and then Liverpool and Wolves had Carlisle teetering, and facing the reality of a long uphill battle to survive.

In late September, the local press reported that Ashman was making an audacious bid to sign John McGovern from Leeds United. McGovern was Brian Clough's pupil, having signed for Clough at Hartlepools in 1965. Clough then took him to Derby with him, where they won the title together in 1972 and again, the two went on their ill-fated sojourn to Leeds United in 1974, when Clough replaced Don Revie as manager. Clough only lasted 44 days in the job and McGovern only played four games for the Yorkshire giants before the whole thing went sour.

Sensing the disharmony Ashman tried to bring the midfield general to Carlisle but instead, McGovern predictably followed his boss to Nottingham Forest. He would go on to captain the Forest side to the First Division title and two European Cup triumphs.

Dennis Martin scores against the eventual Champions Derby in 1974.

Whereas Ashman's intentions were obviously ambitious, all of us Monday-morning-managers were suggesting – even at that early stage – that a goal-scorer was surely more of a priority.

With no obvious candidate on the market, Ashman was left to concentrate on breaking up what was becoming an all too familiar pattern: two or three defeats (usually including the conceding of a late goal somewhere along the line) followed by a stunning result against all the odds. Having been beaten by most of the top sides, Carlisle lined up at home against another contender on 19 October 1974.

Derby County had won the League Championship (their first) under Brian Clough in 1972 and reached the European Cup semi-final the following season. Clough left the club later that same year to be replaced as manager by one of Clough's most influential signings, Dave MacKay.

There was not much reason for optimism among the home fans as Allan Ross, Les O'Neill, Hugh McIlmoyle and Joe Laidlaw were all side-lined through injury.

The game started predictably, with the opposition dictating the play and United struggling to get a foothold in the match. Derby bossed the first half throughout, forcing reserve 'keeper Tommy Clarke into a couple of decent saves. Then on 42 minutes, Dennis Martin and Balderstone combined to set up Ray Train, who had moved forward down the right channel and found himself in the box. Not renowned for his goalscoring, Ray hit an angled drive that found the bottom corner. As things had been so bleak for so long, I am sure it took us some time to realise what had happened: delayed reaction; explosion of noise!

It was with a new-found confidence that the Blues took to the field in the second half. It was also with a new-found confidence that the crowd started to cheer them on. Both parties were rewarded on 66 minutes when Bobby Owen fed Frank Clarke and the striker fired in a shot that hit the base of the post; before we had time to lament our misfortune, there was Dennis Martin to put in the rebound. Four minutes later, it was Clarke who got his just reward with Carlisle's third and the Cumbrians found themselves dominating one of the best teams in the country. Little did we know at the time, but we walked home that night having just witnessed Carlisle hammering the future champions.

But stellar results like this started to become more infrequent as the thin, aging squad fought to keep its head above water. Six consecutive defeats followed the Derby victory: odd goals, late goals, missed opportunities. The once feared pattern was now becoming the norm. Alan Ashman himself later recalled:

'It was tough once the results started going against us. It was like all the players were Cinderella, at 4:38pm every Saturday they would turn into pumpkins and the opposition would snatch late goals. It happened so often that we thought some curse may have been placed on Brunton Park. Dick [Young] had them in doing extra training, but it didn't work.'

The notable highlights among the six defeats included Hughie McIlmoyle scoring what would be his final goal for the club at Sheffield United. Two others were quotes from seasoned pros: Leeds United stalwart Johnny Giles said after his team had snatched a late, undeserved winner, 'I have never been here [Brunton Park] before and I was staggered at Carlisle's show. They did it all didn't they? For some time in the game we did not know where we were. But we won. We have the experience you see.' The other came from managerial legend Bobby Robson who was equally fulsome in his praise of Ashman's charges after the defeat at Ipswich, 'They are a credit to the First Division. They didn't come here to close it up and defend, they came to play. And they allowed us to play'.

That was perhaps the trouble – Carlisle didn't have the savvy (or perhaps the cynicism) of the established teams. Billy Bremner told Allan Ross after the Leeds game that one of the Carlisle players had apologised to him after fouling him. Bremner thought this showed weakness. (You could never imagine Bremner clattering into a 50–50 and then politely asking 'ooh, sorry – did I catch you there?')

Carlisle's push-and-run style was easy on the eye and won them many friends but too often, the Blues were coming out on the wrong end of the all-important result. By early December Carlisle were already second from bottom, and struggling. Midfielder Les O'Neill had scored the goal at Ipswich in the 3–1 defeat and this made him the top scorer with five goals.

Ashman continued to trawl the transfer market to bolster the squad. Two significant deals took place during the autumn period: forward Eddie Prudham came in from Sheffield Wednesday for £35,000 and the terrific Graham 'Tot' Winstanley was sold to Brighton for £20,000.

Tot had graced the blue (and sometimes yellow) jersey in 166 League games for Carlisle since arriving from Newcastle in 1969. Some of the greats from the period – Peter Osgood, Francis Lee, Kenny Dalglish – had all been kept at bay by Winstanley during this time. Understandably, he still lists his winning goal in the epic game with Roma in '72 as the highlight of his career. (Winstanley was destined to return for a second spell at Carlisle in 1979 and play a further 33 games).

He was displaced from the side when Ashman signed Bill Green the previous season. Tot was not only loved by the fans but revered by his colleagues, many of whom give him the ultimate compliment; describing him as 'a pro's pro.'

He only played one game in the top division. Typically, filling in for the injured John Gorman, the ever-willing and versatile Winstanley marked the pacey Neil McNab out of the game as the Blues beat Spurs in the third game of the season to go top. The no-nonsense defender still remembers the game with a smile:

'Alan Ashman came to me before the game and asked if I would fill in at left-back coz John had turned an ankle. I was happy to get a game but then I saw it was McNab playing and knew I was in for a busy afternoon – I mean, how many pigeons can he catch? I made sure the first pigeon he caught looked like my foot, right up his arse!'

After the Ipswich game, the next visitors to The Brunt were Arsenal. This sadly held none of the excitement and expectancy of the Cup tie two seasons earlier. That great Arsenal side had broken up and a poor outfit – themselves struggling toward the bottom of the League – turned up that day. In a bad tempered, scrappy affair, Carlisle finally stopped the rot with a 2–1 victory; the crowd being further buoyed by the sight of new signing Eddie Prudham scoring his first goal.

The Blues could not sustain this form, however – or, indeed, repeat their opening day heroics – as another London visitor, Chelsea, left with all the spoils the following week. This game proved a double whammy for John Gorman, whose high level of consistent excellence over the three previous seasons, was now achieving the national recognition that came with playing in the top division. The Scotland manager Willie Ormond came to Brunton Park to watch Gorman in the Chelsea game.

Sadly, in a rare poor game, John was second best in the Blues' defeat; and just to rub his nose in it, Charlie Cooke – Gorman's direct opponent – was selected for the squad on the strength of his performance that afternoon.

Going into Christmas week, United were in desperate need of a breather; sadly there was no let-up in this League and next up was a trip to the League leaders, Everton. The task was made worse by the fact new striker Prudham was injured and could not travel. The Toffees had only lost one game all season and six minutes in, their prolific striker Bob Latchford duly put them in front. Following the goal, the home side controlled the game comfortably throughout the first half. The second began as a carbon copy, with Latchford making it two after six minutes.

If anyone had said at that point that a further three goals would have been scored in the next 11 minutes, all Carlisle fans would have been fearing the worst. Three goals *were* scored – not by Everton but by United. The first two were courtesy of Prudham's replacement Joe Laidlaw. His first saw Chris Balderstone reverse a pass down the Carlisle right and overlapping full-back Peter Carr sent in a first time cross; Joe met it perfectly and powered a header into the roof of the net. Moments later, John Gorman sent a long diagonal ball forward that caused some hesitation in the Everton defence; the ball broke and Laidlaw fired in a rocket from 30 yards.

From absolutely nowhere, Carlisle were now bossing the game and Everton looked completely shell-shocked. Seven minutes after Laidlaw's second, United moved the ball through midfield and ultimately it went out wide to Balderstone; his inch-perfect cross was met by the perfectly timed run of Les O'Neill and Carlisle's top scorer headed home what proved to be an unlikely winner.

More compliments followed as Liverpool manager Bill Shankly saw the comeback victory, 'They were magnificent,' he said, 'this was a great display and I enjoyed it very much.'

If only United could have exchanged plaudits for points. After the glory of Everton, normal service was resumed when the Blues suffered three, consecutive, agonising last-minute defeats to Newcastle, Burnley and Arsenal. (The Newcastle game saw Allan Ross surpass Ginger Thompson's 376 all-time appearance record for the club).

Frank Clarke scores against League leaders Ipswich in January 1975.

The home crowd were then treated to arguably the most entertaining game of the season when Bobby Robson brought his Ipswich side to Brunton Park. The two teams picked up where they had left off at Portman Road in November: goalmouth action aplenty as Frank Clarke scored against his old team (how does that *always* happen?) and Joe Laidlaw was again on the score sheet as the Blues upped their game to claim the scalp of the team that sat on top of the First Division.

The game was notable also for the appearance of Carlisle-born Kevin Beattie at the heart of the Ipswich defence (Beattie was unquestionably one of best players ever to come from the city), and the fact that the home side did little to assuage the nerves of their fans when they missed a twice taken penalty (that is to say they missed it both times! Bobby Parker and Les O'Neill, being the culprits).

More praise was heaped on the Cumbrians by the *News of the World* correspondant when he wrote the following day:

'Carlisle have not given up the First Division ghost yet. If you don't believe it just ask Ipswich. They went to Brunton Park sitting proudly on top of Division One. But their reputation counted for nothing as Carlisle turned on a performance that made a mockery of their own plight near the foot of the table. Ipswich did not play badly, but they can have no complaints about the result. Carlisle thoroughly deserved the vital two points which gives them great heart for the tough weeks ahead.'

The much needed victory gave the Blues confidence as they turned their attention to the FA Cup.

THERE'S ONLY ONE F IN FULHAM

In over 40 years of watching football, I am of the opinion that players can be split into three distinct categories. The first is sadly the most plentiful, who, like the grey squirrel or the starling, threatens to overwhelm – through sheer weight of numbers – his less numerous and more attractive counterparts. Most common in today's modern game, I refer, of course, to the common or garden *twat!*

Sadly we have all witnessed him at one time or another; he is the badge-kissing mercenary, who frankly does not give a monkey's about the shirt he wears or the plebs he runs towards after scoring a goal; the chances are that he is only interested in his own teammate if his wife is a bit of a hotty. His intentions are to score off the field as much as on it, while raking in vast amounts of cash, before moving on to the next club who have lured him away with a fatter salary and some top typing-pool totty. He is a complete razzermattazer of a man who should be avoided whenever and wherever possible.

The second is the journeyman pro. He is generally a decent bloke who is never going to trouble the top flight or the discerning European observer, but is good enough and dedicated enough to his profession to earn a living by constantly moving around the lower Leagues (you know the old gag: 'He's had more clubs than Jack Nicklaus!'). This man will usually do a job for your club and should be given a decent crack of the whip; with a fair wind he may develop into a bit of a fans' favourite; who knows – perhaps even reaching the much sought after status of 'cult hero'.

But if you are really lucky, you will encounter the rare, apparently near extinct, third species of player. Usually a one club man; reliable, good-humoured who (and here's the rub) has pride in his own efforts and in his club. Being a small town, close-knit-community club, I am delighted to say that Carlisle United has, over the years, had its fair share of this latter category; players who have instantly fallen for the club, the city and the fans. The fans in turn have grown to love – even revere – these players and the appropriately named United have marched on together through thick and (mainly) thin.

One such example is the record appearance holder for the club: the one, the only, the great... Allan Ross. Allan was a good humoured hard-working goalie on the field, and an absolute gentleman off it. Whenever you mention Allan's name to any Carlisle supporter, you sense a lump in the throat and a misting of the eyes – such is the affection for the man. A regular routine of chatting to fans, signing countless autographs, and posing for photos with youngsters in the club car park before the game, became a common occurrence for Rossy. After his retirement he recalled his feelings in 1963 when he was transferred from Luton Town: 'When I came to Carlisle I fell in love with the place.'

I never knew Allan personally but my brother and dad got to know him quite well through their mutual golfing circles, after his playing days were over. Mark, in particular – who was captaining the Wigton Rugby Union team around that time – would recall how Allan always made a point of asking how he had got on in his last game. 'He was always interested in you and what you were doing,' recalls my brother, 'you would never hear him talking about himself or about his own achievements'.

The closest I ever came to Allan was (again, after his retirement) one morning in the Longsowerby area of Carlisle. I was working as a postman at the time and on this particular week I found myself on one of the less salubrious roads in the city. Here on the same road, was Allan Ross, carrying out his work as a rent collector for the City Council. (I wonder if Rooney or Drogba might get a job collecting rent, when they retire?)

To be set apart from their apparent equals, an individual sportsman has to achieve a great deal throughout a lengthy career. But in order to be called 'great' – sitting alongside such longevity and effectiveness – they must possess one prevailing virtue: humility.

You think of Bobby Charlton, of Henry Cooper, of Stirling Moss: they were all fierce competitors in their day, with drive, determination and a will to win, but they possess a humility that sets them apart and puts them head and shoulders above many of their contemporaries. It is the combination of these qualities through which they achieve the status of 'national treasure'. Allan Ross also possessed all of these qualities in spades, and I have no hesitation again in using the word 'great' in relation to him.

I do, however, have a whopper of a confession to make (and for the record – I am welling up with shame as I write this). Because whenever I think of Rossy I immediately think of that bloody quarter-final against Fulham. You see – unlike my dad – I wasn't there the day he saved the penalty at St James' Park to ensure Carlisle's extraordinary passage into the fourth round of the FA Cup in 1968; neither was I at Anfield that time when he kept Liverpool at bay for virtually the whole 90 minutes; and the epic League Cup run of 1969–70 when he performed miracles against Chelsea and West Brom was just a little before my time. But I was at that FA Cup quarter-final at The Brunt when one howler (in my opinion) proved a seminal moment in the club's history.

Perhaps a bit of context is appropriate at this stage. The FA Cup is the oldest and most prestigious domestic Cup competition anywhere in the world. It appears to consist of around 10,000 teams, with the first, opening, preliminary, qualification fixtures for *next* year's Cup Final, beginning the day after the *this* year's Cup Final. At this early stage, it appears to involve pub teams playing 25 aside games in parks around the country with jumpers for goalposts. By about October, the wheat has been segregated from the chaff and we are down to the last 3,000 remaining non-League teams.

Then, just as there is a danger that the number of teams left in the competition might drop below four figures, the numbers are bolstered once again by the pros from the lower professional Leagues. Then, after another half a dozen rounds, on the first weekend in January, it really gets serious when the 'big boys' from the two top divisions join the fray.

Nowadays, the top flight clubs view the FA Cup as an optional extra (like power steering or air conditioning – it's great if you've got it but if you haven't, never mind). They generally field scratch sides in the competition as they have other fish to fry (the top clubs are chasing the League and European glory, while the bottom clubs are desperate to avoid relegation from the cash cow that is the Premier League). But in decades past things were different. The country came to a complete standstill as Cup Final weekend – whether your team was in it or not – gripped the nation and was considered the highlight of the sporting year.

This frenzy reached its zenith in the mid '70s. Compounded by the fact that Bill Shankly's Liverpool had an annoying habit of winning the Championship most seasons, most football fans actually put a greater value on winning the FA Cup than the League.

By the time it got to the Final in May, the country was transfixed (probably because every man, woman and child had taken part in that year's competition at some stage). It all started on the Friday night before the match with preview shows on BBC and ITV (long before satellite TV, remember) both of whom would be screening the game live. Then came the big day itself, which started with Cup Final Swap Shop featuring Maggie Philbin and Keith 'Cheggers' Chegwin in front of the two protagonists' town halls, screaming '*Hello Noel!*' over the hundreds of cheering supporters who were not lucky enough to get tickets for the game itself.

Then it was time for Cup Final *Grandstand* (BBC) or Cup Final *World of Sport* (ITV) depending on your preference. Each station had a reporter in one of the camps and no time was wasted in cutting to the teams' hotels where the reporter would be waiting with the squad prepared to ask them several 'how do you feel?' questions. For the players it was then time for their pre-match meal and then a quick change into their Cup Final suits. For the rest of us it was time for Cup Final *It's a Knockout*, where a group of loonies supporting each team would try and balance on some greasy pole while attempting to burst balloons full of water with a cricket bat. Once we had recovered from that it was then time for Cup Final *Mastermind*, where some supporter/contestant would celebrate his pride in knowing what Charles 'Charlie' Charles had eaten for his breakfast prior to the 1932 Final.

As time was now getting on, the stations would then cut across to their respective reporters who were now on the coach with the teams travelling towards Wembley. The same reporter asked the same players more 'how do you feel?' questions.

Quickly back to the studio for a final reminder of the teams' 'road to the Final' before joining the cameras at Wembley itself. The players leave the coach and walk onto the pitch while the cameras scan the swaying banners among the 100,000 spectators (and then the director quickly cuts away when he realises that the particularly funny one has an inappropriate double meaning). The reporters by this time can hardly be heard as they gather a couple of players behind the goals and screams out their ultimate 'how do you feel?' questions above the din of the crowd.

Finally, at a quarter to three, the two teams walk out and the crowd goes wild. You now have a decision to make: do you go with the BBC's David 'one-nil' Coleman, or do you plump for the assured tones of ITV's Brian Moore? Either way, five minutes into the game, and as traditional as *Abide with Me*, Dad always says, 'The game could do with a goal'.

Much as I would grumble at my kill-joy dad, I must confess he was usually right; mostly the games themselves were garbage – both teams so frightened of losing, they became completely inhibited and terrified to take any risks. Upon reflection it was invariably the event that was special, not the match itself. Afterwards, the reporter would be in the tunnel with the players, participating in the usual post-match prattle: more 'how do you feel?' questions; 'over the moon', 'hasn't sunk in yet,' 'sick as a parrot', *blah, blah, blah*. All the while, the players would be bizarrely drinking pints of milk.

That night, you would then tune into *Match of the Day* to see the highlights of something you had just spent eight hours watching, and then for good measure, *The Big Match* on Sunday afternoon would give you the final analysis of the whole experience. And then that was it for another year.

In short, the Cup Final was a big deal in those days and – although younger readers may think I am drinking quite heavily by this point – I state quite categorically, in 1975 Carlisle United were right in among it, threatening to get to Wembley for the first time in their history.

The adventure began on 4 January 1975 when the Blues were drawn away in the third round to Preston North End. This is another great Carlisle Unitedism, as such a tie – over 80 miles away – constitutes a local derby!

Every January, the top flight teams dreaded such ties, as the hard, rutted pitches and the couldn't-give-a toss-about-reputations home crowd quite often brought the 'blue bloods' down to earth with a humiliating crash.

Bobby Charlton's Preston were two Divisions below Carlisle in the third tier of the League, and given the Cumbrians' lowly League position, this was the game earmarked by many a pundit as the classic giant-killing act of the third round. That view was endorsed by the fact that Carlisle had crashed out of the League Cup earlier in the season at lowly Colchester. It seemed that United had enjoyed for years the role of *being* the banana skin that the big clubs slipped on – now in the top flight themselves, the boot was well and truly on the other foot, and it appeared to fit rather uncomfortably.

The Preston tie proved a nervy affair: it was ugly, it was uncomfortable, and Carlisle didn't exactly look like a top flight side, but somehow they got through it, with an opportunist strike from Joe Laidlaw midway through the first half.

Once your team is through, of course, you can then sit back and smugly watch others struggle, actively cheering for the very same underdog you've feared in your own game (there's very little logic involved in being a football fan!). On this third-round occasion, it was Burnley and Tottenham that had succumbed to lower League opposition. *Shame.*

With the Preston tripping hazard successfully averted, the fourth round draw brought Alan Ashman's former side, West Bromwich Albion to Brunton Park. 'Of course the Cup is important,' said the boss in his pre-game press conference. 'There is a lot at stake for our club. It can bring in much needed cash that could come in handy for First Division survival.'

West Brom had descended from the heights achieved during Ashman's tenure and found themselves in the League below Carlisle, but with an experienced playing staff, coupled with the home side's fragile confidence, it was another potential upset. Fifteen thousand turned up on a dreich January afternoon to witness their team throw off the shackles of their League problems. The Baggies (more commonly known in those days as the Throstles) gave as good as they got for long periods, but goals from Frank Clarke, Joe Laidlaw and Bobby Owen saw the Blues home 3–2.

The victory put United into the fifth round draw for only the fourth time in their history, and with Newcastle, Liverpool and Chelsea all biting the dust along with West Brom in round four, the fans who had hitherto been occupied with their team's fight for survival in the League, started to take more of an interest in the Cup.

Unlike today, when FA Cup ties are played throughout the weekend, in the mid '70s all the games were played on the Saturday afternoon and the draw was made that evening. It was with great excitement then that we all got home from the West Brom game and put Grandstand on to see who was left in the famous velvet bag. Big guns Leeds, Everton and Ipswich all came out early so they had been avoided; the tension mounted and hearts started beating a bit quicker. Then it came: some old geezer squinted horribly at the number on the ball he'd just drawn out of the bag and announced: 'Number 17'; the brains of the operation with the pen and the clipboard, said 'Mansfield Town…will play…?' – inviting the other old guy to draw the away side – 'Number Twenty-Three,' '…Carlisle United…Mansfield Town versus Carlisle United.'

Mansfield Town? We can win this thing!

Mansfield were in the bottom tier of the Football League and as the game approached, Carlisle could put their fading League form to one side as a genuine opportunity for Cup success beckoned. The pundits, of course, saw the tie as another opportunity to see a top flight side humiliated by a lower League outfit. They may have been the only team from the bottom division left in the competition, but they were top of the League and had only suffered two defeats from 29 games all season. They were unbeaten in 18 and, with their confidence high, the media fancied an upset.

Evidence of this came when it was announced that the game was to be covered on *Match of the Day*. If you are a follower of a team given the 'favourites' tag in a Cup tie and you discover the game is going to be televised, you always know the press, media and other fans all fancy an upset. (The other worry sign is when you do not know the result and you tune it to the highlights show to find 'your' game is on first – you know you are in big trouble then!)

It can sometimes work in your favour, however, as there is so much hype and expectation about the 'underdogs', the game itself does not live up to expectation and – much to everyone else's disappointment – the 'favourites' triumph after all and leave the field with an apparent nonchalant air and their best what-was-all-the-fuss-about walk.

So it was to be with this game at Mansfield. In the build-up Alan Ashman spoke for both players and fans when he said, 'We're putting all the worries of the League to the back of our minds this week and we'll be concentrating on getting into the sixth round of the Cup.'

On the day of the game, Brian Clough was being interviewed in the lunchtime preview show and made no effort to hide his view that the Stags would triumph, particularly highlighting the weakness of Blues stand-in left-back Eddie Spearritt as a weak-link (John Gorman was out injured). What Clough did not dwell on was the fact that he had fallen out with the Carlisle player when he was Clough's captain during his brief spell at Brighton.

The Mansfield manager Dave Smith also got lost in the hype when he let it be known that that they had the champagne on ice in the dressing room, in preparation for their post-match celebrations.

Sure enough, when the whistle blew, the Stags came racing out of the blocks and put their illustrious visitors under pressure. 'Just keep it tight for the first 20 minutes,' is the old cliché and Blues' skipper Bill Green marshalled the defence well; a smart save

Bobby Owen rifles in the winner at Mansfield in the cup run of 1975.

from Alan Ross on 16 minutes kept the scores level; then three minutes later, Carlisle got the breakthrough, when Bobby Owen connected with a right foot drive into the bottom corner. Perfect.

Credit to Mansfield, who rallied well after the knock-back and built up the pressure as the game moved into the final quarter. But the Cumbrians triumphed and made it through to the sixth round of the FA Cup for the first time in their history. So it was in the Blues' dressing room where the celebrations took place, and it was Ross that revealed Dave Smith's cardinal sin of assuming the outcome had negated the need for Alan Ashman's team talk before the game.

Everton and Derby County – two teams at the top of the League – were knocked out that day: it really was up for grabs now. That night was the usual routine of crowding round the telly to see who we would get in the next round. Of course, you now know the answer: Fulham at home. It could not have been any better.

Bobby Parker reflects on the feeling in the camp at the time, in spite of the indifferent League form:

'The FA Cup games stick in my mind as being the most memorable throughout the season. Although we were struggling towards the bottom of the League, we all thought it was going to be our year in the Cup – we all had a really good feeling about it. It's difficult to explain but as some of the other teams dropped by the wayside we seemed to get stronger as the competition went on. I think it also helped by giving us a little respite from the League and we seemed to thrive on the pressure being off.'

Then it came – Saturday 8 March 1975 – a day that will live in infamy! (Well okay, that's maybe overstating it but trust me, it turned out to be a pretty crappy day.)

As a kid I was beside myself at the thought of my team getting through to the semi-final of the FA Cup. What my elders and betters knew mattered little to me, but had I taken time to read the match-day programme it would have given me pause for thought. In it, Ivor Broadis wrote (as a fan) of *his* similar dream to mine: 'Personally, I would swap a place at Wembley in to the Final for another 42 games against the Liverpools, Newcastles and Manchesters of the soccer world if it was possible.' But unlike me, he had seen it all before and followed the sentiment up with a cautionary note, 'When you reach this stage of the competition there are no first and second division clubs…just teams.'

Fulham arrived in good form; they had remained unbeaten in the League for a month and had caused a major upset in the last round when they beat top-flight League leaders Everton at Goodison Park. They brought 5,000 fans with them and took to the field wearing a snazzy AC Milan-style kit of red and black stripes. Among their number were former England captains Bobby Moore and Alan Mullery; although in the autumn of their respective careers, they were still useful operatives. They also had a star centre-forward, Viv Busby, who looked like he was a member of a Bee Gees tribute band – it was Busby who had scored two goals at Everton that took them through.

Then there was *their* goalie: a guy called Peter Mellor. On his last visit to Brunton Park, two years earlier, Mellor had gifted Carlisle one of their three goals and the Blues had run out easy winners. Two years on and he still had the swimmer's physique and this, coupled with his blond locks, gave him that appearance of a Viking prince; but never mind all that tosh, unknown to us (and probably to him) the git was about to play the game of his life.

A crowd of over 21,500 – along with the *Big Match* TV cameras – crammed into The Brunt to witness the biggest Cup tie since the West Brom League Cup semi-final five years earlier. Like then, we could smell Wembley (or was I just passing that toilet block again). Either way, we had a great chance. An even greater chance when you consider – notwithstanding their win over Everton – Fulham were in the League below us.

The game got under way.

Ten minutes in and Carlisle worked a nice move that resulted in Joe Laidlaw catching a volley sweetly that arrowed towards the bottom corner of the Waterworks' goal; Mellor dived full length to turn it round the post with a brilliant one-handed save. Collective comments around the ground included – 'great shot Joe'; and 'a good save mate'.

Then on the half hour, a free kick in the inside-right channel was beautifully delivered by Chris Balderstone to the back post; skipper Bill Green had spun and evaded his marker and met the ball as it dropped, with a stunning diving header. The defenders may have been oblivious to the big centre-half ghosting round the back, but Mellor was not – he scampered across his goalline and plunged to his right to push

Peter Mellor and his defenders in action again during the Fulham game.

Green's goal-bound effort behind for another corner. 'Oooo, hard luck Bill', and 'another good save mate!'

With five minutes to go to the break, the Londoners coughed up possession for the umpteenth time – would the pressure finally tell? Ray Train fed Balderstone who sent in another pinpoint ball for Bobby Owen but Mellor was there to block again and shovel it behind for yet another corner that came to nothing.

Despite the latest near miss, it's half-time and things are going okay: still goalless but we're well on top and the lads will be attacking the Warwick Road End in the second half so we'll see the goals close up. As the three 1974–75 season hits blared out (FYI: *Tiger Feet, Billy Don't Be a Hero* and *Sugar Baby Love*), Mark and I chatted about where the semi-finals might be: the usual venues of Hillsborough and Villa Park? Or maybe somewhere different like Highbury or Elland Road. Of course, it all depends on who we draw.

And who *would* we get in the draw? In one of the other quarter-finals that day, Arsenal were at home to West Ham – like this one, another home banker. I wondered if I would be treated to my ultimate footballing Utopia: my everyday club against my fantasy/glamour team in the semi-final of the FA Cup; oh what the hell, why not the Final itself? I squinted at the scoreboard at the Waterworks End of the ground that listed the half-time scores. The various games being played on the given day were listed against various letters (so you had to buy a programme to see which game corresponded to which letter!) The Arsenal/West Ham game was letter C (buggered if I could see it).

Still, must not get ahead of ourselves. Half-time apple devoured (even a trip to the 'toilets' avoided), and it was time for the second half. It started much as the first had finished – if anything Carlisle were upping the pressure and another almighty 'YEAH-ORRR' moment came on the hour when the ball broke to Les O'Neill about 20 yards out – he met it full on the laces and fired in a laser that was destined for the top corner; we were all in mid-air celebrating when Mellor somehow appeared from nowhere to tip the ball over the bar (I swear the ball was actually behind him when he got a piece of it!). 'I thought it was in,' recalls Les, 'I was wheeling away in celebration as soon as I hit it.' The collective comments around the ground were starting to become a little less charitable: 'You spawny git!'

Then something happened in the 67th minute that will – like the turd in the Paddock 'toilets' *c.*1971 – live in my memory for time immemorial. The ball broke Fulham's way on the halfway line and Bee Gees wannabe, Viv Busby got it through the inside-right channel as they attacked the Waterworks End. He stole a yard on Blues' left-back John Gorman and attempted to fire in a low cross through that horrible corridor between the 'keeper and the defence, for the left-winger, Jimmy Conway to run on to. But Busby appeared to scuff his connection and the ball's apparent lack of pace appeared to influence what happened next, as everything seemed to decelerate into a bizarre, slow-motion sequence.

Peter Carr, the United right-back was on the six-yard line facing his own goal and shielding Conway, who was coming in from their left; Carr waited for Allan Ross to take charge and clear his lines but his 'keeper hesitated momentarily, as if mesmerised by the slow moving ball. Finally, after what seemed like an eternity, Ross took a panic-ridden swing at the ball and miskicked horribly; it squirted into the path of the oncoming Fulham striker Les Barrett, who himself seemed to make a poor connection, but he managed to scrape the ball goal-ward, and it dribbled excruciatingly over the line and into the Carlisle net.

It was one of those moments when a football crowd collectively holds its breath for a millisecond; a millisecond later, the 5,000 Fulham fans erupted into a roar of delight, while the 16-odd thousand rest of us stood watching in uncomprehending, open-mouthed silence. What happened? Did the linesman flag?

The red and black huddle of players in front of the euphoric travelling fans at the far end of the ground confirmed, if confirmation were needed, that the goal stood.

It was at that very moment that the dream was over – as if everyone knew the Cup dream was ending and the League campaign would drift away. The body language of the players appeared to change instantly: their fragile confidence was shot, the minds and the hearts were willing, but the bodies would not conform as nerves and fear threatened to stifle them. The crowd were no better: we still cheered the lads on, but the once confident roars of encouragement now seemed to get stuck in your throat and came out as an apologetic murmur. Was there anyone there that day that honestly believed we were going to turn it round after that goal was scored?

Maybe: we won a corner with around 10 minutes to go. Not a bad delivery to which Bobby Owen made reasonable contact; but Mellor sprawled full length again. Rebound? No, he held on. 'You ab-so-lute TeWWAT!'

The minutes started to tick by at twice the speed; Carlisle could not string two passes together; all the 50–50s were being lost; possession was being sacrificed on piece. The crowd continued to try and hide their disappointment, but whatever cheering went on began to sound like desperate cries for help.

In those days there was only 10 minutes taken at half-time so each game was scheduled to finish at 20-to-five. I turned to Mark and asked what time it was, not really wanting to know the answer. 'Nearly quarter-to,' was his ominous reply.

It occurs to me that before a Cup tie, managers, players and supporters all trot out the old cliché about 'how we don't want a replay as it will drain the players and clog up the fixture list'. Equally, we all know that when you're 1–0 down at quarter-to-five, that's a load of bollocks; you would give anything for another game. In a time before the fourth official and his 'red number', effectively we were playing in time that didn't exist. One chance…please…just one chance.

At last Carlisle strung two passes together and the overlapping Peter Carr was found on the right hand side; blue jerseys piled forward into the box…this was it, the last chance: Carr sent the ball in but every United player – his confidence dented and too afraid to take a risk – left it for one another. The outstanding Mellor came off his line and plucked the ball out of the air, unchallenged. The deflation felt by the home supporters was audible.

Clutching the ball to his chest as if it was his first-born, the 'keeper looked suspiciously to each side of him, until he was satisfied that all the players had left his area. Then with a couple of bounces of the ball, he launched it up-field; it was the classic signal for the referee to blow his whistle and the three long shrills duly pierced the afternoon air. It was over.

The sad anorak that is your average football fan feels gutted at any loss; that feeling is exacerbated when your team loses a really big game that does not come around very often. When you add to the mix the fact that your team should have won that game, the feeling in the pit of your stomach is almost unbearable. So it was that afternoon against Fulham as we stared at the departing players in abject disappointment.

On the field the magnanimous Allan Ross went over to congratulate the magnificent Peter Mellor. Les O'Neill was slumped in disappointment on his haunches; Alan Mullery came over to commiserate with him.

'You were robbed mate – that was the equivalent of GBH,' said Mullery, helping his adversary to his feet.

'How many games-a-season does Mellor play like that?' asked a distraught O'Neill.

'Not many!' replied Mullery.

The magnanimous Ross congratulates the magnificent Mellor after the Fulham quarter final – Ray Train leaves them to it.

The Fulham boss was Alec Stock. He was so old, if they ever made one of those 1970s mini-series about the Old Testament, Alec Stock would have been cast in the part of Methuselah's Dad. But he knew a thing or two about the game and in his post-match interview he paid tribute to his 'keeper. 'It was two magnificent saves by Mellor that won the match for us, not the gift goal' he said. (Two saves? And the rest mate!)

The Fulham chairman meanwhile was comedian Tommy Trinder whose favourite catchphrase throughout the '50s and '60s was, 'You lucky, lucky people!' (Hmm!)

In his post-match interview, poor Allan Ross accepted full responsibility for the defeat and described the goal as the worst moment of his 12 years at Brunton Park. Others pointed out that had it not been for his brilliance in the away ties at Preston and Mansfield, Carlisle would not have even reached the sixth round; but characteristically, Rossy shrugged off the words of consolation and apologised for his error. Two years later, with in excess of 450 games under his belt for the club, Allan reflected on the magnitude of his despair:

'I don't think I have ever been so low [as a result of the Fulham game]. Everything had gone mentally. I was a wreck. The lot went – not just my confidence – I was on the verge of packing in football altogether. If I think something has been my fault, I will hold my hands up and say so. That honesty was what made me stand in front of the TV cameras and admit my mistake after the Fulham game. Watching the game – and that goal – again on TV nearly killed me. It was bad enough having made the mistake in the first place without having it rubbed in by the commentators.'

As disappointed as supporters were that day, I speak for all Carlisle United fans when I say that Allan Ross never has anything to apologise for.

John Gorman still remembers the feeling of desolation in the dressing room afterward:

'We couldn't believe it. We played well on the day and had been all over them. Les had a couple of great efforts but Mellor had an incredible game. We should have won and I am confident we would have beaten Birmingham in the semi-final as we'd already beaten them in the League.'

The game proved a great tale of what-might-have-been in the history of the club and, for the players – even today – it remains one of the great regrets of their careers. Skipper Bill Green:

'I was talking to Les [O'Neill] about it only last year. We were really confident going into the match because we had beaten them twice the previous season. Mellor played the game of his life: I had two headers he kept out. All these years later, we still can't believe what happened that day.'

So Fulham left The Brunt, its fans and players to contemplate their uphill battle against relegation that afternoon, while they marched into the semi-final.

We trudged home, gutted after another defeat. Mam and our younger sisters were there, not understanding or caring about our abject disappointment. It was one of those times when you envy the non-football fan their ambivalence – I was only a kid but I had already been drawn into the cruel inexplicable world of this stupid game.

And then it happens: in a sympathetic but unconcerned effort to placate the obsessive footy fan, the loved one comes out with the dreaded phrase you least want to hear…'Never mind, it's only a game'. I felt like Charlie Brown when he runs up to kick the football, only to have Lucy pull it away at the last moment: Aaarrrrggghhh!

Trying not to trip over my bottom lip, we put the telly on only to find out that Arsenal had also been beaten 2–0 at home to West Ham. Again: AAARRRRGGGHHH!

As suspected, Fulham overcame Birmingham City in the semi-final after a replay. So it was the Cottagers and not the Cumbrians that graced the Wembley turf on that sunny afternoon in May 1975. And wouldn't you just know it, they played West Ham; those two quarter-final ties had indeed produced the two finalists as I'd hoped, but not the two that I wanted!

At Wembley, the Hammers had a young 19-year-old called Mervyn Day in goal (20 years later, he would manage Carlisle United). His opposite number, of course, was United's nemesis, Peter Mellor who, on the day, let one through his legs and then parried one to the feet of the centre-forward as West Ham ran out 2–0 winners.

Cheers Pete.

THE SLIPPERY SLOPE

Maybe I am looking through glasses that always appear rosier in retrospect but I believe the defeat to Fulham was a seminal moment in the history of Carlisle United. Had we won that game, who knows how things would have worked out: an upturn in fortune and confidence? Wembley? Survival? As it was, the players trudged off that day and the fans trudged off home all knowing that the likelihood was that the dream was coming to an end.

The following week saw the team slump to another home defeat, this time to fellow strugglers Luton Town. The loss was Carlisle's seventh consecutive defeat (including the Cup tie) and succeeded in cutting United adrift at the bottom of the League.

Just when the inevitable seemed – well – inevitable, the Blues pulled off one of the stellar results of the season when two Joe Laidlaw goals secured victory away at Manchester City. In classic Carlisle fashion, however, it was followed by two further defeats, the first at Stoke who inflicted the heaviest reversal of the season with a 5–2 win at the Victoria Ground.

Although Carlisle suffered 25 defeats by the season's end, it is generally accepted that Stoke were the only team to dominate them in both games. Their 2–0 victory at Brunton Park could have been so much more, while the five goals at Stoke probably represented the true difference between the two teams. How ironic it was that during the season of Alan Ashman's greatest achievement (leading a club such as Carlisle into the top flight), it was his old mentor Tony Waddington that should put him in his place.

The one last hurrah probably came at home to Everton in late March. Ashman brought Tommy Clarke back to give the beleaguered Allan Ross a break. United had achieved probably the result of the season at Goodison in December, and a Joe Laidlaw penalty, and goals from Frank Clarke and Dennis Martin completed a famous double. The victory set in motion a respectable seven-game end-of-season sequence that saw the Blues lose only one game (away to Liverpool) but it was far too late to prevent the drop.

Nine months earlier, the Chelsea players applauded Carlisle onto the field at Stamford Bridge prior to the opening game of the season. In the final game of the season it was the United players who formed a guard of honour and applauded the

FOURTH, FIRST + FULHAM

Derby County players onto the Baseball Ground as the Rams celebrated their second title in four years. The game had a real end-of-term feel to it with few chances being created by either side. Almost inevitably, a goalless draw was played out; but it did give Carlisle the honour of taking three-out-of-four points off the champions.

Could it have been any different? Maybe we are kidding ourselves into believing it could. If only we had signed a proven goalscorer; if only we could have held on to leads; if only we could have defended to the ninetieth minute and beyond. (Six games were lost by the odd goal, conceded in the last five minutes. It became a self-fulfilling prophecy: we fear we will concede late on and continually think about it until it inevitably happens.)

But as we all know, the League does not lie and the upstarts from Cumbria finished bottom when the points were totted up. The manager summed up his thoughts by saying, 'We were relegated at the end of the season, but for me, if I had managed to bring a couple of extra players we would have stood a better chance of surviving.'

Hughie McIlmoyle gave his assessment years later:

'I think the team lacked a little bit of concentration and because they gave everything they ran out of steam. I don't think the strikers gave the defenders much to hold on to. Carlisle paid £60,000 for Bobby Parker at the start of the season. He was a terrific buy. He played hundreds of games and that particular season he and Bill Green were probably the two most consistent players. They were outstanding but instead of spending what to them was big money in defence they should have gone the other way and bought a striker to get some goals.'

It is interesting to look at the League standings at the end of the 1974–75 season. Luton, who had come up with Carlisle, not surprisingly kept them company on the way back down. Of the three London giants, Chelsea were actually relegated alongside the two one-season wonders. Tottenham Hotspur finished one place and one point above Chelsea (Spurs finished only five points above Carlisle – remember those six points dropped to late goals?); while a poor Arsenal team finished a lowly 16th.

Instead of the teams we know today dominating the title race, it was left to the relatively small provincial clubs to lead the way: not only did Derby win the League, Ipswich Town finished third, while Stoke City, Sheffield United (under Workington's old boss Ken Furphy), Middlesbrough and Burnley all enjoyed top half finishes. Only Liverpool, Everton, Manchester City and Leeds United represented the 'big boys' (Manchester United were not even in the Division – they had been relegated while Carlisle had been promoted the previous season. The two now also swapped places – United have never looked back since. Manchester that is!)

In all fairness, it is hard to see how Carlisle could have sustained a top-flight existence. The squad was small and was without a reserve team. As a consequence, the squad players that came in like Mike Barry, Mike McCartney and Eddie Spearritt, were way short of experience and match practice at that level; expecting them to achieve something that the 'first choice' players were struggling with, was clearly wishful thinking. When I interviewed him for this book, John Gorman also revealed that he played most of the season with a stomach injury and resorted to having injections between games to keep him going. (Mention should also be made of third-choice 'keeper Peter McLachlan who never actually got a game in the top flight.)

It wasn't just the staff resources that were thin – with average crowds (even in the First Division) of fewer than 15,000, financial resources were also at a premium and were hardly conducive to sustaining a club in the top division.

The problem is that once you are on the slippery slope – as many other teams before and since Carlisle have discovered – it is difficult to arrest the slide. For younger readers, perhaps the best comparison I can draw is with the Blackpool side that played in the Premier League during the 2010–11 season. Like the Carlisle side of 1974–75, they were great to watch; like Carlisle, they were everyone's second favourite team; but like Carlisle, they lacked that certain top-flight savvy and ended up being relegated as a result.

Once the season finished, it was time to reassess the merits of the squad. Hughie McIlmoyle finally hung up his boots for good, while Chris Balderstone ended his 10 years at the club and went to Fourth Division Doncaster Rovers for a final season in the game. Reserve goalkeepers Tom Clarke and Peter McLachlan were given free transfers. Veteran 'keeper Allan Ross was given a two-year contract but it was thought he would play a supporting role to a new stopper come August.

As the break-up of the rest of the team looked inevitable, the board made a decision that bucked the 10-year trend of buying small and selling big, presumably in an attempt to bounce straight back to the top flight. Their decision involved skipper Bill Green, who recalls the events of the close season of 1975:

'At the end of the First Division season there were a couple of enquiries from Newcastle and then from Spurs who actually tabled a £165,000 offer. I met with Alan Ashman who said he knew it was a good opportunity and he couldn't stand in my way – he informed me that there was a board meeting that night to discuss the offer but it seemed cut and dried. I went in to see him the next morning and I knew right away that it had been rejected – the reason given that it was too close to the start of the season and they couldn't get a replacement. I had a great time at Carlisle but like all players I was ambitious and was really disappointed.'

The 1975–76 season loomed with the club having only signed one player – as suspected, a new goalkeeper – Darlington's Martin Burleigh. Burleigh turned out to be a decent goalie but at the time it was all pretty uninspiring.

August brought good Texaco Cup wins against Newcastle and Sunderland which gave us all cause for optimism, but a tame opening day draw followed by four consecutive defeats gave us all a rude awakening as last year's heroes sat ignominiously at the bottom of the table.

By mid-October, United had only won two games and rumours abound about the manager's position. Some weeks earlier Alan Ashman had rebuked his players and called for more effort; none was apparently forthcoming and after another uninspiring draw at home to Luton – when the Hatters fortunately missed a last minute penalty – Ashman tendered his resignation. It was a sad end to an on-off association, as player and manager, with the club that had dated back over two decades.

It later became clear that the inner demons we all face at one time or another had niggled away at the Carlisle-great, as he revealed in a period of self-analysis years later:

'Looking back I didn't handle the situation well. It seemed clear to me that I was going to be sacked. I had lost a lot of the players in the dressing room. It's one of those things you just know. It was time to go. I should really have talked it over with those who mattered at the club, but I just wanted to get away, get out of football for a while. I was ashamed of myself. I felt as though I had let the whole city down. I didn't like going out in public. It was an awful feeling.'

Dick Young stepped into the manager's seat on a caretaker basis and then, it was announced that Mr Dependable had finally landed the job permanently, at the ripe old age of 57 and having been at the club for 20 years.

Dick's first couple of decisions proved popular with the home fans. First, he reinstated Allan Ross to the first team, in place of the beleaguered Martin Burleigh. Secondly, after scouring the transfer market to freshen up the forward line, he pulled a masterstroke by re-signing 'Our George' to the club in early December 1975.

George McVitie was the darling of the Brunton Park crowd in the latter half of the 1960s. Signed as one of the first apprentices for the club along with Mike Green earlier in the decade, his wizardry on the wing was invariably the catalyst for the crowd to get on their feet and become the proverbial '12th man'. He was a dream for any striker to play with as Hughie McIlmoyle recalls:

'George's strengths were the way he could carry the ball through and his crossing ability. He could cross the ball on the run, which is something not all wingers can do. A lot of them nowadays sprint down the wing and then stop the ball to cross it – for me a winger should cross the ball as he is running and George was outstanding at that.'

It was Bob Stokoe who had sold McVitie in the early weeks of the 1970–71 season for £30,000. The team were having their pre-match meal before a game at Leicester, when the manager took the winger to one side and told him to get his things together as he had accepted an offer from Alan Ashman at West Brom. 'I didn't want to go,' recalls George, 'but if the two clubs agreed, the players had little choice.

After a three year stint in the West Midlands, George moved to Oldham, where he had been an integral part of the Latics' Third Division title-winning team of 1973–74. Now, at 27, he re-signed for his hometown club for £12,000.

The new manager and the new arrival between them seemed to give a little bit of hope and inspiration to the team as they went six games undefeated for the only time in the season, which took them to 15th in the table as the New Year dawned.

But whatever fragile confidence there was evaporated and the club slid further down the table in the second half of the campaign, registering only four wins from their last 18 games. The fans' misery wasn't helped when the popular Ray Train moved to Sunderland at the beginning of the run-in. He was replaced in the squad by Hamilton Academical's Phil Bonnyman.

The agony went all the way to the final day of the season when thankfully, Frank Clarke and McVitie scored to secure one of those four wins against Plymouth Argyle, and with it, Second Division survival, with a paltry 37 points – four above the drop zone.

Plymouth themselves had had a modest season but after the previous promotion campaign when they won the Third Division title, they were perhaps just happy to retain their second tier status. The driving force behind their success had been a prolific strike partnership of Paul Mariner and one-time Carlisle target Billy Rafferty; the two had proved a perfect foil for one another and had racked up 47 goals between them for the Pilgrims in the Championship-winning season.

For the final game of the 1975–76 campaign manager Tony Waiters left Rafferty out of the team, telling the striker that he wanted to give some of his youngsters a game, given that safety had been secured a couple of weeks earlier.

A week or so into the close season, Billy was travelling north to visit his parents in Scotland. He recalls the trip:

'As we passed Carlisle on the motorway I remember commenting to my wife how unusual it was that I was left out of that last match. Thinking no more about it we carried on our way. We arrived at my parents' house and as I was walking up the garden path, I could hear the phone ringing. My mum opened the door and picked up the phone at the same time. "It's your manager Tony Waiters who wants to speak to you", she said. My first reaction was "Oh no, he doesn't want me to go back to Plymouth does he?" It turned out that he was actually phoning to tell me he had agreed terms with Carlisle United, which was a bit of a bombshell as Paul and I had had two years where we did so well together.'

Rafferty's initial reluctance was understandable, as the football rumour-mill had one of the country's top strike partnerships both being linked with the likes of Liverpool, West Ham and Ipswich. Moreover, his dilemma was fuelled by his previous experience with Carlisle three years earlier when he balked at making the move to

Brunton Park. He subsequently regretted his decision (as did the club) but now, three years on, the player was considering a move back up north once more.

Sadly, he did not get the opportunity to haggle with the chairman who had contributed to his looking elsewhere in '73 – George Sheffield died after a short illness in May 1976, ending a 16-year spell in the top job.

Also, at the time of Billy Rafferty's transfer *into* the club, significant negotiations were taking place elsewhere that would see another popular player *leave* Brunton Park. The previous close season, Carlisle had turned down an offer of £165,000 for skipper Bill Green; now, a year on, the club had accepted an offer of half that figure for the centre-half from West Ham. Bill recalled how disappointed he was with the 'Spurs move' 12 months earlier, he then recalled how this was compounded by a sub-standard season, 'I don't think I reached the heights that season of the previous two – it wasn't through a lack of desire but maybe it was just something sub-consciously.'

The fans' disappointment at the loss of the skipper was assuaged somewhat with the news that Rafferty had agreed to sign. Green's replacement at the other end of the field meanwhile was St Johnstone's Ian MacDonald. Other comings and goings included Eddie Spearritt and Joe Laidlaw (out) and John Latham and John Smith (in). Dick Young had also made a bid to sign Oxford United's Mick Tait, but his offer was given short shrift.

With his wheeling and dealing virtually complete Young took his charges down to Southampton for the opening League fixture of the 1976–77 season. Carlisle already had a win under their belts at this stage having won at Southport in the League Cup with new boy Rafferty getting both goals. Now it was on to the Dell.

In the final game of the previous season Southampton had caused one of the biggest Cup upsets of all time by beating Manchester United in the FA Cup Final. On the stifling hot bright August afternoon therefore, there was a real carnival atmosphere as the players were doing a lap of honour before the game with the old trophy.

George McVitie remembers when the players came out into the small area seeing a '…sea of red and white with a sprinkling of Carlisle supporters'. The whole place was bouncing as the tannoy blared out *When the Saints Go Marching In*. Billy Rafferty takes up the story:

> *'I remember kicking off, tapping it to Bobby Owen; Bobby rolled it back to Les O'Neill, Les played it back again to Ian MacDonald to give him a touch, Ian rolled it back to Rossy. Rossy then rolled the ball out to John Gorman (John always had to beat someone!), so he beat the right winger, then hit a long ball up front, Bobby won the header – he touched it on, it bounced once and from about 25 yards I volleyed it right into the top corner. It was 32 seconds – the ground went silent, they just couldn't believe it.'*

(This is another great paradox of the football fan. In such circumstances, you can both empathise with them, while simultaneously pissing yourself laughing at them.

For me, Billy's recollection conjures up a priceless image of the home fans interrupting themselves mid-chant…'Oh when the Saints go mar…awe shit!')

Despite Southampton equalising, Rafferty scored again in the second half to give the visitors an unexpected opening day victory. McVitie recalls Mike Channon and Peter Osgood coming into the away dressing room after the game and giving the Carlisle lads a few crates of beer '…for the journey home. They had been inundated with gifts before the game as Cup winners'.

Shortly after the victory on the south coast, United travelled to Highbury to play Arsenal in the League Cup. After a dreadful start which saw them 3–0 down after 20 minutes, the Cumbrians rallied and got two back before time beat them in what was a tight encounter in the end.

The respectable performance away to one of the 'big boys' should have given the team some cause for optimism, but sadly the season started to mirror the previous campaign. It would be a further three weeks before the next victory was forthcoming (at home to Burnley) and by 20 November the club had only registered one further League victory. What's more, by 20 November the team were playing under a new manager.

The strain had been telling on Dick Young for some time and the team that was in transition simply could not deliver for their boss. On 9 November Young told the *Evening News* of the crisis talks that were going to take place in the camp:

'We are to have a long talk about things. I have to try and get the players to realise the position we are now in. In the end it's up to the players. We have lost our last three games and are now at the wrong end of the table – but we don't want to be there. It's a year since I took over as manager and today we are as badly off as we were then. We'll have this long talk about things in the hope that the players will pull their socks up before it's too late. It's the players out on the field who can ultimately sort things out, nobody else.'

The talks obviously did not go well: the following day Young offered his resignation and the Board accepted, although it was agreed that Young should continue as assistant manager, and he should stay in charge until a new team boss was named.

To make matters worse, the following day, the fantastic John Gorman was transferred to Tottenham Hotspur for £60,000 (Young's last purchase was full-back Steve Hoolickin which paved the way for Gorman's exit). Gorman – frustrated by the team's decline and his own ambition – had put in a transfer request at the end of the previous season but, with no offers forthcoming, he started the season with Carlisle in his usual immaculate form. Like Green, he finally got his deserved move back to the top division.

To make matters *even* worse, the following game, which was billed as a make-or-break trip to fellow strugglers Oldham resulted in a 4–1 drubbing.

The new manager – or should that be player-manager – was North East hero Bobby Moncur. Moncur came in from Sunderland but had enjoyed a long and distinguished career at the heart of Newcastle's defence. It was hoped that his skill and experience, allied to the ever-reliable Bobby Parker, could help their inexperienced colleagues and cut out some of the naive mistakes that were costing valuable points. The theory was one thing, the practice was something else – a couple of defeats were followed by a couple of victories as the club moved towards the vital holiday period.

First up – a week before Christmas – was a home game with another struggler, Cardiff City. George McVitie was back in the team after a spell out through injury and he celebrated his return with a terrific goal in an even first half. Whatever was said in the Welsh dressing room at half-time, however, altered the complexion of the game completely – as the game moved into the last quarter of an hour, the Bluebirds were 3–1 up and playing their hosts off the park. On 79 minutes McVitie was withdrawn and replaced with John Latham.

At the start of play, the combination of a dreich, cold afternoon, a poorly performing team and the last Saturday before Christmas had reduced the gate to a modest 5,934. As the substitution was being made, many started to drift away in disappointment. Billy Rafferty was standing in the centre circle watching scores of fans streaming out. He remembered that night was supposed to be the staff Christmas party and thought 'This is going to be a good night!'.

On came Latham and the game restarted. Four minutes later Carlisle won a rare corner; Latham took it and Frank Clarke's scrambled effort towards goal was collected by Rafferty who swivelled and hammered it in for what even he believed at the time was a rather undeserved consolation, given Cardiff's second half dominance.

The Carlisle players trotted back to the halfway line while the Cardiff defenders were puzzling over how this lot were within a goal of them all of a sudden. With a minute to go Phil Bonnyman went through on the left as two defenders got in a tangle; Rafferty charged on to it ('the next time I touched the ball' he recalls) and hammered a first time effort with his left foot into the bottom corner. Incredibly, the scores were level.

Deep into injury time and Phil Bonnyman again went on a run, this time down the right wing; he crossed and there was the master-marksman who had stolen a march on his defender and allowed the ball to drift across his body – Rafferty made perfect contact with his left foot and guided it in past a distraught Ron Healy. Today, Billy remembers his famous hat-trick with an equal amount of pride and hilarity:

'For a centre-forward it is something you would dream about, like Roy of the Rovers. I can remember their players. I had known Ron Healy after he had had a brief spell at Coventry. When I walked over to shake hands I can't tell you what he said – all of their players were just devastated because they had played so well. With 20 minutes to go the crowd were just streaming out. And yet when I speak to people,

Billy Rafferty scoring his famous hat-trick against Cardiff in December 1976.

there's never a week goes by when someone says "Oh yes, I was still there, Billy – I stayed to the end". The number of people that have said that to me, there must have been about 15,000 there that day!'

It's confession time again for me: I honestly cannot remember if I was there or not! If I was, I definitely would have been there at the end because we never left early (honest Billy!). But given that I cannot remember it, I have to conclude that I probably wasn't there for some reason.

However, one game that Mark and I definitely attended came four months later. We are now in our late 40s but to this day, we still talk about 'The Wolves Game!'

Sadly, the unlikely victory over Cardiff did little to arrest the slide; it was followed by 16 games that returned only three victories. By the time League leaders Wolves came to town on Tuesday 19 April 1977, the Blues were in the bottom three and with only six games left, were staring down the barrel.

During the dismal run, Dick Young finally secured the signing from Oxford of Mick Tait. Tait was a tough-tackling midfielder who, it was hoped, would fill the 'Ray Train role' alongside Les O'Neill in the engine room. By April 1977 it looked as though we needed Red Adair and John Wayne in there with them.

Wolves were storming away at the top of the League and there was absolutely nothing in the form book to suggest this would be anything but another victory on their way to the title. But when was there any logic in this daft game?

For a game to be truly memorable, there are a number of ingredients required. Perhaps first and foremost is the David and Goliath scenario (as we have seen, there have been plenty of those over the years). Then there is a good atmosphere – a noisy crowd has to be a prerequisite for a great game. It is usually best when the contest is at night – the benefits of this are twofold: the best atmospheres are almost always generated under lights, and the pitch 'has a top on it', either through an April shower or the descending dew (with a bit of luck, this will hopefully lead to a bit of slithery chaos in the opposition defence). The final two ingredients are a ref that favours the bigger team, leading fans and players of the smaller team to adopt a 'world's against us' mentality; and last but by no means least, a dramatic finish in your favour.

Ladies and gentleman, I give you…The Wolves Game.

The day started well with the news that 19-goal Billy Rafferty passed a fitness test and was good to go.

Over 8,500 turned up to see the game get under way with the League leaders dominating possession as expected; as early as the second minute, John Richards hit their first shot just wide. Then, against the run of play, in the sixth minute George McVitie sent in a left wing corner – Mick Tait and Ian MacDonald had drawn the Wolves defence out of position and who else but Rafferty powered in his 20th of the season.

Undeterred, Wolves resumed their slick passing game and Martin Patching, Steve Daley, Richards again, and John McAlle all went close before Kenny Hibbitt had an effort smothered by Allan Ross; as the ball squirmed clear Patching played a neat chip towards the empty goal, but Les O'Neill was there to race back and head it out from under his own bar.

The game was ebbing and flowing by this point and Dennis Martin ghosted in from his wide position to power a Bonnyman cross just wide. Bonnyman and Rafferty threatened again before a soft concession undid Carlisle's good work. Alan Sunderland sent in a ball from the right and Ross let it slip from his grasp; it was all the encouragement Hibbitt needed and he was on it in a flash to ram in the equaliser. The goal spurred Wolves on and the Blues did well to make it to the break all square.

At half-time, Bobby Moncur instructed Les O'Neill to stick closely to Kenny Hibbitt who was increasingly running the show. On the terraces, we were all buzzing with the exhilarating game that was taking place before us – which was in marked contrast to some of the turgid games we had seen during the run-in.

The players re-emerged and picked up where they had left off. Richards and Willie Carr both wasted good chances for the visitors, while Bonnyman had a superb 30-yard drive tipped over and Mick Tait saw his header from a McVitie corner being deflected

Les O'Neill slams in the winner in the Wolves game.

just the wrong side of the post. A goalmouth scramble moments later resulted in Bonnyman's goal-bound shot being blocked on the line by Geoff Palmer and McDonald's diving header from a trademark McVitie cross shaved the woodwork.

As the epic seemed to be drifting towards stalemate, the crowd were fired up again with some agricultural challenges by Palmer and Frank Munro on poor Mike McCartney. 'OFF, OFF, OFF!' we all chanted as the ref bottled it. But justice was done with three minutes to go.

For once, O'Neill neglected his man-marking duties and found space with a forward run down the inside left channel; Bonnyman spotted Les's run towards the edge of the box and sent through a slide-rule pass for the midfielder to run on to; O'Neill hammered the ball past Gary Pierce without breaking stride. *We went nuts!*

The final whistle signalled the perfect end to the best game seen at The Brunt for 12 months or more. The hero of the hour described his first goal of the season afterwards:

> *'I'd been marking Hibbitt all the second half and had felt a bit stifled. Then this huge space opened up in front of me and I decided to make for it. Phil Bonnyman saw me move and played through a brilliant pass – it was magic and I was clear. The 'keeper got a hand to my shot and I thought for a moment that it wasn't going to go in, but it did and I felt 10 feet tall.'*

The whole team had made a mockery of their League position with the full-back pairing of Steve Hoolickin and Mike McCartney in outstanding form, while the magician that was George McVitie was a delight to watch as he teased and tormented *his* full-back. Manager Bobby Moncur could scarcely conceal his pleasure when he emerged from the victorious dressing room.

'These are amongst the better moments in football. When your team can win in a game like that. I was delighted with the way everyone battled and particularly as we had been given the run-around in the first half, we came back to win and win well. It was a night just perfect for a football match and it was a game to savour. I feel I must mention our fans – they were magnificent. They were always behind us and it was the best support we have had since I've been here. It was a great night all round.'

The terrific victory was followed up by another excellent display against fellow strugglers Plymouth – Billy Rafferty tormented his former club with a 3–1 win. Strangely the game against the Pilgrims was the first of (the final) five games, all against opposition at the bottom of the League. After the Plymouth victory Carlisle were one of five teams on 31 points – five points above the doomed Hereford United. Nervy goalless draws at both Leyton Orient and Hereford were acceptable with a home game against Bristol Rovers to come.

An early John Latham goal against the Pirates took the pressure off Carlisle in the early stages as the team settled into a controlling position against a poor Rovers team. When their cumbersome defender Stuart Taylor put through his own goal, we all thought things were cut and dried at half-time.

The Blues continued to control the game in the second half. With 10 minutes to go, in desperation, the Bristol manager waved the giant Taylor forward for a last hurrah and the move immediately paid dividends with what we hoped was a consolation. Encouraged by the return on the manager's gamble, Rovers started loading Hail Mary balls into the box for the big man to get on the end of. Whether he got on the end of them or not, it was enough to cause panic in the Blues' defence. With 89 minutes on the clock, things were starting to look decidedly uncomfortable, although Carlisle were still 2–1 up. The visitors won a corner in the last minute and everybody piled in: the scramble resulted in Carlisle's net bulging for the second time in 10 minutes – we could not believe it.

By this point we were watching the game through our fingers – surely it could not happen could it? This being football, of course it could – from the restart, Bristol won it back and lumped it forward; confusion reigned once more and the ball, incredibly, was lashed past Allan Ross for the winner.

All the good work against Wolves and Plymouth had been negated by two last minute goals against one of the worst teams in the League. It was almost as though it was the Cardiff game in reverse – one team dominating, while the other nicks the points at the end with late goals.

And speaking of Cardiff, the return fixture was at Ninnian Park on the final day of the season, in a winner-takes-all encounter (or perhaps loser-loses-all would be a better description). Carlisle needed to win the game to retain their Second Division status.

In a tetchy, ill-tempered game, the Bluebirds got off to a great start and piled the pressure on their visitors with a goal after only five minutes. Carlisle countered straight from the restart. Mick Tait played the ball forward to Billy Rafferty, who carried it square and laid the ball back to Les O'Neill who, without checking his stride, volleyed ferociously into the top corner of the net from 25 yards. 'It was one of my best ever,' recalls Les, 'I caught it right on the laces.' It proved to be his last goal in what was to be his last game for the club.

The referee's erratic display culminated in an outrageous decision in the second half that threatened to seal United's fate. A long punt forward by the home side saw Cardiff front-man Campbell barge Bobby Parker off his feet; going down under the challenge from the advancing Ross, Mr Homewood not only ignored Carlisle's appeals for a free kick, he pointed to the spot for a Cardiff penalty. Buchanan struck the penalty hard and low to the 'keeper's right but justice was seen to be done when Rossy dived low to beat out the shot, for the umpteenth penalty save of his career.

United had the Cardiff goal under almost constant siege during the final quarter but goalline clearances and near misses sadly do not count and the final whistle meant Carlisle had to rely on matters elsewhere to save their Second Division status. How ironic that they should be waiting 24 hours later for a result to come through from Brisbane Road, where they desperately hoped Orient would fail to win to give them the result they needed, just as had been the case in May 1974, when the two were vying for promotion to the top flight.

This time it did not go Carlisle's way and Orient's draw meant that, after 12 years in the top two divisions, the Cumbrians were once again consigned to lower League football (Cardiff, Orient and Carlisle all finished on the same number of points – United went down on goal difference).

The final noteworthy tilt at a giant windmill came in January 1978 when the club drew Cup holders Manchester United in the third round of the FA Cup. The city was buzzing for weeks before the tie that rolled back the years.

Game day arrived and, as we lived quite close to the ground, several cars carrying visiting fans decided our small housing estate would be a good parking location. We lived in a tiny cul-de-sac and unusually, this mini came driving up and parked directly outside our house. Dad jumped up and went over to the front window to give the occupants a '…if you think you're gonna park there…' mouthful. The occupants turned out to be a bunch of mulletted Mancs – they looked like a cross between the Ant Hill Mob and the Bay City Rollers. About 28 of them piled out of this mini. When one of them gave a menacing Neanderthal stare our way, Dad's clenched fist turned into a cheery wave: 'Your car'll be alright there lads; I'll keep an eye on it for you!' Off they went and our windows avoided being potted.

At the ground meanwhile, The Brunt was jammed to capacity for the first time in a long time. Bobby Parker remembers it vividly:

'We really fancied our chances. The atmosphere that day was fantastic – the best I'd known at the club. We couldn't believe it when we came out and saw the place packed.'

The game kicked off and threatened to be the classic anti-climax when Lou Macari put the favourites 1–0 up in the first minute. But Carlisle rallied and seven minutes later Ian MacDonald headed in the equaliser. With the Blues starting to get on top, Brian Greenhoff had the home crowd howling on 35 minutes when he brought down Phil Bonnyman on the edge of the box, earning himself a booking in the process. Ten minutes later came one of the seminal moments in the game. With a Manchester player being caught offside, MacDonald spotted Rafferty's run and took a quick free kick over the top; Greenhoff was beaten and instinctively stuck his arm up and stopped the ball. The crowd exploded and the referee had no choice but to send him off. Greenhoff left the field in tears.

With the Blues sensing their chance in the second half they piled forward in wave after wave of attack; Mick Tait had a couple of one-on-ones, but it was an incident involving George McVitie that caused the biggest uproar. George weaved a bit of magic only to be scythed down in the box by David McCreary. Unbelievably the

George McVitie is brought down against Man United in 1978 – no penalty?

referee claimed the winger dived and waved away the appeals (I suppose two massive decisions *against* Man Utd was too much to ask for).

Carlisle battered Manchester for the whole of the second half without getting the deserved winner. Billy Rafferty summed up the feeling in the dressing room afterwards:

> *'It was amazing having come in after playing Man United and having drawn and yet we were so disappointed because it could easily have been four or five one.'*

As is often the case, the replay was a different matter. Carlisle were again excellent but naive defending allowed the Red Devils to keep the Cumbrians at arm's length. A two-goal half-time lead was pegged back by a Mick Tait strike but then more silly goals took it to 4–1. The consolation was that Billy Rafferty scored the goal of the game after a slick move from a counter attack. Rafferty's goal made the *Match of the Day* shortlist for Goal of the Month. Billy was on fire, Billy was great, Billy could do anything...

Billy was sold to Wolves two months later (that buggered it). His outstanding Carlisle career had seen him score 27 goals in 72 games in a team on the decline. Rafferty had been watched for several months by Wolves boss Sammy Chung and his displays against Manchester United clinched a deserved move to the First Division where he helped the Molineux club avoid relegation.

As for the team he left behind, the Manchester tie proved the last 'near miss' and virtually signalled the end of the golden era of the club.

THE BLUES BROTHERS

Of course, there would be other adventures for Carlisle United following the period covered in this book. There would even be a positive blip in the early 1980s when a Beardsley-inspired United won promotion back to the Second Division.

But most of the exploits in the decades that followed, would take place back in the lower Leagues: there would be trials and tribulations, titles and traumas, unlikely last day escapes and bizarre penalty shoot-outs. The club would finally find the holy grail of Wembley (and Cardiff), albeit in the lower-league Cup competition; and there was even the ignominy of a season outside of the Football League.

But whatever adventures have taken place in the past 30 years – or those that will take place in the next 30 for that matter – there is no doubt the club will never again experience times like those covered in this volume. The face of the game has changed so much; the gap between the Premier League and the Championship alone is cavernous; the other two divisions increasingly appear to make up the numbers. While the rich get richer, the poor have to make their own arrangements.

It seems that for a club to have any kind of sustained success today it requires the intervention of a wealthy benefactor – usually some obscure oligarch from an otherwise Third World corner of the planet. And let's be brutally honest about it, even if the hitherto unknown Sheikh A-Leg from Timbuk-three with a shed-full of cash did decide to point his private jet in the direction of Britain, there would surely be other more attractive airstrips than that of Crosby-on-Eden to attract his attention. The best a club like Carlisle can hope for is to sneak into the Championship via the Play-offs – and even then, whether they could maintain such a status would remain to be seen.

So why was it so different then? How come a small club from a sleepy backwater managed to punch way above its weight for so long and generally put the fear of God into teams that in theory should have brushed them aside without a second thought? Call it fate, call it fortune, call it providence, call it what you like – the fact is that the club and the whole city just managed to find the right formula and maintain it for more than a decade.

My own theory is that it came from a sense of community; from the very top with the chairman and the club officials, down to the supporters on the terraces, not to mention the players on the field. Everyone had a sense of belonging to the city and bought into the idea that there was nothing (and no one) to fear. As a result everyone gradually realised that great things could be achieved. It's as though everybody from E.G. Sheffield to Harry (the lift man at Binns) all had a role to play: we all understood it and played it to its maximum potential.

Today, you often hear about businesses and organisations taking a balanced scorecard approach to management – that is balancing the finances, the resources, the performance, and the customer satisfaction – so that they all complement one other to produce a successful, sustainable venture. In football, the demand from the fans for success now *and* sustainability makes this balance incredibly difficult to strike.

Often chairmen become hostages to fortune by spending beyond their means in an effort to achieve short term success. (A classic example would be Leeds United of around 10 years ago, when their strap-line appeared to read: 'We are Leeds – we buy anything that moves!' This took them to the Champions League semi-final but when the money dried up and success eluded them, the club imploded and dropped like a stone through the Leagues.)

The flip side is the club who play the long game by ensuring the finances are sound and nurture young talent for the future. (The classic example of this is probably Arsène Wenger and Arsenal who always balance the books, buy relatively small, and have managed a move to a new stadium during the worst financial crisis in living memory – but they never actually win anything! While other clubs parade their trophies in May, Arsenal parade their balance sheet. Their strap-line could almost be: 'Why win something today, when you can admire the potential tomorrow!') In either scenario, the customer satisfaction is bound to suffer; or in football terms – the natives will eventually get restless.

I've just thought of another example – that of the owner who buys the club, strips it bare of any assets, and flogs the family silver before buggering off into the sunset (remind you of anyone?).

In the 1950s and '60s, no one had ever heard of the 'balanced scorecard', or 'due diligence', or a 'fit and proper persons test' (whatever that means). People running football clubs appeared to simply follow the lead of the previous generation dating back over half a century.

But there were a few exceptions – those that broke away from the ordinary usually did so behind a kind of Pied Piper character that players and fans alike latched onto and followed through as one to almost inevitable success. Whether they be a visionary in the boardroom, a tactical genius in the dugout, or a talisman of the field, these decision making risk takers acted as catalysts for their club's achievements in the years that followed: you think of Wolves and you immediately think of Billy Wright; you think of Liverpool and you think of Shankly; Ipswich and Ramsey; Leeds and Revie.

E.G. Sheffield would probably be horrified if I called him a visionary, let alone a Pied Piper figure such was his quiet, almost shy persona. But as far as Carlisle United is concerned, it is surely no coincidence that the foundations for the 'golden era' were excavated when George Sheffield became chairman in 1959.

Like everyone in positions of authority, he had his critics and detractors, but his ability to inspire others to follow his lead produced short, medium *and* long term rewards for the club.

His stated aim was to bring financial stability to the club and with it, a basis to move it forward. Momentum (and money) was generated almost immediately when Andrew Jenkins and David Dent were appointed to their respective roles. It was virtually unprecedented at the time to have young whippersnappers with their new-fangled ideas running Football League clubs. The two hit it off immediately and their innovative ideas and vision for the club appeared to complement the frugality and experience of George Sheffield and his contemporaries perfectly. When Sheffield died in May 1976 David Dent paid tribute to him in the local press:

'I became secretary shortly after Mr Sheffield became chairman. In that time, I've built up a wonderful understanding and working relationship. There were several qualities Mr Sheffield will be remembered for. Firstly, there was his absolute and total sincerity and honesty in all his dealings. One was always left with a total belief in his word – his word could be taken as a gentleman. Then he had this very great ability to make people work for him out of affection. One always wanted to work for him. He also had an enormous calming influence that he could give to any situation. He always had the ability to prevent situations getting out of hand. He was a very effective chairman who, though a quiet man, commanded great respect and his approach had a lot to do with the success the club had in his 16 years in the role.'

Coincidentally, the club's success started to unravel around the time of his passing – it would be relegated back to the lower Leagues at the end of the following season.

Going back to where it all began in the early '60s, the initiatives to generate more income into the club (like the weekly raffle) proved the most significant. Today, this sounds almost comically obvious, but not back then, when an attitude of 'we've never done this before' pervaded.

The generating of extra income into the club had a twofold benefit for the manager: he had more money to spend on a better quality of player; and secondly – in a [pre-agent] era when players' attitudes were very different to what they are today – he could entice the player to the remote city with the promise of a good quality house, purchased by the club. Current chairman Andrew Jenkins explains:

'It was a conscious decision – we kept buying houses, and every time we sold a player we would pay off the mortgage. It was all about building the club – living

within its means and not paying what we couldn't afford. Besides, the players were easy to handle in those days, they just wanted to play.'

(Unlike today apparently, when it seems that half of them don't seem bothered if they play or not – as long as they have the big contract, who cares?)

In an age when community spirit was more prevalent than it is today, this resulted in players living next door to the supporter who was cheering him on every Saturday. The children of the player and the fan meanwhile would become friends and go to school together, while the wives would be involved in neighbourhood activities. I can remember instances of this first-hand: our family home was in a small estate at the bottom of Warwick Road, on which there were three or four club houses. At one time or another [full-back] Joe Davies and his wife Rose, and [midfielder] Mike Sutton and his wife would get involved in organising dances and fêtes. With no apparent sense of hierarchy, club officials David Dent and later Colin Hutchinson also lived on the same estate.

And so it was in other areas – Harraby, Stanwix and Belle Vue all had players living within close proximity to one another and the supporters. First Division skipper Bill Green summed it up when he recalled his time in the city, 'Everybody lived round about. You saw people who would chat about the games'.

Stan Bowles recalled his own experience of his time in Carlisle in his autobiography:

'The people were great – when they could get out of their houses – but the weather was bloody awful. Some of the nicest memories of Carlisle revolve around the park opposite my house. Every Friday evening before a home game, the local kids would come knocking on my door, saying, "D'you fancy a kick about Stan?" I always did for an hour or so. It was just great fun.'

Stan's generosity is reflected by all of his contemporaries, many of whom were more than happy to give their time and share with me their experiences at the club. As I have stated earlier I was lucky enough to meet some of my childhood heroes among them, Les O'Neill. It was actually my second ever meeting with the great man – the first came in 1975. Les's career had reached its high watermark as he was playing in the top division of the English League but even then, he took the time to accept my school's invitation to present me and my teammates with winners' medals after our historic triumph in the Carlisle and District Primary Schools' Five-a-side Cup (Whadya mean I am overstating it?).

You know those really swanky awards dos at the top hotels where everyone gets togged up in their finest evening wear? Well it was nothing like that; instead it was a fish and chip supper in the school hall. Then, as now (and like so many of his colleagues) Les was great and was genuinely interested in the kids and their parents.

Emulating my heroes for the school team in 1975 (seated second left).

(Little did either of us know that that night was destined to be the high watermark of *my* footballing career as well. Mind you, I once did 22 keepy-uppies in 1977 – 23 if you count the ricochet off next door's car).

But all of this is to digress. This sense of community and camaraderie had been developed long before Bill, Stan and Les's time. Peter McConnell reflected on his arrival in 1962:

> *'It took a little bit of time to adjust to the smaller ground, but I quickly learned that they were some of the most loyal supporters in the country. Although the gates were only averaging around the 5,000 mark when I arrived there was still plenty of passion and noise from the terraces. The people were great inside and outside the ground.'*

During the decade, at one time or another, McConnell used to share a car to Brunton Park with neighbours Tommy Passmoor, Frank Large and Tommy Murray, all of whom lived at Belle Vue. 'Players were all on the same wages so there were no prima donnas,' he recalls.

Another way players and fans got to know each other was through working together. In an era when players were paid only a nominal wage in the close season, they took summer jobs to supplement their modest income (Peter McConnell drove Pioneer Foods' delivery van, for example). And when supporters were not actually working *with* the players, they were doing jobs *for* them: my dad – a joiner by trade –

remembers putting some windows in for Ginger Thompson, as a 'foreigner' at his house on Melbourne Road in the early '60s.

(Perhaps the best close-season story involves that most popular of players, Frank Large. Frank got a summer job working as a drayman for a local brewery. Legend has it that he showed the same enthusiasm and application for the job as he did on the field – the regular guys could not keep up with their temporary colleague as he ran up and down from the lorry to the cellar and back again carrying two barrels of beer to their one on his shoulders! The human bulldozer – giving it Large, as always.)

Players would go out for a coffee one day a week together after training and go out for a pint one night a week. The inner sanctum would include two or three supporters who had grown to know the players as mates.

There is no finer example of this than local builder Geoff Thomlinson – if anyone deserves the title of 'Mr Carlisle United' it's Geoff. When I interviewed him for this book we worked out that he had missed four Carlisle United games in 54 years (that is not a misprint – 54 years!); and just to clarify, that is home and away, friendly games and matches abroad. When he missed a game at Walsall a few years ago, due to an accident and subsequent 20-mile tailback on the M6, it actually made the local news – no one remembers the result but everyone knows that Geoff missed the game!

Geoff is a joiner by trade (he was my own dad's apprentice at local firm Barwick Bros. back in the early '60s) and has run his own building firm for many years. Before setting up his own business, and after completing his apprenticeship, he worked for another firm where he got to know [keeper] Joe Dean, who was a brickie, and [defender] Stan Ternent who had trained as a joiner – both of whom were working there during their summer hiatus from the game. When Geoff left to set up his own business, the two players got him a repair job at Brunton Park.

Before long, Geoff was virtually part of the set-up, doing regular maintenance jobs at the ground and at the club houses. The following summer he actually employed Stan and Tot Winstanley during the close season.

Perhaps the best example of this fan/player camaraderie came when Geoff and his mates travelled to Italy for the Anglo-Italian Tournament. Staying in Sorrento, they travelled by train to Rome knowing full well they could not get back to their digs due to the lateness of the game in the Italian capital. After one of the most famous results in the club's history, Stan Ternent and Tot Winstanley allowed him to bunk down on their hotel floor, while Frank Barton and Allan Ross put the other guys up. The following morning – while everyone was tucking into breakfast – the then caretaker manager Dick Young announced to everyone's amusement, 'We had a great result last night, and it seems that we've signed three new players!'

Fans like Geoff would join the players for drinks at the Harraby Inn (for those living in the south and east of the city), or the Museum Pub (for the Bell Vue crowd), or for a game of dominoes at the King's Head on a Sunday lunchtime.

It's probably because of this sense of community that players like Stan Bowles, Bob Hatton, Frank Large, Billy Rafferty and Ronnie Simpson – all of whom played less than 100 games for the club – are held in as much regard as the likes of Chris Balderstone, George McVitie, Bobby Parker, Allan Ross and Ginger Thompson, who racked up around 2,000 appearances between them.

It's testimony to this feeling of belonging that many players chose to return to the city after their playing days were over, to enjoy their retirement. Others, of course, were local lads to start with and many still contribute to the club and the city (and the odd book!) today. Perhaps the most notable football-related contribution came from Ginger Thompson and his former teammate George Walker, who founded Carlisle City Football Club in 1975 (City remain one of the top amateur sides in the area).

Another characteristic of the period – despite the fact that managers and players came and went – was that the majority of the back room staff remained stable throughout. David Dent's assistant Jean Hewer kept the office running efficiently ('...she was brilliant,' recalls journalist Ross Brewster, 'she would deal with calls for the players and anything else that came in'); Herbert Nicholson was the physiotherapist for years; and, after his playing days were cut short through injury, Hugh Neil continued with the club as chief scout.

Even downstairs in the tea room, there was an old boy called Kit Robinson who would be there with his world-weary look, making the lads a cuppa while all he got in return was a degree of leg-pulling about his age and lack of mobility. It all contributed to a good-natured, informal atmosphere.

The final piece in the Brunton Park jigsaw was the playing surface produced by groundsman Ted Swainson and his assistant Robin Dalton. At a time when some pitches – most notably Derby County's Baseball Ground – resembled areas of Northern France *c.*1916, the lush, green pitch produced by Messrs Swainson and Dalton was smoother than a Barry White concert.

This all suited Carlisle's passing style perfectly. *It*, of course, was instilled into the successive generations of players by trainer Dick Young. When Hughie McIlmoyle signed for the first time 1963 he was struck by Young's different approach to that of his previous clubs:

> *Normally at clubs I had been at, pre-season was everything about strength and endurance. At Carlisle it was different – the footballs were out every day and Dick Young was always there looking to get the games and ball skills going. "Pass the ball", Dick would constantly shout.*

When Hughie's 'townsman' Billy Rafferty (they were both born in Port Glasgow) signed 13 years later he couldn't believe the skill displayed by his new colleagues. The common denominator, of course, was Dick Young.

The 1960s had started with the tremendous Tottenham Hotspur team that had pioneered the 'push and run' style of play to great effect (they were the first team in the twentieth century to win the League and Cup double and followed it up the following season by retaining the FA Cup). Dick Young was a great advocate of this style and for the next 20 years he would encourage his Carlisle players to play with an elegance that was rare in the lower Leagues. 'The ball is round,' was his mantra, 'pass it along the ground'.

It was all about possession – one of his stock phrases was 'I don't mind if you run up Warwick Road, down Botchergate and then back down Greystone Road, as long as you've still got possession of the ball when you get back!' He would lead training with two-men teams doing basic skills three times a week: short passing, trapping the ball, longer passing, chest trapping.

George McVitie, who grew up at the club, watched with some amusement as players who were transferred in looked quizzically at the trainer:

'Some of the players who came in wondered about this old bloke rabbiting on about the same thing day after day. When they came to leave the club the same players couldn't thank him enough for having progressed their careers. Many players loved coming back and always made a point of seeking out Dick or asking after him. I remember Bob Hatton came back with Birmingham and was genuinely upset that Dick wasn't there [he was ill] – he made a point of asking me to pass on his regards. All the managers that worked with Dick wanted to take him with them but Dick always wanted to stay with the club he loved.'

George's comments were echoed by all the players who helped with this book: Les O'Neill said, 'Dick Young is like God to me,' while John Gorman perhaps paid the ultimate tribute by saying, 'I learned more from Dick Young than I did from Jock Stein'.

The managers Dick worked for were interesting characters too. Different maybe, but in the main, each kept up the impetus. Alan Ashman's understated style was to gather the players in the Central Hotel on the Viaduct on match days for the pre-match meal around 1:30. He would then give the players a glass of sherry and talk to them quietly about the opposition. They would then make their way down to the ground and Dick would get them revved up. The two complemented each other perfectly. Andrew Jenkins also remembers Ashman's eye for a player:

'He signed Hughie and the likes of Baldy and Willie Carlin. He was very thorough looking into a player's background and visualising how they would fit into the team. I used to go with him to places like Queen of the South and he would say "I fancy that player or this player." He was a really good judge of a player.'

Fifty years as director and current chairman Andrew Jenkins.

Before some accuse me of sycophancy as far as Alan Ashman is concerned, in the interest of fairness and balance, it is perhaps appropriate to take a moment and look at one of his failures in the transfer market – I suppose if you are going to screw up, you might as well screw up big!

It was 1972 and Stan Bowles had just given the greatest cameo performance in the club's history (he only played 33 games) before being sold for a club record fee. The fans were naturally disappointed but buoyed by the news that the boss intended to buy big and replace him.

The player in question had caught Ashman's eye during a pre-season friendly at Boghead Park (*honest!*) against newly promoted Dumbarton. The strike force for the home side was made up of Roy McCormack and Kenny Wilson, who had scored over 100 goals between them in the previous two seasons. Wilson also scored in the 3–2 defeat of Carlisle and Ashman decided to make his move by smashing the club's transfer record and securing the part-time joiner's services for £36,000.

The move proved a disaster, with Wilson clearly out of his depth in the English Second Division. Fans always give the new guy a bit of slack but as Christmas approached and Kenny had yet to score, rumours abound that Ashman had signed the wrong guy – it should have been McCormack!

Then on Boxing Day 1972, an event as rare as the birth of a baby 'Giant' panda occurred at The Brunt. Carlisle were putting in one of their best performances of the season and were destroying Preston North End 5–1 with 15 minutes to go. Almost 10,000 supporters witnessed what happened next.

Dennis Martin broke free down the right, attacking the Warwick Road End; with a snake-hips swivel he split the defence with a pinpoint pass to the blue jersey that had timed his run to perfection to beat the offside trap – Kenny Wilson! The whole ground held its breath as Kenny bore down on goal in another one of those excruciating slow-motion sequences.

North End 'keeper Alan Kelly came out to narrow the angle and Wilson hammered it goalwards (some cruelly claim that Kenny closed his eyes as he hit it – I know we all did). The ball cannoned against the 'keeper but had enough momentum to loop over the stopper and into the net. If it wasn't already a Bank Holiday, I feel sure one would have been declared there and then.

As somebody once said – football's a funny old game isn't it? Leading the Preston attack that day, and witnessing the momentous event at the other end (Wilson's only ever goal for the club) was none other than the great Hughie McIlmoyle! (McIlmoyle moved from Middlesbrough to Preston in 1971). So there you have it – McIlmoyle and Wilson scored 77 goals between them for Carlisle United.

Later Dick Young reported:

'Kenny was a nice bloke but he simply wasn't up to the type of game we played. Alan regretted signing him. I advised against it but he felt that the player was

more than able to do it for us. He never settled in Carlisle and was really out of his depth.'

Wilson moved on before the season was out. At the end of the following season, as the club prepared for life in the top flight, Ashman restored his reputation in the transfer market when he topped Wilson's fee by spending £52,000 on Coventry defender Bobby Parker.

Unbeknown to Bobby and the supporters then, by the time his career was completed at Carlisle, the defender would have started 373 games (one short of outfield appearance record-holder Ginger Thompson). But similarly to Bill Green's arrival 12 months earlier, Parker wondered which planet he had landed on when the train pulled into Carlisle Station:

'When I came up I was shocked. I was met by Dick Young who was a one off! We went down to Brunton Park and I thought it was something out of Dad's Army! I was used to the fantastic facilities at Coventry and all we had here was Bitts Park and the Sheep Mount. In order to sort out the paperwork Dick sent me up town for something to eat. I didn't know Carlisle and didn't know where I was going! I wandered up Warwick Road asking people where I could get something to eat.'

Meanwhile back at Brunton Park, the club had asked builder and fan Geoff Thomlinson to re-fit the dressing rooms in readiness for the new season. Stan Ternent and Tot Winstanley were training in the mornings and then labouring for Geoff in the afternoon, who recalls with some hilarity:

'We were playing Tottenham in three weeks and the dressing room was just bare bricks. Dick Young picked this panel that was like hard board with a grey effect and a chicken design – bloody horrible it was but that's what he picked! Dick would come in and ask if there was any panelling left. He took all these off-cuts from the dressing room and he was doing something at home and he was about 18' square short – so I had to go out and buy a sheet so Dick could finish his job at home! Herbert Nicholson was as bad – it was a laugh a minute.'

Bobby returned from having his Wimpy burger at the Crescent and signed up. Both he and the dressing rooms were ready in time for the new season. (It could surely only happen at Carlisle.)

The other big player to sign for the Blues before the First Division season, of course, was Hughie McIlmoyle. It was the second time Ashman signed the player (the first being in 1963) but the third time in all that McIlmoyle had signed for the club. The other occasion was in 1967 when the player was at Bristol City and the Carlisle manager was in need of some fire power.

The manager in question was Ashman's first successor Tim Ward but the fact that the move was completed was down to another key member of the 'Carlisle family,' Ivor Broadis, who had advised the player two years earlier to complete his move away from Brunton Park to top-flight Wolves. Bristol and Carlisle agreed a fee and Hughie drove up from Bristol on Friday 22 September 1967.

Former player and manager Broadis was now a journalist, of course, and he waited with his colleagues outside the players' entrance, as the talks progressed inside, to get the lowdown on the new signing. Sure enough McIlmoyle appeared after a while and told the waiting pressmen that the deal was off due to a disagreement over personal terms. Everyone disbursed somewhat disappointed.

Ivor mulled over the strange events during lunch and thought that something didn't add up – Hughie loved Carlisle, so why couldn't an agreement be reached? He went to visit the player at his hotel.

Hughie explained that the club were not prepared to break the wage structure and that getting one salary in the winter for playing and then a reduced salary in the summer would be too big of a drop. Ivor asked if he would accept the same gross payment over the year divided equally over the 12 months – the player had a chat with his wife and they agreed that would be acceptable. Fan, friend and confidant then became savvy journalist once more, as the man himself explains:

'I then rang up Tim Ward and explained what I had agreed in principle with Hughie. He said he would speak with the chairman. I then spoke with George Sheffield who agreed but I said Hughie wouldn't sign until nine o'clock that night. The chairman asked why and I told him that the other papers closed down at nine but The Journal *(my paper) worked on so we would get the exclusive.'*

The player, the journalist, the manager and the chairman met up at nine o'clock as arranged and the signing took place. The following day – while most of the papers reported the breakdown in negotiations – every tree on Warwick Road wore a *Journal* poster which screamed 'McIlmoyle signs and plays today!' McIlmoyle did play and scored in his second debut for the club in a 2–1 defeat of Huddersfield.

The signing proved a rare high-spot for Tim Ward who many felt was simply not cut out to be an operator in the ruthless world of football management. Mind you, he didn't help himself at times: independently of one another George McVitie and Peter McConnell both related one bizarre early season half-time tale.

The team had played awfully and had conceded four in the first half. Dick Young was doing his nut as the players sat with their heads down like naughty schoolboys. Suddenly the dressing room hushed as the manager walked in; Ward scanned the dressing room before walking over to [cricketer] Chris Balderstone to inform him that Gary Sobers had just been out for a duck during the Fifth Test between England and the West Indies at the Oval. With all the players looking on in open-mouthed incredulity, Dick Young virtually exploded at his manager and the players at the same time. (FYI – England won by an innings and 34 runs.)

The following season, during the only real slump the club endured during this successful period, 'Gentleman Tim' left the club, having lost the supporters' backing. Ivor Broadis expressed his sympathy for Ward in his programme notes before the following game:

> *'One sentence he spoke to me this week after the smoke had cleared away, probably holds the key. He told me "I don't think I would ever have had the public behind me, however long I stayed". Some managers are able to shed the worries, ignore the abuse when things are going wrong. A deeply sensitive man, Tim Ward was unable to.'*

If Ashman and Ward were mild-mannered in their approach, the two that followed were in complete contrast. Following Ward's departure Bob Stokoe took control and succeeded in saving the club from relegation. His Cup and League exploits in the seasons that followed left the club in a healthy state but his handling of players was not to everyone's taste; to this day, there appear to be as many players that loathe Stokoe as love him.

An example of Stokoe's unpredictable approach came in the last minute in a rip-roaring encounter with Birmingham City at Brunton Park in 1970. The game had seen the lead change hands on two or three occasions, and as Birmingham won a corner in the dying seconds, Carlisle were leading by the odd goal in seven. The cross came over but instead of catching the ball Allan Ross opted to punch it clear; George McVitie was standing on the edge of the D when the ball flew through the air towards him. George takes up the story:

> *'As the ball was coming down I could hear Stokoe above the noise of the crowd! He was about 50 yards away and I could hear him screaming at Rossy [for not catching it] and then at me!'*

George, being George, brought the ball down: chest, trap, swivel and clear down the line to a blue jersey. At that point, the referee blew for time and Carlisle had won. George resumes the tale:

> *'I had actually cleared it and we had won but I could still hear Bob effing and jeffing about how we should have cleared it to Row Z. As everyone was trooping off I was shaking hands with the Birmingham players and shaking hands with the referee; I think I was shaking hands with everyone in the crowd because I knew what was coming! Anyway I finally plucked up courage and went into the dressing room where Bob's got Rossy by the scruff of the neck screaming at him about how he should have *****well caught it instead of *****well punching it back into the *****well crowd of players where anything could have *****well happened!'*

George managed to creep into the dressing room on tip-toe and slide unseen into the bath.

When Bob left Ian MacFarlane (who had been interviewed when Stokoe got the job in '68) joined. His no nonsense approach with players, journalist and fans (and bookmakers come to think of it) became legendary. Andrew Jenkins remembers one game at Sunderland where MacFarlane was getting all sorts of abuse in the dugout from the nearby Roker Park crowd due to his previous association with rivals Middlesbrough. 'He didn't care at all, he was carrying a cheque and just turned round and waved it at them!' (Here is another example of all's-fair-in-love-war-and-football, as MacFarlane went on to manage the Roker Park club in a caretaker capacity in 1976.)

But for many players, they appreciated the know-where-you-stand approach of MacFarlane. For the supporters, they just wanted to see a winning team, so when the big Scot was relieved of his duties in 1972, the natives were decidedly unimpressed. The fans – the paying customers – are often regarded as amenable, gullible idiots to be used and abused by the club they love. We need not have worried on this occasion, however, because Alan Ashman came back to replace MacFarlane and the rest, as they say, is history.

Like all football fans, I am a dreamy romantic (or looney, depending on your view) who believes the good times are just around the corner. Perhaps my earlier predictions about the club's future status will prove inaccurate; with a new stadium in the offing, and (as these words are written) the club sitting in the play-off positions, I may be forced to eat my words – I hope so. But whatever the future holds, United fans should always treasure the 'golden era' of the club. For every player who pulled on the blue shirt during this part of the club's long journey – thanks for the memories. Bless you boys!

PRINCIPLE SOURCES

Books

Cowing, Ronald; Lawson, Martin; Willcox, Bill. *The Carlisle United Story* (Lakeland Publications, 1974).

Hall, Andy. *Carlisle United on This Day: History, Facts and Figures from Every Day of the Year* (Pitch Publishing Ltd, 2008).

Harrison, Paul. *Carlisle's Cult Heroes* (Know the Score Books, 2007).

Harrison, Paul. *The Lads in Blue: Complete History of Carlisle United* (Yore Publications, 1995).

McConnell, Peter. *Nice One Skip – From Elland Road to Brunton Park* (Andy Hall, 2008).

Porter, Alan. *The Sporting Life: Chris Balderstone* (Elaine Humes, 2002).

Routledge, Gordon. *McIlmoyle – The Legend of Brunton Park* (Arthuret Publishers, 2004).

Steele, David. *Carlisle United: A Season in the Sun 1974–1975* (Desert Island Football Histories, 2006).

Wild, K.A. *Carlisle United, Fifty Seasons On* (1985).

Printed Papers

Carlisle United programmes
Cumberland News
Evening News
Evening News & Star

Interviews with players, supporters, journalists and club officials

Ross Brewster	Andrew Jenkins	Billy Rafferty
Ivor Broadis	Hugh McIlmoyle*	David Steele
Paul Daley	Peter McConnell*	Geoff Thomlinson
Peter Garbutt	George McVitie	Graham Winstanley
John Gorman*	Les O'Neill	
Bill Green*	Bobby Parker	

* Telephone interviews

Websites

www.carlisleunited.co.uk

www.neilbrown.newcastlefans.com/carlisle/carlisle

www.newsandstar.co.uk

www.soccerbase.com

www.statto.com

www.thebeautifulhistory.wordpress.com

www.wikipedia.com

18588902R00110

Printed in Poland
by Amazon Fulfillment
Poland Sp. z o.o., Wrocław